Praise, Praise, Praise for Decks & Patios For Dummies!

"Thorough and thoughtful, with plenty of solid, 'on the ground' advice. Bob Beckstrom will have you thinking like a landscape architect, a carpenter, a mason, an artist. If you're considering finally living to the limits of your lot line, this book is required reading; it's the guidebook to turning your yard into your favorite getaway destination."

— Bill Crosby, Editorial Director, ImproveNet

"*Decks & Patios For Dummies* is a concise, well-put-together summary of everything do-it-yourselfers need to know about building their dream decks."

— Pamela Allsebrook, Publicity Manager, California Redwood Association

"This is an exceptionally complete guide. It treats decks and patios not as isolated projects but as features that should fit with the entire property, and it helps homeowners avoid later disappointments by covering details often overlooked in the eagerness to enjoy outdoor living. You know a book is thorough when it goes so far as to recommend that, before digging post holes by hand, you do some physical workouts!"

— Huck DeVenzio, Advertising Manager, Wolmanized wood

"On behalf of the Association of Construction Inspectors, I fully endorse *Decks & Patios For Dummies*. I have reviewed selected chapters and feel it is an excellent publication for the industry."

— Robert G. Johnson, Executive Director, Association of Construction Inspectors

D1227757

Praise, Praise, Praise for the NGA's Lawn Care For Dummies and Annuals For Dummies!

"*Lawn Care For Dummies* fulfills a real need for the do-it-yourselfer by providing the how-to's of lawn care in an easy-to-understand format. Unlike many other books, *Lawn Care For Dummies* covers the basics of grass establishment, growth, and care in an enjoyable, non-technical fashion. I would recommend this book to anyone starting a new lawn or intent on improving an existing one."

— Kevin N. Morris, Director, National Turfgrass Evaluation Program

"Sure to become many a homeowner's dog-eared favorite, *Lawn Care For Dummies* answers the common and not-so-common questions we all have from time to time about caring for grass. With its friend-talking-to-a-friend style of writing, the advice is easy to understand and put to use. If you don't have about 20 years to spend on lawn-care guesswork or trials and errors, this is one book you should have, keep handy, and use often."

— Doug Fender, Executive Director, Turf Resource Center, Rolling Meadows, Illinois

"*Annuals For Dummies* is a masterful blend of tips, tricks, and techniques that even an experienced gardener can use to create a successful and spectacular flower garden. It's like having a garden designer at your fingertips."

— Doug Jimerson, Editor-in-Chief, *Garden Escape,* www.garden.com

"The subject of annuals was just waiting for the straightforward, quiet-humor delivery of Californian Bill Marken. (The "Californian" tag is part of Bill's mastery: In growing annuals year-round, mild-climate gardeners accumulate twice the lifetime experience available to cold-winter people.) In small takes, the book gives you the full range of instructions for growing and displaying these charming one-act plants."

— Joseph F. Williamson, Former Garden Editor and Managing Editor, *Sunset Magazine*

DECKS & PATIOS FOR DUMMIES®

DECKS & PATIOS FOR DUMMIES®

by Robert J. Beckstrom
&
the Editors of The National Gardening Association

IDG Books Worldwide, Inc.
An International Data Group Company

Foster City, CA ♦ Chicago, IL ♦ Indianapolis, IN ♦ Southlake, TX

Decks & Patios For Dummies®

Published by
IDG Books Worldwide, Inc.
An International Data Group Company
919 E. Hillsdale Blvd.
Suite 400
Foster City, CA 94404
www.idgbooks.com (IDG Books Worldwide Web site)
www.dummies.com (Dummies Press Web site)

Library of Congress Catalog Card No.: 98-84304

ISBN: 0-7645-5075-6

Printed in the United States of America

10 9 8 7 6 5 4 3 2 1

1E/RW/QT/ZY/IN

Distributed in the United States by IDG Books Worldwide, Inc.

Distributed by Macmillan Canada for Canada; by Transworld Publishers Limited in the United Kingdom; by IDG Norge Books for Norway; by IDG Sweden Books for Sweden; by Woodslane Pty. Ltd. for Australia; by Woodslane Enterprises Ltd. for New Zealand; by Longman Singapore Publishers Ltd. for Singapore, Malaysia, Thailand, and Indonesia; by Simron Pty. Ltd. for South Africa; by Toppan Company Ltd. for Japan; by Distribuidora Cuspide for Argentina; by Livraria Cultura for Brazil; by Ediciencia S.A. for Ecuador; by Addison-Wesley Publishing Company for Korea; by Ediciones ZETA S.C.R. Ltda. for Peru; by WS Computer Publishing Corporation, Inc., for the Philippines; by Unalis Corporation for Taiwan; by Contemporanea de Ediciones for Venezuela; by Computer Book & Magazine Store for Puerto Rico; by Express Computer Distributors for the Caribbean and West Indies. Authorized Sales Agent: Anthony Rudkin Associates for the Middle East and North Africa.

For general information on IDG Books Worldwide's books in the U.S., please call our Consumer Customer Service department at 800-762-2974. For reseller information, including discounts and premium sales, please call our Reseller Customer Service department at 800-434-3422.

For information on where to purchase IDG Books Worldwide's books outside the U.S., please contact our International Sales department at 650-655-3200 or fax 650-655-3295.

For information on foreign language translations, please contact our Foreign & Subsidiary Rights department at 650-655-3021 or fax 650-655-3281.

For sales inquiries and special prices for bulk quantities, please contact our Sales department at 650-655-3200 or write to the address above.

For information on using IDG Books Worldwide's books in the classroom or for ordering examination copies, please contact our Educational Sales department at 800-434-2086 or fax 817-251-8174.

For press review copies, author interviews, or other publicity information, please contact our Public Relations department at 650-655-3000 or fax 650-655-3299.

For authorization to photocopy items for corporate, personal, or educational use, please contact Copyright Clearance Center, 222 Rosewood Drive, Danvers, MA 01923, or fax 978-750-4470.

is a trademark under exclusive license to IDG Books Worldwide, Inc., from International Data Group, Inc.

About the Authors

Robert J. Beckstrom is a licensed general contractor living in northern California. He enjoys building things, spending time outdoors, and sharing what he's learned with other people. His first building experience was as a VISTA volunteer in 1968 as the coordinator of a self-help housing project in rural Alaska. He taught elementary school for 10 years; has taught adult courses in house building and remodeling at The Owner Builder Center in Berkeley, California; has written and edited extensively on home-improvement topics; and has built a few decks and patios along the way.

The National Gardening Association is the largest member-based, nonprofit organization of home gardeners in the United States. Founded in 1972 (as "Gardens for All") to spearhead the community gardening movement, today's National Gardening Association is best known for its bimonthly magazine, *National Gardening* ($18 per year). Reporting on all aspects of home gardening, each issue is read by some half-million gardeners worldwide. The magazine is supplemented by online efforts at www.garden.org and on America Online.

Other NGA activities include:

- ✔ *Growing Ideas* **newsletter and GrowLab** (funded in part by the National Science Foundation) provides kindergarten through grade 8 science-based, gardening-centered curricula and products.
- ✔ **The National Gardening Survey** (conducted by The Gallup Organization, Inc.) is the most detailed research about gardeners and gardening in North America.
- ✔ **Youth Garden Grants** — every year the NGA awards grants of gardening tools and seeds worth more than $500 each to schools, youth groups, and community organizations.

Mission statement: "The mission of The National Gardening Association is to sustain the essential values of life and community, renewing the fundamental links between people, plants, and the earth. Through gardening, we promote environmental responsibility, advance multidisciplinary learning and scientific literacy, and create partnerships that restore and enhance communities."

For more information about The National Gardening Association, write to us at 180 Flynn Ave., Burlington, Vermont, 050401 U.S.A. Or get in touch with us by calling 1-800-LETSGRO (1-800-538-7476) or by sending e-mail to nga@garden.org.

ABOUT IDG BOOKS WORLDWIDE

Welcome to the world of IDG Books Worldwide.

IDG Books Worldwide, Inc., is a subsidiary of International Data Group, the world's largest publisher of computer-related information and the leading global provider of information services on information technology. IDG was founded more than 25 years ago and now employs more than 8,500 people worldwide. IDG publishes more than 275 computer publications in over 75 countries (see listing below). More than 60 million people read one or more IDG publications each month.

Launched in 1990, IDG Books Worldwide is today the #1 publisher of best-selling computer books in the United States. We are proud to have received eight awards from the Computer Press Association in recognition of editorial excellence and three from *Computer Currents'* First Annual Readers' Choice Awards. Our best-selling ...*For Dummies*® series has more than 30 million copies in print with translations in 30 languages. IDG Books Worldwide, through a joint venture with IDG's Hi-Tech Beijing, became the first U.S. publisher to publish a computer book in the People's Republic of China. In record time, IDG Books Worldwide has become the first choice for millions of readers around the world who want to learn how to better manage their businesses.

Our mission is simple: Every one of our books is designed to bring extra value and skill-building instructions to the reader. Our books are written by experts who understand and care about our readers. The knowledge base of our editorial staff comes from years of experience in publishing, education, and journalism — experience we use to produce books for the '90s. In short, we care about books, so we attract the best people. We devote special attention to details such as audience, interior design, use of icons, and illustrations. And because we use an efficient process of authoring, editing, and desktop publishing our books electronically, we can spend more time ensuring superior content and spend less time on the technicalities of making books.

You can count on our commitment to deliver high-quality books at competitive prices on topics you want to read about. At IDG Books Worldwide, we continue in the IDG tradition of delivering quality for more than 25 years. You'll find no better book on a subject than one from IDG Books Worldwide.

John Kilcullen
CEO
IDG Books Worldwide, Inc.

Steven Berkowitz
President and Publisher
IDG Books Worldwide, Inc.

Eighth Annual
Computer Press
Awards ≥1992

Ninth Annual
Computer Press
Awards ≥1993

Tenth Annual
Computer Press
Awards ≥1994

Eleventh Annual
Computer Press
Awards ≥1995

Dedication

This book is dedicated to the imagination, ingenuity, and resourcefulness of every homeowner who believes that making this world a better place to live usually starts in your own backyard.

Acknowledgments

Bob Beckstrom: Besides learning about decks and patios from the school of hard knocks, I am indebted to a number of contractors, building inspectors, teachers, homeowners, and family members who have shared valuable information with me through the years, starting with my father, Randy; my brother, Lyle; and my brother-in-law, Jerry Hiner. My wife Linda has been a constant support for me in writing this book. I am deeply grateful to many colleagues and acquaintances in the design and building trades, many of whom may be surprised to know how much they have inspired and enlightened me: Michael Hamman for his wealth of knowledge about concrete technology; Redwood Kardon for his useful tips as a building inspector; Dan Fuller for his contracting and carpentry skills; Bob Mannix for his probing mind that constantly seeks better ways to do things; Bob Lombardi for his enthusiasm about design; Glen Kitzenberger for his patient teaching skills; Roger Grizzle for his builder insights; Jon Larson for his inspired designs; Michael Landis for his dedication to outdoor beautification; fellow teachers and staff members of the Owner Builder Center; and a great number of do-it-yourself homeowners whom I have had the pleasure to work with — and always learn something from — as we've built decks together.

I also wish to acknowledge the pleasure that I've had working on this book with project editor Rev Mengle and copy editor Bill Barton, and the support I received from Bill Marken of The National Gardening Association.

Michael MacCaskey, Editor-in-Chief of The National Gardening Association thanks author Bob Beckstrom and the entire staff of IDG Books Worldwide, Inc. We especially thank the IDG Books Chicago-based staff: Publisher Kathy Welton, Executive Editor Sarah Kennedy, and Acquisitions Coordinator Ann Miller. Thanks are also due to this book's able project editor, Indianapolis-based Rev Mengle. Also thanks to my good California friends of many years, Lance Walheim and Michael Landis, for their encouragement of this book; to Lincoln Prescott, for additional fact-checking; and to Bill Marken, NGA's ...For Dummies series editor. At NGA, thanks to David Els, President, and Larry Sommers, Associate Publisher.

Publisher's Acknowledgments

We're proud of this book; please send us your comments about it by using the IDG Books World-wide Registration Card at the back of the book or by e-mailing us at `feedback/dummies@idgbooks.com`.

Some of the people who helped bring this book to market include the following:

Acquisitions, Development, and Editorial

Project Editor: Rev Mengle

Executive Editor: Sarah Kennedy

Permissions Editor: Heather H. Dismore

Copy Editor: William A. Barton

General Reviewer: G. Gibbons

Editorial Manager: Leah P. Cameron

Editorial Assistants: Paul E. Kuzmic, Donna Love

Photo credits: All photos by Crandall & Crandall Photography except for Figure 15-1 (R. Todd Davis) and Figure 17-6 (Michael S. Thompson)

Illustrator: Mark R. Zahnd

Production

Project Coordinator: Regina Snyder

Layout and Graphics: Lou Boudreau, Linda M. Boyer, J. Tyler Connor, Angela F. Hunckler, Jane E. Martin, Drew R. Moore, Brent Savage, Janet Seib, M. Anne Sipahimalani, Michael A. Sullivan

Proofreaders: Christine Berman, Kelli Botta, Melissa Buddendeck, Michelle Croninger, Nancy Price, Rebecca Senninger, Janet M. Withers

Indexer: Infodex Indexing Services, Inc.

Special Help

Tamara Castleman, Senior Copy Editor; Patricia Yuu Pan, Copy Editor; Stephanie Koutek, Copy Editor

---

General and Administrative

IDG Books Worldwide, Inc.: John Kilcullen, CEO; Steven Berkowitz, President and Publisher

IDG Books Technology Publishing: Brenda McLaughlin, Senior Vice President and Group Publisher

Dummies Technology Press and Dummies Editorial: Diane Graves Steele, Vice President and Associate Publisher; Mary Bednarek, Acquisitions and Product Development Director; Kristin A. Cocks, Editorial Director

Dummies Trade Press: Kathleen A. Welton, Vice President and Publisher; Kevin Thornton, Acquisitions Manager

IDG Books Production for Dummies Press: Beth Jenkins Roberts, Production Director; Cindy L. Phipps, Manager of Project Coordination, Production Proofreading, and Indexing; Kathie S. Schutte, Supervisor of Page Layout; Shelley Lea, Supervisor of Graphics and Design; Debbie J. Gates, Production Systems Specialist; Robert Springer, Supervisor of Proofreading; Debbie Stailey, Special Projects Coordinator; Tony Augsburger, Supervisor of Reprints and Bluelines; Leslie Popplewell, Media Archive Coordinator

Dummies Packaging and Book Design: Patti Crane, Packaging Specialist; Kavish + Kavish, Cover Design

◆

The publisher would like to give special thanks to Patrick J. McGovern, without whom this book would not have been possible.

◆

Contents at a Glance

Cartoons at a Glance

By Rich Tennant

page 71

page 5

page 277

page 191

page 321

Fax: 978-546-7747 • E-mail: the5wave@tiac.net

Table of Contents

Introduction

*I*t's Sunday afternoon and my editor wants this introduction for a deadline tomorrow. I'm staring at a blank computer screen and thinking of writing about the joys of do-it-yourself building or about the role of decks and patios in American life. I remember seeing some statistics a few months ago that showed how Americans, over the decades, are spending increasingly more time indoors than outdoors (shopping malls, offices, commuting, TV-watching, net-surfing, and so on). I also recall other surveys that show gardening to be the most popular hobby in America today, and that home-improvement projects have shifted dramatically from sprucing up the interior of the house to creating knockout backyards.

This all seems like interesting stuff, but I can't figure out how to turn it into a gripping introduction. So I think I'll go outside and sit for a while on our patio where I wrote a few chapters of this book (the ones I didn't write late at night just before deadlines). It's January, between rainstorms that roll in off the Pacific Ocean every few days and soak the California countryside where my wife and I live. I need my sweater, but I'm comfortable. Our patio is nothing fancy — just ordinary gray concrete with a few trees and bushes around it, and a simple board fence along two sides. But it faces the sun and has charming views of the nearby vineyards, homes, and hills.

As I sit here on this wintry day I notice that the ground is covered with soggy leaves from the bleak trees. I hear some birds rustling among the leaves, and I become fascinated watching them forage for food. I also notice spectacular clouds swirling above, and revel in the warm sun as it peeks through them. I'm gaining a whole new perspective: What book? What deadline? I'm thinking about balmy summer evenings and dinner parties, daytime barbecues, friends who have sat around this weather-beaten table, and the fact that my wife and I eat all of our meals out here from May through September. I'm also thinking about patios and decks that I've built or enjoyed through the years. It seems strange, but in every case I recall laughter, sparkling conversation, good times, a vacation atmosphere. People coming together and enjoying life together. The same thing happens in-doors, of course, but somehow people feel more alive and attuned to their senses when they spend time outdoors. That's what this book is really about — making daily life richer. I hope that's what it does for you.

How to Use This Book

This book is packed with information about all aspects of decks and patios, from design through construction. I started writing with Chapter 1, but that doesn't mean you have to start reading there. This book is written so that you can start wherever you want, with the topic that interests you. If the topic requires that you know something covered elsewhere in the book, I summarize it for you and direct you to the appropriate chapter for more information. Before you start digging up the yard for your footings or foundations, however, take a look at Chapter 8 (if you're building a deck) or Chapter 15 (if you're building a patio). Those two chapters tell you a little about getting the proper permits and making preparations for your project.

How This Book Is Organized

This book follows a straightforward, sequential order, starting with design information and proceeding through construction techniques for decks, patios, and related structures. I present much of the information in a step-by-step format, making it easy for you to follow and to refer to when you begin your project. To further simplify the book, I group the chapters into five parts.

Part I: Design Basics

These chapters cover such basic issues as how large to make your deck or patio, where to place it in the yard, and how to give it some pizzazz. This part points out common pitfalls and expensive errors. You'll find dozens of design ideas and checklists to help you evaluate your design.

Part II: Building a Deck

This part presents all the information you need to build a complete deck, from choosing the lumber to applying a finish. You figure out how to string layout lines, dig footing holes, build forms for the concrete piers, and attach the deck to the house. You also determine which size joists to use, which side of the decking boards to expose, how to build stairs and safe railings, how to choose a stain or sealer, and much more.

Part III: Building a Patio

Even if picks, shovels, and wheelbarrows aren't your thing, you'll find out what it takes to build any type of patio — concrete, brick, pavers, stone, or tile. These chapters guide you through all of the steps for building a beautiful and lasting patio.

Part IV: Deck & Patio Amenities

Say you've already got a deck or a patio at your house. Does this book have anything for you? You bet. In this part you'll find instructions and tips on adding everything from overhead coverings to planters to barbecues. These chapters show you how to turn your deck or patio from being just the scene of a party into the main attraction.

Part V: The Part of Tens

Whether you're looking for unique ideas to enhance your project or ways to save money, this compendium of tips offers all kinds of unusual and essential information. Use this part to break logjams in the design process or to transform your deck or patio from drab to dramatic.

Icons Used in This Book

The icons in this book highlight different kinds of important information. Here's the rundown:

When you see this icon, I'm sharing a shortcut or a bit of useful information that I've picked up over the years.

You don't exactly have to tie a string around your finger when you see one of these icons, but don't overlook the important information the icon points out.

Building decks and patios is simple, but making a mistake while in the process is also simple. This icon points out stupid pitfalls you should avoid.

Some mistakes you can make while building a deck or patio are more serious. Take heed of the warnings given in these paragraphs.

I'll be honest: Building a deck or patio — at least, building one the *correct* way — isn't cheap. But that doesn't mean you can't save a dollar here and there. These icons point out ways to do that.

If you've ever seen the television show *Home Improvement,* you know that the character played by show star Tim Allen would be mighty confused during a conversation with lumber store workers. Well, take a close look at the terms that this icon highlights and you won't have that problem. Argh, argh, argh, argh!

Conventions Used in This Book

Before you begin, this book uses some simple building-trade conventions that you should be aware of. You probably know these, but in the interest of clarity, let me just list them.

- When you see something like *2x4,* it refers to a piece of lumber with a specific thickness and width — in this case, two inches thick by four inches wide. Actually, those are the nominal dimensions, because what you'll get from the lumber yard won't quite be two inches by four inches. But you can read more about that in Chapter 5.

- When I say "1-by lumber" or "2-by lumber," I'm talking about lumber that's one inch by something or two inches by something. So a 2-by board could be a 2x4, a 2x6, a 2x8, or . . . you get the picture.

- Nails have an arcane sizing system based on "pennyweight," an anti-quated British system, with an even more arcane symbol (d) that stands for an even more arcane object: the Roman coin, denarius. Don't ask me how it all came to be, but just know that 4d, 16d, and so on refer to "four-penny" and "sixteen-penny" nails. The good news is that smaller numbers represent smaller nails, larger numbers larger nails, so the system has some logic.

Well, you probably wanted to start building that patio or deck yesterday, so I won't keep you. Turn the page (or turn to whichever chapter you'd like) and get started!

Part I
Design Basics

The 5th Wave · By Rich Tennant

"I think Philip was inspired by our trip last year touring the Great Gothic Decks of Europe."

In this part . . .

The fun part of any project is dreaming about it. You probably have a wish list for your deck or patio. Perhaps you've even started a collection of magazine clippings and snapshots of interesting ideas that may work in your yard. You may even have plans to hire a landscape architect to help you design your project. Or perhaps you're just wondering where to begin.

The four chapters in this part take you through the fascinating process of planning a successful outdoor living space — not a fantasy land for the rich and famous, but a practical and beautiful backyard that you and your family can enjoy for many years to come. None of this process is difficult or requires elaborate work — you just have to be patient and consider as many options as possible. As you read through these chapters, keep a notebook or binder handy to jot down ideas and doodle some sketches as they occur to you. You will find your mind racing along with exciting and creative ideas, so enjoy the ride.

Chapter 1

Creating a Special Outdoor Space

For most people, enjoying the great outdoors means packing up the car and driving all day to a distant destination. But it can also mean staying at home. Whether it's a rooftop in Raleigh, a courtyard in Cleveland, a development in Denver, or acreage in Anchorage, your yard can be your own outdoor escape . . . with all the conveniences of home. The key to this paradise is a well-designed patio or deck, and that's why you're reading this book.

You can see yourself greeting the morning sun with a cup of coffee on your new deck. Or lounging on a beautiful patio with your favorite book. Or entertaining friends for a casual lunch while you watch your youngsters play in the yard. Or dining outdoors on a balmy evening. Or soaking in a steamy spa with snow all around. You see yourself *out there,* and you're ready to build that patio or deck now.

But not so fast. Nothing guarantees that slapping a platform onto the back of your house or pouring a concrete slab next to the lawn brings you Shangri-La. Thousands — probably millions — of homes have a deck or patio that nobody uses. You've seen them: a parking lot for tricycles and little more. Why? Because they're no fun. The answer's that simple. Something went wrong somewhere: wrong size, wrong location, too hot, too chilly, inconvenient, no visual appeal, too many bugs, no privacy, and so on. In a nutshell, poor design. This book can help you figure out what makes a deck or patio great and then show you the planning tools for making *your* deck or patio equally great. The process starts with the total backyard environment.

The Call of the Wild Backyard

A successful deck or patio does not exist in a vacuum. It has a setting, and it needs to feel harmonious with that setting. What is fascinating about decks and patios is that they enjoy a sort of hybrid identity — part fish, part fowl. They're an extension of the house and need to have that connection, but they're also part of the yard, the natural world of the garden — and beyond. Successful decks and patios relate well to both the house and the garden (even if they're not attached to the house) and you must plan them with both environments in mind. Unless you're prepared to make major changes to your house, however, you should focus your initial planning on the yard, because that's where you're creating your new outdoor living space.

Taming the Jungle

What makes a backyard like the one in Figure 1-1 paradise? Although each yard is unique and every homeowner has individual preferences, all successful landscape designs share certain characteristics. These qualities aren't mysterious. Most of them are common sense — many of them so obvious that you could easily overlook them as you become involved in the planning process. Being aware of these qualities helps you make your planning decisions and also helps you to understand why certain yards appeal to you and others don't — or why you're drawn to certain areas of your own yard and not others.

Figure 1-1:
This patio with a deck is a special outdoor space. How many of the design factors that these sections describe can you identify?

Privacy

For a yard to be enjoyed completely, it must have a sense of security and enclosure. History and fiction alike abound with fascinating accounts of walled gardens and secluded retreats — private places for the enjoyment of their owners and guests. The entire yard doesn't need to be screened from public view, especially at the front of the home. Nor should privacy screens be so tall that they block views of the sky and pleasant vistas, making the garden feel threatening and foreboding. Examples of successful screens are shrubs, hedges, fences, walls, and small buildings.

Shrubs and hedges provide soft, natural barriers, but they may not block views completely unless you plant them heavily. Deciduous shrubs, which lose their leaves in the fall, provide a screen during the growing season, when people are most likely to use the yard, and open up the yard to expanded views and increased sunlight during the winter months. They add the extra bonus of flowers, fragrances, and fall colors. Evergreen shrubs create a denser, more permanent screen.

Fences offer more flexibility than plants do as privacy screens. Their placement is not limited by growing conditions. Fences can be as high or as long as you need. They offer more security. The variety of styles is virtually endless, from solid stockade fences to open picket rail designs, and you can paint them to create contrasting accents, leave them natural, or stain them to blend in with the garden. A variation of the fence is a trellis that you cover with vines such as climbing roses or clematis.

Walls of stone, brick, or decorative concrete block offer even more security and durability than fences do. Because they're so substantial, walls only two or three feet high may be sufficient where you don't need a complete visual barrier.

Small buildings, such as garden sheds or pool cabanas, create secure enclosures. In urban areas, neighboring houses may sit on the property line and enclose most of the yard. Although such barriers require special treatments to camouflage or disguise them and reduce their overpowering presence, they can be a welcome design challenge.

Access and convenience

A beautiful yard is hard to enjoy if you must go through a maze of doorways, tread down steep stairs, and walk around corners to get to it. You should have at least one large, inviting transition between the house and yard, such as French doors or a sliding patio door that opens onto a large landing, patio, or deck at floor level. For many homes, an instant improvement to the yard would be to move the kitchen table away from the patio door to make access easier. Ideally, several rooms should have doors to the outdoors. The garden should also be easy to travel in without walking on damp lawns, dusty beds, or uncomfortable surfaces and without taking inconvenient detours to find gates and passageways. Paths and walks should be wide enough and firm enough for comfortable walking. Unlike sidewalks, garden paths and walkways should meander somewhat to reinforce a relaxed, luxurious atmosphere within the garden.

Adaptable spaces

In successful yards, each area of the garden is suitable for its intended uses. An area intended for entertaining, for example, should have facilities for preparing and serving food, ample space for tables and chairs, an attractive setting, smooth paving, and adequate lighting. A children's play area should be visible from the kitchen, equipped with storage and play structures, screened from areas where noise or clutter may be a distraction, and accessible to areas of the house where children can march to and fro. The gardening area must have the requisite sun, shade, and soil conditions for growing the chosen plants. It should also have convenient storage and a network of paths. A utility area should be hidden, convenient to the street, and outfitted with storage facilities. Many of these areas you must devote to a single, specific use, but some areas of a yard should be adaptable for multiple uses, such as a patio that you can use for dining, sunning, or potting plants.

Defined spaces

Variety is the spice of life. Too much of anything in a landscape, whether a large lawn, a monotonous expanse of deck, or an endless profusion of the same plant, leads to a deadly design. But variety for variety's sake is equally dangerous. Yards that succeed have a clear, logical organization of areas. You feel comfortable because areas are delineated and everything is "in the right place." The transitions and flow of spaces are not boringly predictable or jarringly awkward. The overall effect is an enchanting miniature world that you want to explore and in which you feel comfortable spending time.

In practical terms, these sitting areas, gardens, play areas, work areas, and other spaces are *defined*. They're separated from and connected to each other in interesting ways. Some boundaries may consist of a solid barrier, such a fence or lattice screen; other boundaries may be as unobtrusive as a change of surface textures (lawn to gravel, for example), a line of meandering stones, or the perimeter of an overhead canopy. The way that you arrange these elements gives yards their distinctive character, from formal, symmetrical compositions to exuberantly informal arrangements.

Visual appeal

Beautiful yards are . . . well, beautiful. Although you may completely organize and plan a yard for functional uses — and you should — you can't enjoy it very much unless it pleases the eye. You may not have the training and experience of a professional landscape designer, but you can certainly learn a few basic rules and tricks of design that help you compose the various elements of your garden. (See Chapter 3 for information.) Equally important is paying attention to spaces that you enjoy and figuring out why you enjoy them. Do you like things orderly and precise or casual and informal? What colors do you enjoy? Why are some views captivating and others boring? The answers to these questions can give you clues on how to best organize your own yard.

Comfort

Beauty isn't just visual. Your yard may not make the front cover of a glossy magazine, but it may be a place that people love to visit. Conversely, some gardens make stunning photographs but aren't pleasant places in which to spend time.

Why? Although we're strongly aware of visual stimuli, our bodies are far more sensitive to temperature, odors, textures, and sounds than we realize. We also react to visual stimuli in complex ways. A shapely and majestic tree may delight us in a photograph but could make us feel uneasy in our own yard if we respond to it as a towering hazard. As you begin to plan your own landscape, think about places you've visited that you especially enjoy and think about the various sights, sounds, smells, and feelings that contributed to your pleasure. Perhaps the soothing sound of splashing water, the singing of birds, or the crunch of gravel under your feet gave you the most pleasure, even though you were aware of more immediate sensations at the time. Happily, dozens — even hundreds — of such sensations have universal appeal and are easy to duplicate in a garden, from dappled sunlight on summer days to heat reflecting off sun-baked rocks on a crispy fall afternoon.

Besides these individual sensations, you need to consider the overall ambiance of the yard. A yard may feel cozy and protected, stimulating and exciting, or mysterious. Indeed, one person may see a yard as an endless list of chores, and another may see the same yard as a welcome break from housework. All these impressions are powerful, if not easy to identify, and should infuse the design process.

Safety

A safe yard is secure from the outside world and free from dangerous hazards. The most common injuries are from tripping and falling, so you should set up clear paths that are firm, smooth, easy to see (especially at night), and free of head-bumpers. You want to build all structures according to the necessary permits. The yard should remain free of clutter. Swimming pools and spas need to be fenced to keep toddlers away. Electrical outlets and lighting should include protection from shock hazards. Avoid using any plants that may be poisonous to pets or children and securely store all gardening tools and materials.

Personal statement

A successful yard reflects the uniqueness and personality of its owners . . . within limits. Taking into account such factors as resale value, neighborhood restrictions, regional design preferences, code requirements, and good taste, it's still *your* yard, so make it your personal statement. Surround yourself with things that you love. Do you enjoy sports, gardening, cooking, collecting, building, birding, puttering, fishing, stargazing, nurturing children, sculpting, welding, growing food? The list is endless, but the point is to let your yard reflect your own interests and tastes. You don't need to display every geegaw you own, but build into your design something that is you.

Exploring the Primrose Path of Garden Design

Designing a garden, whether in a condominium courtyard or a sprawling estate, is easy if you follow a clear process. Doing so just takes time. Most textbooks of garden design, no matter how formal and complex, use a systematic process similar to the one that I outline in the following section. This process is simply a series of steps — not so much a linear path as an ascending spiral — in which you return to previous steps but always with new input and fresh insights.

The goal is a final site plan with specifications for installing the landscape. The plan may be as simple as an annotated sketch or as complicated as multiple sets of working drawings and specifications, depending on the scope of the work. Although you may be eager to finish the plan and get on with construction, don't overlook the pleasures of the process itself. At this point, you're mainly interested in the broad outlines of a landscape plan so that you can design your deck or patio — but still give yourself as much time as you can. Make sure that you involve everyone in the family. Set aside a desk drawer or portable file for collecting notes, sketches, magazine clippings, photos, product brochures, and so on. Reserve some wall space or even the refrigerator door to hang drawings where family members can doodle their suggestions and responses.

Be prepared for a back-and-forth process with problems to solve and myriad decisions to make. Expect to make tradeoffs. Put the planning on hold if you reach an impasse. Also expect exciting discoveries and breakthroughs that deserve celebrating. Above all, enjoy the adventure as you figure out neat ways to get the most out of your little corner of the world.

A Brief Look at the Process

The process for designing a garden or landscape plan includes these steps:

1. **Establish a ballpark budget and timeline.**

   For most people, the first question is "What is a garden going to cost?" But the question you really should ask first is "How much can I spend?" At the very beginning, set a realistic budget for your backyard landscaping, including your deck or patio project, that is based on what you can afford, not what you think the project will cost. Also establish a desired schedule for completion. These targets are critical guidelines throughout the design process.

2. **Make a plot plan.**

   This plan is an accurate, dimensioned drawing of your entire property, showing all the existing features where they are now.

3. **Analyze the existing site.**

   Look at your entire property with a steely eye to figure out all its assets and liabilities.

4. **Identify functional needs.**

   Make a wish list of all the activities and features you should plan for; then evaluate and prioritize the list. The patio in Figure 1-2, for example, doesn't require a lot of maintenance.

Figure 1-2: For many people, "easy maintenance" would be near the top of their wish list. A low-maintenance deck or patio such as this makes the entire landscape easier to care for.

5. Experiment with various arrangements.

Here is where the list hits the map. You know the site; you know what you want; now figure out where things should go by experimenting with sketches. A quick and easy method is to draw ovals, or *goose eggs*, to represent areas of the yard. (See the section "Drawing Goose Eggs," later in this chapter, for more information.)

6. Establish a preliminary site plan.

Choose the best arrangement of goose eggs and transform it into a dimensioned plan.

7. Refine and revise the plan.

As you plan each element of the landscape, you need to make adjustments to the overall plan.

8. Draw a final site plan.

After everything falls into place and you're satisfied with the scheme, create a dimensioned site plan showing each feature in its place.

9. Create construction drawings and specifications for the "hardscape" features — for example, decks, patios, overheads, walks, and fences.

I'm a professional — I can help

If you need help with your design, many types of professionals are available. Some offer full planning services. Others specialize in particular aspects of a yard, such as decks, patios, fences, swimming pools, irrigation systems, or plant materials. You may want help drafting the final working drawings or a professional critique of your own final plan before you begin construction.

The list of possible resources includes landscape architects, landscape contractors, master gardeners, swimming pool contractors, nursery staff, irrigation suppliers, masonry suppliers, and building materials outlets. The most reliable way to find such help is by word of mouth. Ask friends, neighbors, local nursery personnel, cooperative extension agents, community college instructors, builders, real estate agents, and homeowner associations for recommendations. Be clear about the kind of help that you need. Inquire about the services your contact offers and the fees and follow up on any referrals the contact provides.

Back to reality: Budget, codes, feasibility

Although the design process encourages you to take a wild romp with your imagination, certain realities rein it in. Many of them pop up during your site analysis and experimental layouts, but three predictable realities have a major effect on your design.

One is your *budget,* which should serve as a touchstone during the entire planning process. Start with a determination of how much money you can and are willing to devote to landscaping — or at least to your deck or patio. Then try to determine whether this figure is a prudent investment in your home by asking real estate agents how much the improvements may enhance the value of your home. You probably have a lot of latitude with which to work; just avoid overbuilding for your neighborhood. Of course, don't overlook the intangible benefits you receive. Your landscape is not just a monetary investment; you receive a pleasure payoff. If necessary, adjust your original budget to reflect these investment and lifestyle factors.

The second reality that influences your plans, especially if you're building a deck, patio, pool, or similar structure, is *local regulations.* Most communities have zoning ordinances that specify how far you can set back the house or pertinent structures from the property lines *(setbacks);* what percentage of the property you can cover with improvements *(lot coverage);* and *height restrictions* for fences, sheds, and overheads near property lines. Building codes govern how you must design and build a structure such as a deck or overhead; for example, the building code specifies the minimum depth of footings (concrete supports for posts, piers, or walls) and the required dimensions for stairs. Certain improvements, such as a deck less than 30 inches high or a patio, may be exempt from such regulations.

Your home may also be subject to the Covenants, Conditions, and Restrictions (CC&Rs) of a neighborhood association, which often include strict design guidelines and a design review process for any outdoor improvements. Tree removal, swimming pool fencing, and landscaping along the sidewalk median strip are other improvements that may be subject to regulation. Contact your local building department and neighborhood association to obtain information about codes, ordinances, and other regulations that may affect your project.

Finally, make a realistic assessment of your own abilities and time if you plan to do any of the work yourself. Do you have time to complete your project? Do you have the tools, expertise, and physical stamina to build a deck, patio, fences, walks, and other improvements? Building a deck or patio is certainly within the abilities of most do-it-yourselfers. After reading the construction information in this book, you should have a good idea of what's involved. The level of your abilities and ambition influence many of your planning and design choices.

Making a List, Checking It Twice

Right now, thinking of your yard as a place for outdoor living may be difficult, perhaps because you see it only as an endless list of projects. To break out of that box and to free your creative juices, start with some dreaming or visioning. Forget about tape measures, graph paper, building specs, even your budget and just imagine your yard at its best, where you can fully enjoy outdoor living. What are the things you want to do in your yard? Perhaps you see sumptuous garden parties with a multitude of guests. Or a recreational dreamland complete with a sport court, lap pool, playground, and putting green. Or a miniature Garden of Eden, where you can spend every spare moment you have tending and caring for a profusion of pampered plants.

Do you enjoy growing your own food? Perhaps you have other hobbies, such as woodworking or sculpture, that you want to do outdoors. Or you dream of intimate al fresco dinners away from the television set or a spa where you can relax under the stars after dinner. Perhaps your most compelling wish is for a better view out the kitchen window. Of course, you may also have utilitarian concerns, such as a place for gardening equipment and an area for storing yard waste. If you're an avid builder, you may also need a backyard area for storing construction materials. By thinking about your own wish list, without restrictions, you begin to see many more possibilities for your yard than you'd ever imagined. This stage is the time for your imagination to go wild. The sorting and deleting happens later. You should account for all members of your household in your planning (including future members), whether they participate or not.

Sample wish list

The following list is an example of different activities and features that a family may wish for in designing a yard. This list is by no means exhaustive or typical, but it should get you started on your own list.

- A basketball court
- A birdbath and bird feeder
- Playing surfaces for youngsters
- An outdoor grill
- A potting shed
- Patio space near the garage for working on projects
- Enough lawn for soccer practice
- A deck off the family room
- A private deck or courtyard off the master suite
- A better view of the western hills
- The sound of running water
- Raised planting beds for a vegetable garden
- A small herb garden near the kitchen door
- Shade trees west of the house
- A spa
- A deck or patio for parties
- A place to store pipes and lumber
- A compost pile

As you develop this list, you may be tempted to eliminate certain ideas (your spouse's, for example), but don't toss them out yet. Prioritize the list instead. Start at the top with features that you "absolutely must have." Then go with the "would-be-nice-but" group. Finally, mark the "in-your-dreams" set. This list is sure to change over time. You can set it aside and move on to the plot plan and then return to the list as you get inspired.

Discovering the Plot

Time now to make a *plot plan,* or *base plan,* of your property. (See Chapter 4 for drawing information.) Even if you're designing a backyard deck or patio and nothing more, you should make a scale drawing of your entire lot, including the front yard. For one thing, such a drawing may be a requirement if you need to apply for a building permit. More important, planning a deck or patio is easier if you can see how it relates to the entire property.

What a plot plan includes

A plot plan is simply a map of your property that includes the following elements:

- Property lines
- Fences (which aren't necessarily on property lines) and gates
- House (showing roofline and exterior walls)
- Windows and exterior doors
- Garage and driveway
- Porches, patios, decks, and exterior stairs
- Walks and paths
- Outdoor structures (sheds, gazebos, patio covers)
- Swimming pool, spa
- Outdoor lights and electrical outlets
- Outdoor faucets
- Valves for sprinkler and irrigation systems
- Water meter, gas meter, electric meter, downspouts
- Lawns, trees, shrubs, planting beds
- Septic tank and leach field (area where drainage lines are located)

Taking field measurements

Before you take any field measurements, sketch a rough plan of the property, showing the property lines, house, driveway, and other major features. Then take measurements and add the dimensions to the sketch. Some of the field measurements are easy to take, such as the length of house walls or a straight fence. Start with these. Then draw in other elements and show their locations in relation to known measurements. Indicate the precise location of a tree trunk, for example, by measuring the distance from it to two known points, such as two corners of the house. Include the diameter of tree trunks and the distance from the trunk to the outermost branches.

Do not assume that right angles and parallel lines that walls, fences, driveway, and property lines create are always perfect. The nearest wall of a backyard garage may not be parallel with the rear wall of the house; a driveway may not be perfectly parallel with the property line. In most cases they're reasonably close, but verify the distance between objects with as many measurements as you can.

After you fill in your rough sketch, make a scale drawing of your property that includes all the pertinent features, their dimensions, and the distances between them (see Chapter 4). Draw the plot plan on 24-by 36-inch paper, using a ⅛-inch scale (¼-inch for smaller lots). Make at least two copies.

WATCH OUT

Locating property lines

You don't find your property lines drawn on the ground. If you're lucky, you find *monuments*, or *markers*, at the property corners. These markers may be conspicuous posts driven into the ground, but more likely they're small pipes or brass medallions, often covered by several inches of accumulated soil. Property corners at the street are usually marked by small crosses inscribed in the concrete curb or gutter. Keep in mind that your actual property line may be set back several feet from these markers; check your deed to see whether the street occupies an easement along the front of your property. Refer to your deed's legal description of your property. It may be a "metes and bounds" description based on known landmarks or a reference to a lot number on a subdivision map that's recorded with the appropriate agency, such as the county recorder's or tax assessor's office.

If you can't find your markers easily, ask your immediate neighbors or longtime residents living nearby. As a good-neighbor policy, you may want to conduct the search with your immediate neighbors anyway, especially to clarify the ownership of fences. If you can't verify the property lines, you should hire a surveyor, perhaps sharing the cost with neighbors. If your neighbors refuse to cooperate, you can still hire a surveyor yourself and seek his or her advice about any disputes.

Playing Sherlock

After you have a plot plan, you need to continue your investigation of the property, this time digging deeper for clues to discover and solve design problems. These clues are known as *site conditions,* and your investigation is a *site analysis.* As you work through the following list, you can record your findings on the plot plan itself or attach notes.

North, south, east, west

Draw an arrow indicating true north on your plot plan. If you don't have a compass, check your property deed or a street map of your city for clues. Other clues are the noontime position of the sun (standard time), which is due south, or the position of the North Star (Polaris), which aligns with the two stars forming the lip of the Big Dipper.

Slope

Which way does your property slope and how steeply? First, establish a *benchmark,* or *datum point,* as a reference for vertical measurements. The easiest benchmark is the ground floor of your house, to which you can assign an arbitrary elevation such as 100 feet. First, take vertical measurements to the ground from each doorway and mark the appropriate elevations on your plot plan — for example, 98'6", 95'4", and so on. Then take field measurements of points on your property every 5 to 10 feet and plot them on your plan. Start by driving stakes or placing markers at various points on your property that you also marked on your plan. Include patio, deck, driveway, and similar surfaces. To measure the vertical distance between points, place one end of a 10-foot straightedge on the higher point and, holding the straightedge level, measure down from the other end to the ground (see Figure 1-3).

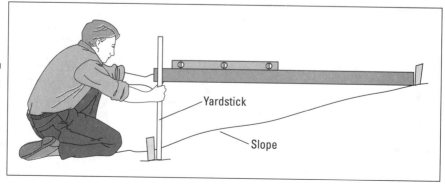

Figure 1-3:
Measuring
the vertical
distance
between
two points.

Yardstick

Slope

A quicker way to take vertical measurements is with a builder's level (an instrument that looks like a telescope on a tripod), which you can rent, or with a hydrolevel (see Chapter 8).

Note: This type of work can be a fun activity for the entire family, especially preadolescents (with sufficient supervision).

After you plot all the elevations on your plan, draw lines connecting any points within one or two inches of the same elevation. Finally, using these points and lines as a guide, draw flowing contour lines to indicate one-foot changes in elevation (two-, three-, or five-foot changes for steeper lots).

Drainage

Mark drainage patterns on your plot plan — places where water flows or collects. Look for catch basins and drain outlets and mark any subsurface drainage lines that you know of. Note any basement or crawlspace moisture problems.

Microclimates

What is the direction of prevailing winds? How does the pattern change over the seasons? Which areas of your property tend to be chilly and damp? Hot and sunny? Is your property in a low area, where pockets of cool air linger for days, or in a higher area that gets steady breezes? How do nearby buildings affect your yard? How do conditions change during the day? Make as many observations as possible over several months, especially at the times when you're most likely to use your yard.

Patterns of sun and shade

The angle of the sun, which has a powerful effect on your yard's climate and comfort, changes dramatically according to the time of day, the season, and your geographic location. The sun doesn't always rise right at due east, for example, and set directly at due west. It does at the equator and on the equinoxes (March 21 and September 21). During the summer, however, the sun rises considerably north of due east and sets considerably north of due west, and the winter sun rises and sets considerably south of those points. These differences can have a dramatic effect on outdoor living. A patio on the north side of your home, for example, is shaded during most of the year but may be exposed to the searing late afternoon sun during the hottest months, as shown in Figure 1-4.

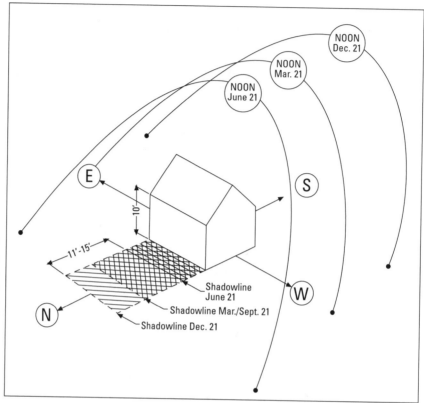

Figure 1-4:
Shade
patterns
change as
the angle of
the sun
changes
through the
seasons.

Besides the sun's movement, the location and height of trees and buildings affect shade patterns, as shown in Figure 1-5. If you can't make measurements and observations over the course of several months, you can easily calculate an object's shade pattern if you know its height and the angle of the sun. The angle of the midday sun, for example, is approximately 85 degrees on June 21 (the summer solstice) along the southern border of the United States (latitude 30 degrees), 65 degrees along the northern border (latitude 50 degrees), and 75 degrees midway between the two borders (latitude 40 degrees). To calculate the length of a tree's shadow, draw a vertical line to scale, representing its height (for example, 30 feet), and a horizontal line at its base. Using a protractor, draw a line from the top of the "tree" to the base line so that the new line measures 65, 75, or 85 degrees at the base. The tree's shadow covers the distance along the base line from the "tree" to this angle.

For example, if the tree's height is represented as x, the shadow lengths are approximately as follows: 85 degrees solar angle = a shadow length of $.1x$; 75 degrees = $.28x$; and 65 degrees = $.5x$. The winter sun angles are approximately 40, 30, and 20 degrees for the Southern, middle, and Northern states,

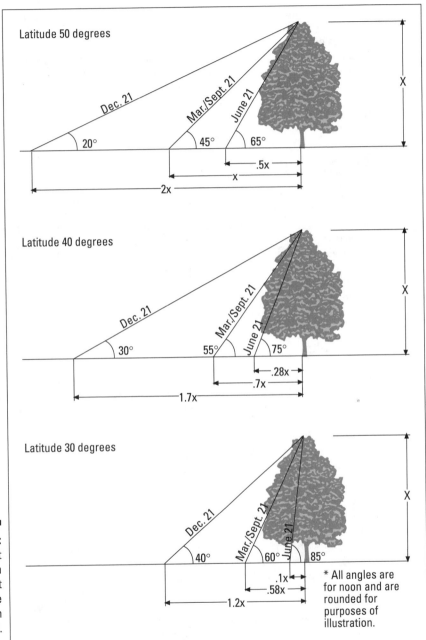

Latitude 50 degrees

Dec. 21
Mar./Sept. 21
June 21
20°
45°
65°
.5x
x
2x
X

Latitude 40 degrees

Dec. 21
Mar./Sept. 21
June 21
30°
55°
75°
.28x
.7x
1.7x
X

Latitude 30 degrees

Dec. 21
Mar./Sept. 21
June 21
40°
60°
85°
.1x
.58x
1.2x
X

* All angles are
for noon and are
rounded for
purposes of
illustration.

Figure 1-5:
Tree height
and sun
angle affect
shade
patterns in
your yard.

respectively, and would cast shadows of 1.2x, 1.7x, and 2x at noon on December 21. These are the shortest shadow lengths of the day. Although you can consult a solar chart that indicates the sun's angle at various times of day and at various latitudes to calculate shadow lengths at different seasons, you can make reasonable estimates based on these noon calculations and the fact that the early morning and late afternoon sun locations are very close to the horizon. (You can find a solar chart in any book about solar design or solar architecture.)

Traffic patterns and access

Notice where doorways, gates, paths, walks, and other "official" traffic routes are located and then observe where people (and pets) actually walk. Do well-traveled shortcuts exist throughout your property? Where should you locate new traffic lanes? What's the easiest way to get from the front of the house to the back, the garage to the kitchen, or the toolshed to the garden? What obstacles interfere with easy access? Where could paths be routed for greater convenience? Can you add doors to the house or move or improve exisiting doors?

Privacy

Which areas of the yard offer the most privacy? The least? You can install screens and fences to provide privacy almost anywhere, but determine as many factors as possible that may affect location. What parts of your neighbors' yards do they use for socializing, children's play, and quiet relaxing? Knowing their patterns of activity enables you to more easily respect their privacy as well as ensure your own.

Views

You have an idea where your million-dollar views are already, but have you really investigated? Grab a chair, set it in various parts of your yard, and sit in it for a while to absorb the different viewpoints. Next, do the same thing with a sturdy stepladder. You may discover peekaboo views of distant hills or lovely trees that would make a perfect background for a small patio or notice distracting buildings or power lines that could spoil views where you thought the raised deck should go. You may also discover that views *toward* your house are a refreshing change from the familiar views out your windows. Consider as many vantage points as possible and note in your plans the good, the bad, and the ugly.

Easements and setbacks

Make sure that you're aware of any easements on your property. An *easement* is the right of someone else to use your land, such as a neighbor who has a driveway on part of your property *(easement appurtenant)* or a utility company that has the right to install and service power lines across your land *(easement in gross)*. Such easements, specified in your deed, guarantee certain rights of usage to the other party. You can't build anything on the easement, even if it hasn't been used for years, unless the easement is legally terminated.

Setbacks also restrict where you can and can't build on your property. A *setback* is the area along the property line where certain structures aren't allowed. Typical setbacks in most communities are 20 feet from the front and back, 6 feet from the sides. After you verify the setbacks in your area, draw them on your plot plan.

Drawing Goose Eggs

"Enough analyzing!" you say. You're bursting with ideas and want to get them on paper to see whether they work. The easiest way to do so is to lay tracing paper over your plot plan and pencil in the broad activity areas that you propose. Ovals (goose eggs) help you isolate different areas and see relationships between them (see Figure 1-6). You can vary the size, orientation, and color of the goose eggs to make visualizing these relationships and connections even easier. After you try a scheme, replace the tracing paper with a fresh piece and start over again. Create as many options as you can. Use the information on your plot plan and site analysis to evaluate ideas. Take your diagrams outside and "test drive" them by walking around the yard.

Sooner or later, you exhaust all the possibilities you can think of and a particular scheme emerges. Voilà! You have a preliminary site plan and you're ready to plan each element in detail, including your deck or patio.

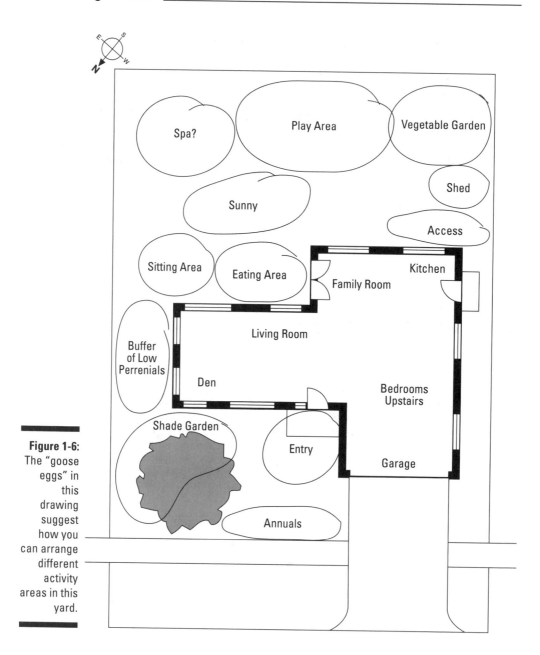

Figure 1-6:
The "goose eggs" in this drawing suggest how you can arrange different activity areas in this yard.

Chapter 2

Locating a Patio or Deck

*W*hich comes first, the deckin' or the egg? The planning process focuses on your entire backyard until you come up with some "goose eggs," as Chapter 1 describes. This goose-egg scheme, or preliminary site plan, is an important tool in designing your deck or patio. It establishes the location and perhaps even suggests the shape and size. But don't get wedded to your proposed site until you evaluate it thoroughly. As you launch into the specifics of deck and patio planning, you may discover some drawbacks to this site or find a better location. If so, you need to go back and redo your goose eggs. That's okay. Design is a back-and-forth process. But for now, set aside the site plan and use this chapter to help you figure out the major design details for the deck or patio itself, starting with a review of the reasons why you want a deck or patio in the first place.

The Joy of Decks, the Oh! in Patio

A deck or patio, well planned and correctly built, adds to the enjoyment of a home in so many ways that it's often the centerpiece of a landscape design and a stage for daily living (see Figure 2-1). It's an outdoor room where your family can enjoy many special moments. It enables you to relax in the comforts of home while surrounded by the delights of nature.

A deck or patio expands your indoor living space. If your home is small or feels cramped, you can add square footage without the disruption and cost of a room addition. Even if the weather doesn't cooperate, just knowing that you have that extra "room" outdoors makes you feel less confined. A tiny room that opens onto outdoor living space doesn't feel tiny anymore, even if the door stays shut.

Figure 2-1:
This deck divides into distinct areas that accommodate a number of different functions.

A deck or patio increases the pleasure of your garden. It brings you closer and makes the garden more accessible. You're likely to spend more time tending plants and keeping the grounds tidy if they're only a few steps away. The more that you observe your plants, the more in tune you become with their growing habits and seasonal changes.

A deck or patio can cover up a garden's problem areas. Every garden has a spot or two where things just don't seem to grow. No problem. Deck that spot or pave it over. You're eliminating an eyesore while preserving the more beautiful parts of your yard at the same time.

Even if you're not an avid gardener, you'd welcome a deck or patio in your yard because it contributes to a low-maintenance landscape. Along with carefully chosen plants, carefree groundcovers, a few walks, and a few container plants, it helps you keep gardening chores to a minimum.

A deck or patio can also solve circulation problems. If strategically located, it consolidates traffic lanes that may require extra walks or paths. On steep sites, a series of cascading deck platforms or small patios eliminates the need for long stair runs, making the yard more accessible and inviting. A patio or deck overcomes bottlenecks where several paths converge, such as at the back door.

Decks and patios aren't just practical; they can be stunningly beautiful. They create an opportunity to combine rich colors, appealing textures, interesting forms, pleasing shapes, and lovely lines into a showpiece of garden design or an architectural enhancement of the house itself. A deck or patio doesn't need to make a bold design statement. The most successful designs are often understated structures of elegant simplicity.

Another bonus of a deck or patio is how much value it adds to a home: a return of around 70 percent to 80 percent of the deck or patio's original cost — and often much higher. A home advertised as a "3BR, 2BA home with 2,000 square feet of living space and 1,200 square feet of decking" has much to offer. Resale value should never be a reason for building your patio or deck in the first place, but it is a nice bonus to the pleasure payoff. Plan your deck or patio project with your own long-term enjoyment in mind, and consider the return on your investment just another of its many benefits.

Evaluating Your Proposed Location

After you complete a preliminary design, ask yourself how well the goose-egg location of your deck or patio works. It probably works fine. You considered a great many factors in choosing it and you aren't likely to discover a major oversight at this point. Nevertheless, a thorough evaluation of this site is worthwhile because you gain valuable information for planning the size, shape, and other details of your deck or patio. Besides, making changes on paper is easier and cheaper than needing to rebuild or abandon an unsatisfactory project. Use the following guidelines as a checklist for your evaluation.

General considerations

As you analyzed your property and arranged your goose eggs, you became familiar with most of the following criteria. (See Chapter 1 for more information.) The following list, which adapts those criteria to deck and patio locations, gives you an opportunity to evaluate your site even more closely:

✔ **Views.** If you're designing a raised deck, make sure that you evaluate views from the same position and eye level that you plan to occupy on the finished deck. Of course, looking out a window or door that opens onto the deck site, especially if the view is straight ahead, gives you a strong clue. But if you're counting on oblique or partially hidden views, such as the one in Figure 2-2, find a tall-enough ladder or scaffold to verify the best site for capturing them. You may also discover an eyesore that you need to screen out.

Figure 2-2:
This deck makes accessible a view that was partially hidden by nearby trees before the deck was built.

✔ **Privacy.** Again, a raised deck can create surprises. If your yard is surrounded by six-foot-tall fences, it probably feels private and secure, but a deck three feet off the ground suddenly puts you onstage. Adequate screening would need to be eight or nine feet tall, which may exceed height restrictions along property lines unless you use trees or shrubs. Ironically, the sense of privacy increases as the deck gets higher, and possibly more visible, because you feel above the world and can screen most of it out by adding a barrier at conventional railing height.

Another privacy problem involves urban backyards surrounded by tall buildings. Here, an overhead screen or wide-spreading tree may be necessary. If so, you must plan it carefully so that it doesn't conflict with limited views, sunlight, or breezes.

✔ **Access.** Is the site convenient to the kitchen? If not, would a kitchen window or other pass-through solve the problem? Is the door wide enough for easy access? Would moving or enlarging the doorway be possible? A design problem for many decks and almost all patios is how to resolve the height difference between floor level and ground level. The most inviting doorway transition is no change in levels at all (except for the threshold and an inch or two drop to keep moisture out), which is easy to attain if you're building a deck at floor level. If you want to drop the deck for privacy or build a patio on the ground, you need to plan stairs or descending platforms. Try to avoid stairs at the door — one step is acceptable if necessary — by planning a landing at floor level. The minimum size requirement for landings is that they be as wide as the staircase or door served and at least three feet deep, but plan your landing as large as possible so that someone can linger without creating congestion (at least six feet by six feet).

Consider, too, access to other parts of the property. A ground-level patio offers unlimited possibilities, but a raised deck requires careful planning. If you plan stairs for a beeline to the garden, what about getting to the garage or side yards? And how does the stair location affect activities and furniture placement on the deck itself? Consider also that outdoor stairs need to be broader, wider, and less steep than indoor stairs, whenever possible, to take advantage of the wide-open spaces and a more relaxed pace. (See Chapters 5, 12, and 21 for more information about stairs.)

✔ **Sun, wind, and rain.** If you live where endless days of balmy sunshine prevail, you have some flexibility in locating your deck. If the weather is blistering, blustery, or blizzardy, you want to squeeze every bit of advantage from the microclimates on your site. (See Chapter 1 for more information about microclimates.) Plan with the seasons in mind. You may expect to use your deck or patio most during the summer, but you may stretch out the enjoyment by adjusting the site to sun and shade patterns for other seasons. For one thing, the long days of summer spread plenty of pleasantness all around. Other seasons are more stingy. And in some regions, because of coastal fog, unbearable summer heat, or other unique conditions, being outdoors in the spring or fall is more comfortable than in the summer.

If you're not ruling out winter altogether, think of sunny decks at ski resorts. You may find that a deck on the south side of your house captures just enough winter sun — especially in February and March — to extend your outdoor living season. If you live in snow country, avoid placing a deck where roof avalanches could pile up and collapse the deck.

Be wary of decks and patios set on the north side of the house. These moss collectors may seem comfortable on hot summer mornings, but on summer evenings, they heat up; during most of the year, they're damp and unappealing. Be equally cautious about placing a patio in a low spot on your property, where chilly air may gravitate. You may solve the problem by incorporating a raised deck or an outdoor fireplace into the design. On the other hand, a raised deck is exposed to prevailing winds and may be undesirable on certain sides of the house. Notice patterns of frost around your yard — where it thaws and evaporates quickly and where it lingers all day.

✔ **Slopes, soils, and drainage.** You can design a deck for virtually any slope, no matter how steep, although the deck may require an engineered structural system. If you plan a patio that depends on a retaining wall to hold back a slope, be aware that a wall more than three feet high sustains tremendous pressures; hire professionals to engineer and construct such walls if you lack experience. Look for suspicious soil conditions anywhere you plan to build, such as fill that may not be compacted correctly or persistent seepage. If you're building over prime top soil, try to use the soil by moving it to other parts of your yard. A patio next to the house must never divert water toward the foundation. Make sure that the ground surrounding a patio site is low enough to accept runoff. If not, you need to install subsurface drainage lines. The ground at a deck site should also slope away from the house. If your deck covers an existing patio, make sure that the patio slopes away from the house. Otherwise, remove it and regrade the site.

✔ **Available space.** Even if your property seems like a sprawling estate, the actual land available for building may be very small. Setbacks, easements, septic tank clearances, traffic paths, buried utilities, and similar obstacles define this "building envelope." Happily, many of these restrictions don't pertain to a patio or ground-hugging deck, although total lot coverage may be an issue. If you're planning a raised deck that aligns with the side of your house, make sure that your community hasn't expanded the setback requirement since you built or bought your home. If your home was built 4 feet from the side property line, for example, and your community now requires a 6- or 10-foot setback, you can't "grandfather" the deck into the old setback alignment just because the house is there without first obtaining a variance.

✔ **Construction logistics.** Can you get the materials to the job site? For a modest deck, this issue is not significant, but if your project requires tons of patio pavers, a truckload of 20-foot deck boards, or a large backhoe, make sure that the site is accessible. You may need to negotiate access through your neighbor's yard, clean out your cluttered garage, or remove some fence panels and sacrifice a flower bed or two. Builders have been known to transport lumber through the house or hoist pallets of stone over the roof using a rented crane. Interestingly, the heaviest material to transport and place is also the easiest — concrete — thanks to pump trucks with long hoses or booms. If your project involves extensive excavating or grading, you can rent a very small tractor, complete with front loader and backhoe, that's only three feet wide.

Specific situations

Some locations present unique challenges or opportunities for designing and building a patio or deck. Check the following list for your location to see whether you haven't yet considered any of these design issues:

✔ **Attached or not?** Consider how future remodeling plans may affect an attached deck or patio. May a kitchen remodel change door and window locations? May a room addition encroach on the patio or deck? May new French doors off the master bedroom or a new chimney for a fireplace affect the deck? Consider also how a second-floor deck or a deck over basement windows may darken the rooms below. Look for gas or electric meters, utility chases, downspouts, exhaust vents, an air conditioning unit, and similar obstacles that could interfere with attaching your deck to the house. Does the roof overhang provide enough headroom for a raised deck?

✔ **Backyard.** Most decks and patios end up in the backyard. Besides construction logistics (as I describe in the preceding section), you usually find no particular drawbacks to this location and a great many advantages. If the side yards have better views or solar exposure, however, and you chose the backyard only because of available space, you may figure out a way to bend your deck or patio around the corner to take advantage of these benefits. If your backyard has a patio or deck that you want to replace, don't overlook the "two-fer" option: two decks or patios (or one each) for the effort of one. In other words, spruce up the old one, build a new one elsewhere, and link them with a nice path or stairway.

✔ **Grotto.** A shady grove or secret nook is perfect for a small, intimate patio or deck. If you have such a site, try to preserve its charm and utilize the least attractive parts of it. A natural clearing may seem like the logical place to build a patio, for example, but you may get better results by pruning some trees and fitting a low deck among them.

✔ **Steep sites.** Decks on steep sites present several design challenges. Footings must be deeper than for level sites and, for certain soil conditions, must be tied together at grade level with a grid of reinforced concrete beams (check local building requirements). Access between the deck and the ground below may not be possible except by stairs directed back toward the upper slope or, in extreme cases, through the house. The underside of the deck, unless it has an elegant structural system, is not very attractive. Camouflage or conceal it with lattice, plants, trees, or similar screens. Avoid solid enclosures unless they blend with the siding of the house.

✔ **Small spaces.** If you need to shoehorn a patio or deck into a small space, you can use design tricks to create the illusion of greater space. The deck or patio itself must be a minimum size (see the following section, "Considering Size"). One trick is to manipulate scale. Choose small, modular surface materials, such as brick, tile, or narrow deck boards. Use delicate furniture of modest proportions (chairs with low backs, for example). Plant flowers and shrubs in small containers and choose small, fine-textured plants. Another trick is to create a path to nowhere — a path that dead-ends around a corner but gives the illusion of leading to some distant place. Minimize the effect of tall fences and walls by attaching lattice or other visual distractions to the lower portion and leaving the upper portion blank.

✔ **Vast spaces.** Most sites don't have this problem, but if your deck or patio is open to unbounded vistas, you must design it to keep the space from overwhelming it. You can solve this problem by keeping the deck or patio at human scale (unlimited space doesn't mean unlimited deck or patio size) and by defining areas with simple borders, low walls or railings, clustered furniture arrangements, plants, and overheads.

✔ **Swimming pool.** If your yard has a pool or you intend to install one, you must decide whether the swimming pool is a dominant or subordinate element of your design. If it's the centerpiece, plan the paving and landscaping features so that they're balanced around it. If you desire a less formal arrangement or don't want the pool to overpower your yard, locate the patio or deck so that it becomes the focal point instead. A common problem with pools surrounded by patios is the large expanse of unrelieved space, which can be broken up by planters, overheads, changes in deck level, and contrasting textures and colors.

Safety is another issue. Your yard may already be fenced, but if you have toddlers, you should place an additional fence between the house and pool. A patio that functions as your main family gathering place should also be close to the house, not poolside.

✔ **Side yard.** A side yard, which presents the same design challenges as other small spaces (see the paragraph on small spaces earlier in this list), is a perfect location for a secondary deck or patio. Side yards tend to be thoroughfares, so you must account for unobstructed traffic lanes, but you may find space for a private sitting area off a bedroom or bathroom. Setback or lot-line requirements may restrict your design, especially if you plan a tall fence or overhead, but bushes, vines, and other plants may provide sufficient privacy or shade.

✔ **Front yard.** Backyards aren't necessarily the best location for decks and patios. Views, sun patterns, or a convenient kitchen may beckon you to the front yard instead. The main design challenge for an entry patio, enclosed courtyard, or front deck is privacy. Walls and solid fences block noise and create privacy, but they may block desirable views or be restricted by zoning laws. If your property is above street level, a low screen should be adequate for privacy. Make sure that a sheltered courtyard doesn't provide a hiding place for intruders by installing a security gate or restricting all access completely except through the house. An option for small front yards is to gate the driveway and include it as part of a patio. To soften the effect, plant groundcover in driveway cracks or replace the paving with turf blocks (pavers that have open grids for planting grass or groundcovers, which are designed for traffic).

✔ **Balcony or rooftop.** Balconies and rooftop decks, perched above the cares of the world, claim delightful but challenging locations. You must integrate both into the structure of the house, and both require careful planning. Although some balconies are small enough to hang from the house wall, primarily as decoration, most require joists installed between the existing floor joists. Thus, the floor joists must run at a right angle to, not parallel with, the wall intended for the balcony location. A roof, which is usually designed for loads of only 15 to 30 pounds per square foot (psf), isn't strong enough to support a rooftop deck or patio unless you reinforce the rafters and supporting walls to support 40 to 50 psf. Rooftop decks also require roofing membranes durable enough for the extra wear and tear and a sloped surface for adequate drainage. Plumbing vents and chimneys must be at least 10 feet away from the deck. Finally, if you're planning a balcony or rooftop deck near a property line, you need to check your community's setback requirements to see whether they've changed since your home was built. (See the paragraph on available space in the preceding section.)

Considering Size

Location, size, and shape are interrelated elements of design and can influence each other. After you establish the location for your deck or patio, you may find that certain site conditions, such as a setback or swimming pool, dictate some of its dimensions, lines, or angles. As you consider size and shape in greater detail, they, in turn, may influence the final location. Design is a fluid process (or, more accurately, a juggling act).

As for size, you have no fast rules except the Goldilocks rule: "not too large, not too small, but just right." Use the following principles to find the just-right size:

- As a rule, make outdoor living spaces slightly larger than equivalent indoor rooms intended for the same use. If your family room is 18 feet by 22 feet in size, for example, a deck or patio for similar activities should be approximately 20 by 24 feet, or 480 square feet. If a breakfast nook is 10 feet square, a 12-foot-square deck or patio is just large enough for the same function.

- Patio furniture, which is designed for leisure living, tends to be slightly larger than indoor furniture.

- Use the standard dimensions and clearances shown in Figure 2-3 as a guide for planning specific areas.

- Plan with furniture arrangements and traffic paths in mind to ensure enough room for them. If these areas, combined, result in a sprawling parking lot, break it up by using planters, alcoves, dividers, benches, and so on. (See the following section, "Considering Shape," for more information.)

- Consider the size of your home and yard and design accordingly to keep your deck or patio in scale (see Figure 2-4). A large home may overwhelm a small deck or patio, even if the latter's large enough for its purpose. A small home may make a comfortably-sized design feel inappropriately large. Avoid "wall-to-wall" decks and patios that span the entire back of the home. They feel out of proportion. (For information about proportion and scale, see Chapter 3.)

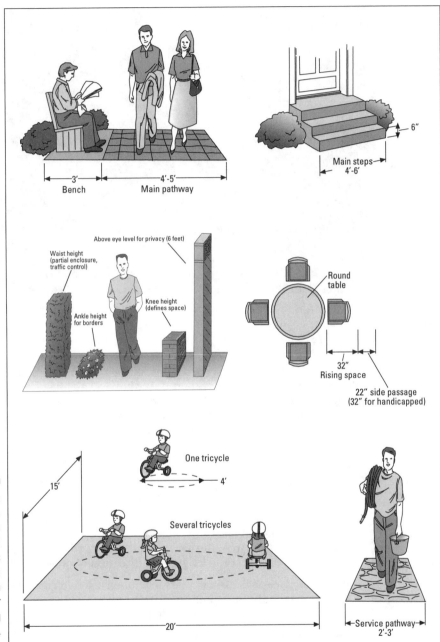

6″

Main steps
4′-6′

3′
Bench

4′-5′
Main pathway

Above eye level for privacy (6 feet)

Waist height
(partial enclosure,
traffic control)

Knee height
(defines space)

Ankle height
for borders

Round
table

32″
Rising space

22″ side passage
(32″ for handicapped)

One tricycle

4′

15′

Several tricycles

20′

Service pathway
2′-3′

Figure 2-3:
These
dimensions
and
clearances
help you
plan
outdoor
living
spaces.

Figure 2-4:
The size of
this patio is
appropriate
for the size
of the home
and yard.

Considering Shape

Now the fun begins. Squares, rectangles, curves, zigzags, L shapes, T shapes, angles, circles, free-forms — you probably have a kaleidoscope of shapes swirling around in your head. The choices may seem unlimited and bewildering but you already have some strong clues for finding the best shape for your patio or deck. Site conditions, furniture arrangements, access points, and your own preferences give you a starting point. The size and shape of a courtyard patio or of a deck tucked into the alcove of a U-shaped house, for example, are defined by the walls that enclose it. Use the following suggestions for additional clues to define the rest of the shape:

- ✔ Align the sides of your deck or patio with existing features. The house probably defines at least one edge. A swimming pool, jogs in fence lines, a prominent tree, the garage wall, doors, windows, and similar features may suggest the length and direction of other sides.

- ✔ If your landscape is formal, plan a symmetrical deck or patio laid out along a clear axis, or center line. Use an eye-catching focal point, such as a swimming pool or remarkable tree, to define the axis.

- ✔ Employ a modular grid to define edges and shapes. Formal designs have a strong grid pattern, often visible as rows of contrasting materials, such as bricks. Informal designs may also employ a less-obvious grid. Base the grid on repetitive features of the house, such as posts that support a porch roof or rows of windows or on 8- or 10-foot modules. Follow the same grid structure in placing planters, benches, indentations, and similar elements.

✔ Look for existing shapes to duplicate or mirror. Most are squares and rectangles, but if your home or yard already has some octagons, triangles, or circles, you may want to carry these patterns into your design. Nature may also suggest shapes. An expansive horizon dominates an ocean view; a long deck railing would mirror that horizon. A curving brook or ditch, on the other hand, may suggest a serpentine shape.

✔ Angles are interesting but should be logical. The angled side of a deck or patio makes sense if it orients you to a breathtaking view, redirects your path to some stairs, or connects two prominent features. Angles also soften corners. Restrict angles to families of 90, 45, and 22$\frac{1}{2}$ degrees or to 90, 60, and 30 degrees.

✔ Consider the effect of shapes. Long lines and rectangles suggest serenity. Zigzags and sharp angles are bold and dramatic but could be disturbing. Curves are restful. Full circles can be restful if you're centered in them, unsettling if you aren't.

✔ Not all decks and patios are regular geometric shapes. Some are free-form, a curved and seemingly random and spontaneous shape. Such shapes blend well into natural settings. Patios lend themselves to this shape more than decks because of construction logistics and the strong rectilinear patterns of decking boards. Most free-form patios are based on some type of elliptical or kidney shape.

✔ Use the principles of proportion and scale to refine the basic shape. (See Chapter 3 for more information.)

As you make sketches and take measurements, you can easily get locked into a plan, or "bird's-eye," perspective. This perspective is necessary for planning and communicating about outdoor spaces, but if you restrict your imagination to this two-dimensional world, you may end up with a deck or patio that's immensely appealing in aerial photographs but isn't a satisfying place to spend time. Architects and designers refer to a "sense of place" as the defining quality of successful design. They're referring not only to the uniqueness of the space, but also to the harmonious blending of all dimensions, perspectives, and senses. Try to visualize yourself in, not above, the spaces that you plan.

Chapter 3

Looking with a Designer's Eye

● ●

● ●

*A*great location, the ideal size, a perfect shape — these three elements give your deck or patio a basic form for you to work with. You may be eager to plan construction details and select materials as soon as you reach this point of your planning, but you'd end up with only a diamond in the rough. Instead, you should look at this basic form with a designer's eye and refine it. What can give your deck or patio a sense of style? What enhances your design and gives it the polish you desire?

This part of designing is fun. You do it all the time. Whether deciding what to wear in the morning, setting the table for guests, arranging furniture, or picking out a new car, you make conscious choices to create the best effect. As with clothing, entertaining, or cars, outdoor design can be as homespun or as sophisticated as you want. Considering the money and care that you invest in your home, you probably want your deck or patio to be as elegant, livable, and enjoyable as possible — which doesn't mean complicated or expensive. Stylish, elegant designs are often very simple (but not simplistic). This chapter can help you find a style that suits your yard, home, and personal taste.

More Than a Floor

Think of your deck or patio not as a platform but as an outdoor room with floor, walls, ceiling, and furnishings. The colors, textures, shapes, dimensions, and proportions of these elements should harmonize with each other.

The decking or paving (the floor) is the largest surface and sets the tone. It can be a dominant feature with bold or contrasting materials to attract the eye or a subtle background element that blends in with the setting. Either way, the deck or patio floor unifies the space and has the same effect as floor coverings in interior rooms. (For detailed information about selecting deck or patio materials, see Chapters 6 and 15.)

The "walls" give a sense of enclosure. Most locations have an existing wall or two, such as a house wall, fence, or adjacent building, that may provide enough privacy and security. Consider how they can fit into your deck or patio design and plan decorative treatments such as lattice screens or plants to soften their effect. You can define walls for the open sides of the patio or deck very loosely by using plants, railings, steps, borders, paving edges, benches, planters, and similar features. In small yards, the transition from patio or deck to lawn is the only "wall" you need. Larger yards or open vistas may require a low wall, bench, railing, or similar barrier to make the patio or deck feel safe and inviting and to frame the views.

For a sensational ceiling, you can't top the wide-open sky. The appeal of most decks and patios depends on it. But "wide-open" and "sensational" can also mean blistering sunshine, stormy skies, or just an uneasy, disquieting immensity. Plan a few patio umbrellas, a canopy of tree branches, or an overhead structure to relieve such effects. These features can be as open and airy or as closed and protecting as you want. As with the floor and walls, consider how these overhead elements fit into the overall design.

Using the Formal Elements of Design

"I don't know anything about design, but I know what I like" is a common response to formal design. Indeed, you don't need to memorize an encyclopedia of design terms to have some basic tools for refining your deck or patio plan. The following sections cover a few of the time-honored design principles that you can use to refine your design. Some of these principles pertain to your basic design, others to your choices of materials and details. Although you don't have the training and experience to use these principles as skillfully as a professional designer, you certainly do have familiarity with the site and the time for testing ideas.

Unity

A well-designed deck or patio feels as if it "belongs." A logical location, comfortable size, and suitable shape contribute to this feeling, but colors, textures, overall style, and finish details enhance it. Choose a deck finish that matches or complements the house colors. Choose patio materials that reflect patterns and textures in the house. Outline the patio or deck with flower beds, contrasting paving materials, or a gravel border to create a clean, crisp look. Soften abrupt transitions and sharp corners with plants. As you observe yards that you enjoy, notice which features make a deck or patio fit in with the house and yard (see Figure 3-1).

The overall style of a patio or deck, whether formal or informal, traditional or modern, should also be unified with its surroundings. If your home has a casual, relaxed feeling to it, a free-form patio or a deck with lively angles and transitions would fit in. If your home is formal in style, a symmetrical deck or patio is more appropriate. The materials, colors, and textures should also be uniform and regular, not meandering or random.

Figure 3-1:
The colors, lines, forms, and scale of this deck blend with elements of the house and garden to create a unified whole.

Proportion and scale

How large is too large? Size is relative. Your deck or patio design may be ideal for outdoor living but it could be out of *scale* (too large or too small for the setting) or one of its dimensions or features may be out of *proportion* (ratio of a part to the whole).

You can evaluate proportion and scale in several ways. The first and most important test is human scale, to which you've already given some thought. People require a predictable amount of space for standing, sitting, reclining, stretching, reaching, strolling, and so on, as well as for more abstract needs such as security, intimacy, and autonomy. Designers use standard dimensions, for example, to plan spaces for such activities as reclining (seven feet by three feet, or 21 square feet), dining (eight square feet for a table and four chairs), passage (a two- to three-foot width), or parties (18 square feet per person, or 450 square feet for 25 people). (See Figure 2-3, showing standard clearances and dimensions, in Chapter 2.) Smaller dimensions than these don't work; larger dimensions may work but don't "feel right." (Why isn't anyone at this party?)

Another test for scale and proportion is to compare the size of your deck or patio with surrounding features, such as the house, a lawn, a swimming pool, or a large tree. Use scale drawings to help you visualize relative sizes or take photos of the site and superimpose cutout shapes over them. Or, using stakes and strings, plot the outline of your project on the site and view it from different angles.

If you want a more objective measurement for testing proportion, use the *golden mean*. This 5:7 ratio, used in Classical design, fixes the ideal dimensions of a rectangle (five feet of width for every seven feet of length) but is also useful for determining other relationships. If the back of your house is 35 feet wide, for example, make an attached deck or patio 25 feet wide and approximately 18 feet deep. (To calculate the 5:7 ratio, divide the larger number by 7 and multiply that answer by 5.) An overhead shade structure for this deck would cover 18 feet of the 25-foot width and be approximately 13 feet high (13:18 = approximately 5:7). These proportions don't always work — the 13-foot height, for example, may be excessive for the roof height of the house — but they give you another tool for testing your design.

Because proportion and scale depend more on perception than on actual dimensions, you can use many visual tricks to expand or diminish a sense of space. Small decks and patios, for example, look larger if the design is simple and uncluttered. Use small-dimensioned paving, such as brick, tile, or narrow deck boards. Plan the foreground, middle ground, and background plants so that their overall sizes increase toward the distance and the foliage becomes increasingly fine-textured.

Large decks and patios lend themselves to grand design: broad stairs, generous-sized planters, multiple levels or activity areas, and large-scale furniture. Plan the direction of decking boards to your best advantage. Boards laid across the line of vision shorten perceived distances; boards laid in the same direction as the line of vision magnify the straight-ahead view and make the deck seem narrower. Vary the direction of boards to define different parts of a deck and break up the space.

Color

Color is a strong design element. Interior decorators find that color is the first thing you perceive as you enter a room and that it leaves the most lasting impression. For outdoor spaces, nature sets the tone, so earth colors and neutrals, such as tans, grays, browns, and terra-cotta hues, are always appropriate for a deck or patio. Choose colors that blend with your house or, if the deck or patio is clearly part of the home's architecture, use exact house colors to reinforce the connection visually.

If you're familiar with formal color principles, such as complementary schemes, you can make use of them to plan.

In choosing colors for patio materials and deck finishes, consider glare and heat absorption. A dark patio exposed to direct sunshine can become unbearably hot in the summer (but may be comfortable in winter). The effect is not as severe with decks, because wood doesn't retain heat as well as masonry does. A light-colored patio or deck may produce too much glare, both outside and inside the house.

Contrast

Contrast is another powerful design element (see Figure 3-2). Decks and patios are large surfaces that benefit from contrasting colors, shapes, and materials. A gray concrete patio with a brick border, a deck finished with two different stain or paint colors, a flagstone patio bordered by a bed of red flowers, and a brick patio with a wooden retaining wall are all examples of the use of contrast. The trick is to keep things in check (remember unity?). Too much contrast creates chaos. Use high contrast, which is most effective if you use it sparingly, to accent one or two focal points. A white statue in a garden dominated by green, for example, or a white railing around a nicely shaped deck are effective focal points.

Figure 3-2:
Light and
dark colors
contrast
nicely in
this patio.

Coming to Your Senses

Think about all your senses — sights, sounds, smells, and body comfort — as you refine your design. (See Chapter 1 for more information on sensual experiences and comfort.) If unwanted noises plague your site, plan a fountain or a small pond and waterfall to provide a constantly soothing background sound. Plan birdbaths and feeders to attract songbirds. Consider building a solid wall or fence just high enough to block out noises at patio or deck level. Such a barrier must extend to the ground and not have any openings.

If persistent breezes spoil a sunny location, plan a windbreak. The most effective design is a baffle that breaks up the wind rather than a solid barrier that may cause irritating eddies behind it. If your patio or deck location is chronically cool, plan dark paving to absorb the sun's heat. Plan a covered, protected area of the patio, maybe with a fireplace, as a refuge for chilly evenings. If temperatures are likely to swing to the other extreme, plan shade trees and sun shades. Orient them toward the southwest, west, and northwest sides of the space, where they can shield it from the afternoon sun.

As you plan flowers and plants, choose some for their fragrance. Use the following list for ideas to start your own. Consult with your local nursery or plant supplier to select those plants that are the most suitable for your area.

- Bay laurel
- Citrus
- Daylily *(Hemerocallis)*
- Dianthus
- English lavender
- Iris
- Jasmine
- Lily
- Peony
- Phlox
- Rose varieties noted for their fragrance, especially heritage roses such as the apothecary's rose *(Rosa gallica,* "Officianalis"), the Bourbon roses, and others
- Rosemary
- Sage
- Wormwood
- Yarrow *(Achillea millefolium)*

The visual effect of the design also goes a long way toward making the area a comfortable place to be. Unity, harmony, smooth transitions, and similar characteristics of good design are more than visual tricks; they create a sense of well-being. Pay attention to details. Avoid sharp edges, distracting eyesores, surfaces that may seem especially hard or slippery, low overheads, unobstructed views of work that you need to do, and other disquieting features.

Historical and Regional Connections

Designers have been creating beautiful outdoor living spaces for centuries in places as widespread as Egypt, Japan, and England. You're not likely to re-create Spain's Alhambra or Canada's Buchert Gardens in your own yard, but you can borrow elements from a particular regional or historical style that you admire. Japanese gardens, for example, have distinctive characteristics that many American gardeners capture in their designs. English cottage gardens, French formal gardens, and Mediterranean courtyards (see Figure 3-3) are other examples of distinctive styles. The United States is home to several distinct regional styles.

Figure 3-3:
This patio reflects a Mediterranean heritage.

Of course, your own home, yard, and neighborhood define much of your deck or patio's style. If your neighborhood has a strong unifying character, you shouldn't deviate far from it. If it has a wide variety of styles, as most do, you may want to use elements from the following list of selected styles to suggest a particular design heritage.

The following list of garden styles, although not definitive, captures some of the distinctive characteristics of each style that might be useful in planning your own patio or deck:

- **Japanese/Asian:** Serene; minimalist; groomed greenery; patios of gray stone; natural wood; decks with clean, simple lines, either stained dark or painted gray (sometimes black); use of natural objects for focal point; skillful use of contrast; balanced but asymmetrical.

- **English:** Patios made of brick or quarried stone; profuse flowers; intimate sitting areas.

- **French:** Symmetrical, formal; often arranged around a central fountain or circular planting bed; brick, gravel, white flowers.

- ✔ **Mediterranean:** Stone; earth colors; dry but diverse plantings; Classical influences (columns, sculptures, balustrades); sense of permanence.

- ✔ **Eastern U.S.:** Patios or decks abutting the house; patio materials include brick, limestone, bluestone, granite; large, deciduous shade trees; few shade structures.

- ✔ **Southern U.S.:** Extensive shade structures; tropical or humidity-loving plants; swimming pool; brick; formal, with Classical or French (New Orleans) influence; decks of cypress or pressure-treated pine.

- ✔ **Western U.S.:** Natural feeling; open space; extensive use of wood, logs; decks over steep slopes; indigenous plants; planters and flower boxes.

- ✔ **Southwestern U.S.:** Drought-resistant landscaping; walls, arbors to create feeling of courtyard; burnt-orange, pink, and terra-cotta colors; extensive use of colored concrete and stucco-covered block; ceramic tile; swimming pools; fountains; bold with large spaces; shade structures.

- ✔ **Northwestern U.S.:** Deciduous and evergreen forested look; profuse flowers: roses, rhododendrons, azaleas, tulips; Japanese influence; gravel and boulders placed among plants and paved areas; the garden and nature dominate; small shelters to protect from rain.

Add-Ons, Options, and Features

Designing a new deck or patio can be like buying a new car. After you decide on the basic model, size, and color, you can choose optional features. The best time to plan for them is now, before you build the deck or patio, to make sure that they fit into your design. The lists of options in the following sections help you decide on your own list.

Cooking and food preparation

Even if your deck or patio is only steps from the kitchen, you probably want at least an outdoor grill, as shown in Figure 3-4. Locate it away from traffic areas and downwind from windows and doors. Don't place the grill inside an unvented enclosure or under low-hanging tree branches. Avoid placing a charcoal grill on a deck unless the grill has at least two feet of clearance all around and the deck surface is protected by bricks or similar fireproof materials. Portable gas grills are more versatile. Although they can stand alone, gas grills are more attractive and easier to use if you set them into a permanent enclosure with countertops close at hand (see Chapter 24). Avid cooks may prefer a complete barbecue unit with a large fire pit, a grill that you can raise and lower, a rotisserie, and a smoker for meats and fish.

For more remote locations, such as a poolside patio, consider a minikitchen, complete with sink, grill, counters, cabinets, and a refrigerator. Protect it from rain and snow with an overhead structure and plan at least one wall behind it — or at least provide weatherproof enclosures for the cabinets and appliances. Use tile or similar durable materials for countertops. Plan the location of plumbing, electrical wiring, and gas lines carefully before you build the patio or deck.

Lighting

Lighting is necessary for the safety and usability of your deck or patio and contributes to its overall ambiance. At the bare minimum, plan lighting for doorways, stairs, and main traffic areas, and whatever else local building codes may require. Avoid floodlights or harsh overhead fixtures, which cause glare and ruin a sense of intimacy with the outdoor setting. A low-voltage landscape lighting system is perfect for most deck and patio needs. Such a system enables you to place fixtures in many strategic locations, especially close to the ground where they can illuminate stairs, paths, and plants in soft pools of light. For interesting effects, use strings of minilights to accentuate trees and outline deck railings. Use 120-volt (standard house voltage) lights for doorways and cooking areas. For information about selecting and installing lighting equipment, see Chapter 25.

Electrical outlets

Plan at least one electrical receptacle, ideally as close to the cooking area as possible. It must be protected with a ground-fault circuit interrupter (GFCI) and a moisture-proof cover. (Check with your local building department for other electrical code requirements.) An outdoor outlet is fairly easy to install on the exterior wall of your home or garage, where you can tap into an outdoor light fixture or interior general-purpose circuit. For remote locations, plan to run underground wiring. Use cable designated UF and buried at least 12 inches deep (providing the circuit rating does not exceed 20 amps), or run Type TW or THW wire through a metal or plastic conduit buried at least 12 or 18 inches deep, respectively. You must enclose wires in a metal conduit where they emerge from the ground, and all conduit connectors must be liquid-tight.

Stereo speakers

The main considerations for planning outdoor speakers (besides choosing what to play) are location, weather, and independent volume control. If you place the speakers near the house, avoid aiming them toward nearby neighbors' houses. By using compact outdoor speakers designed for direct weather exposure, you can place them anywhere, such as in an arbor or tree, where you can direct them downward toward the patio or deck. Run wires along deck joists, fences, railings, garden walls, and similar paths. Avoid cutting corners or suspending them overhead, where they're too conspicuous. Wireless speakers also are an option. Some music systems have an independent volume control for remote speakers. Others have only an on-off switch, but you can attach a separate volume control to the wires running to the outdoor speakers.

Make sure that you check with your neighbors for an acceptable volume level. The sound from your music system should *not* be heard within their homes.

Water faucets

Plan at least one hose bibb that's easy to reach from your deck or patio for watering plants and cleaning. (See Chapter 25 for information about irrigation systems.) If you're attaching a deck to the house that requires relocating an existing hose bibb, extend it to the outside edge of the deck where it's convenient to the garden as well. If you plan a cooking center or a potting bench, include a sink and faucet with at least cold water. Drain the sink directly to the garden or a gravel "dry well," unless you intend to dispose of food scraps or wash dishes in the sink. For climates with freezing winters, install a drain-down valve to drain water from all exposed pipes before winter.

Spas

Spas are available in a wide range of shapes, sizes, installation formats, and prices. If you price a spa, figure the added costs of utility hookups, fences, safety equipment, privacy screens, lighting, maintenance, freeze protection, and similar necessities.

Consult the manufacturer's specifications and local codes for installation requirements.

Plan the spa location for convenient barefoot access to the bedroom and bathroom areas of the house. Make sure that the surrounding patio surface is a nonslippery material that slopes away from the spa at a quarter of an inch per foot. If you live in snow country, don't place the spa directly under the roof eaves. Avoid placing a spa near tall plants that shed leaves, needles, seeds, or pods. If you intend to use the spa frequently, keep it away from beds of plants that spilled water may damage. Instead, use containers that you can move or repot easily.

You can install spas in the ground or above ground. Plan an in-ground installation where water doesn't drain into the spa from surrounding areas. Make sure that the spa's excavation doesn't interrupt underground utility lines (a wise precaution for any project that involves digging). Avoid placing the spa under a tree, where roots may cause problems. You can integrate above-ground spas into their setting by using low walls, platforms, or low benches.

A deck spa requires careful planning. Decks are designed to support 40 to 50 pounds per square foot (psf), but a spa filled with water and bathers weighs approximately 200 psf. Try to set the spa into the deck so that it can rest on a concrete slab or a sand base on the ground. Otherwise, consult an architect or structural engineer about the best way to reinforce the deck to support the spa.

If the spa is a focal point of your design, you can dress it up with a gazebo, pavilion, or overhead shade structure. If you prefer that the spa blend into its surroundings, screen it from view, disguise it with a low wall that matches the patio paving, or surround it with rocks, plants, and a waterfall to resemble a natural pool.

In addition to the spa itself, consider the support equipment (pump, filter, air blower, heater, and so on). Follow all manufacturer's recommendations. Most suggest locating the equipment within 10 to 15 feet of the spa and as close as possible to the same level as the spa floor. Plan a weatherproof enclosure with a concrete floor and easy access. Garage locations have special requirements, including a wall between the parking area and the spa equipment and a separate door for the equipment. If the spa is a portable unit with the equipment built into it, all you need to provide are utility lines and unobstructed access to the equipment.

Fountains and pools

Water features range from small, wall-hung fountains that you can order out of a catalog to large ponds full of aquatic plants and exotic fish. Because water attracts the eye and splashing water is a soothing sound, any water feature is likely to become the focal point of your patio or deck (see Figure 3-5). You can make a small fountain of your own design out of almost any material imaginable, from bamboo buckets to cast-off cattle troughs, or create a very small pond by using a polyvinyl chloride (PVC) liner. You need a pump to circulate the water and, for ponds, a filter to keep it clean. Most small pumps are submersible units with an intake opening built into them and an outlet to which you attach a pipe or tubing. You can create a trickle, a spill, or a spray arrangement. Locate an electrical outlet with GFCI protection close to the fountain. Have landscaping professionals design and install large pools or ponds.

If your patio or deck is a formal design, place the fountain or pool along the central axis. Squares, octagons, and circles are excellent shapes for such features. Informal designs permit looser arrangements, such as a free-form pond and waterfall in a natural setting or a classical fountain placed under an arbor. Include underwater lighting in your pool plan. Make sure that you fence the pond or pool area to prevent toddlers from wandering in.

Figure 3-5: The spa is clearly the focal point of this deck.

Overheads

Don't let sun, wind, or rain spoil your patio parties. Plan a roof. Overhead structures vary, from wispy frameworks that barely suggest protection to massive, retractable roofs. Most are a criss-cross design of increasingly smaller structural members intended for shade or pure decoration.

You need to consider several factors in designing an overhead. Overall size should be in proportion to the deck or patio. (See the section "Proportion and scale" earlier in this chapter for more information.) Plan about 8 feet of headroom (the overall height often being 12 to 20 inches higher), but consider the direction and angle of the sun to make sure that it doesn't dip below the overhead during hot summer afternoons or become blocked by the overhead during short winter days. (See Chapter 2 for more information on evaluating the location of your deck and patio and how sun and shade may affect it.)

Most overheads consist of vertical posts holding up beams that, in turn, support rafters covered by an open framework or solid roofing. Each of these elements offers many design options. The posts can be single pieces of lumber, built-up assemblies of lumber, round columns, pipes, concrete cylinders, or boxlike structures covered with stucco or wood siding. The screening material can be lattice, lath, 2-by lumber set on edge, fabric, shade cloth, clear plastic panels, woven reeds, or deciduous vines. Choose a design, colors, and materials that blend with your overall design. For construction details and more design options, see Chapter 22.

Storage

Storage is necessary for comfortable outdoor living, but it tends to be an afterthought in the design process (if you consider it at all). Many items that you use outdoors you can store in the garage or basement, such as seasonal patio furniture, but some things need permanent storage space near the deck or patio. These include barbecue equipment, spa or swimming-pool gear, outdoor toys, sports gear, hoses, gardening tools, and so on.

By thinking about such needs during the design process, you can work large storage units into your plan. A shed or free-standing cabinet, for example, can act as part of a privacy screen. Built-in benches can accommodate storage space for cushions or toys. A low cabinet attached to the house wall can double as storage and counter space. If your yard lacks a strong focal point, plan a decorative or whimsical shed — a reproduction of a Japanese teahouse, for example — to double as an eye-catcher and storage space.

The unused area below a deck is particularly suited for storage, especially pipes, lumber, bricks, roof gutters, firewood, and other bulky items. Store objects above the ground, protect them from rain and snow, and block them from view with screens or plants. (See Chapter 23 for more information about storage.)

Furniture

Outdoor furniture vies with interior furnishings for design appeal . . . and prices. Your options are more varied than ever before. Visit showrooms and patio-furniture outlets early in the planning process to see what's available. Besides price and design appeal, consider size, durability, movability, and versatility. Large, heavy items are appropriate if you plan separate dining areas, conversation areas, and lounging areas, where furniture has a permanent home. If your design requires adapting the same space to different uses or you plan to store the furniture during winter, choose light, portable styles. Consider heat retention. A black wrought-iron chair that's been sitting in the sun all day is anything but comfortable. Make sure that legs or feet are broad enough not to lodge in cracks between deck boards or patio paving. Consult with your furniture dealer about maintenance and durability. You can scrub or hose off most quality furniture. Some is vulnerable to rust, and some species of wood furniture don't weather gracefully and must be refinished every year.

Plan built-in benches as space dividers and backup seating. As with outdoor furniture, the choices are abundant, from prefabricated park benches made from cast concrete or stone slabs to one-of-a-kind designs to match existing features of the site. (See Chapters 12 and 21 for design and construction information.)

Softscaping

Patios, decks, and other structures are the "hardscape" features of a landscape design; plants are the "softscape." The two elements harmonize and interact with each other much as dancers do. You have many ways to work plants into your deck or patio design, from a few low-maintenance containers to a completely integrated scheme of permanent planting beds. (Where does the patio stop and the garden begin?) The following tips can help you decide where to put the plants:

- ✔ **Use plants for screens.** Plant a leafy vine or mass of dense shrubs for a privacy screen or to block an undesirable view.

- ✔ **Use plants to make walls interesting.** Conceal or break up a monotonous wall or fence with vines, espaliered trees, shrubs, and flowers.

✔ **Use plants to divide the patio or deck into areas.** Leave open spaces between deck sections or blocks of paving or build raised planters to define areas.

✔ **Use plants to smooth transitions.** Edges and corners seem unnatural in a garden setting. Use plants to conceal or soften the transition lines between house and deck, between patio and lawn, between the deck and the ground.

✔ **Use plants to unify your design.** Tie your deck or patio to the garden by using a few of the same plants.

✔ **Use plants for accents.** Plants provide a spot of color here, an interesting form there, a pleasant distraction elsewhere. Use plants to bring variety and interest to your design. Start with container plants, which you can move around and experiment with.

✔ **Use plants to create perspective.** Create "compositions" of foreground, middle ground, and background by strategically placing tall, medium, and short plants in appropriate locations. One "composition" is sufficient for a small yard, but two or three such arrangements in a larger yard keep areas distinct from one another.

Plants are dynamic. They grow and change with the seasons and require maintenance. They also require specific growing conditions, such as sunlight and shade. Finally, they offer unlimited varieties of color, texture, form, size, and fragrance. With so many variables to consider, how can you choose what to plant? Use the following tips to help you decide which plants to use:

✔ **Define the purpose of each planting bed or other plant location.** Do you need tall, bunched plants for a privacy screen? A broad tree for shade? An interesting mix of colors and textures for decoration? A medium-sized plant to establish middle ground? By defining the purpose of plants, you can specify their characteristics (how tall, how wide, how dense, how colorful, how fast- or slow-growing, and so on).

✔ **Identify the growing conditions of each planting area.** Does the area receive morning sun, afternoon sun, partial sun; can plants grow in containers or open beds; is the soil moist, dry, fast- or slow-draining; can you provide irrigation?

✔ **Determine the level of care you're willing to give.** Roses need pruning and fussing; ivy doesn't. Some trees shed leaves or needles that need constant sweeping. Some annuals need only a squirt of water now and then and that's all. Choose plants that match your level of enthusiasm.

✔ **Steal shamelessly.** Ideas, that is. You don't need to study horticulture for four years to figure out what to plant. Take a walk around your neighborhood with a notepad, cheery smile, and perhaps a plant book. Talk to people. Ask questions. If your patio or deck site is sunny, stay on the sunny side of the street. Take the same notebook into town and see what's planted at restaurants, shops, plazas, and — of course — nurseries.

✔ **Consult plant lists.** Gardening books, CD-ROMs, Web sites, garden clubs, and similar venues abound with plant lists tailored to specific criteria, such as geographic region and plant characteristics. Determine your criteria for a particular plant (for example, tree, deciduous, umbrella-shaped, 20 feet tall, no seeds or pods, fast-growing, adapted to your climate zone), search for lists that include those criteria, and note any plants that show up in all the relevant lists.

Wheelchair access

At some time or other, almost everyone experiences limited mobility because of aging, accidents, pregnancy, disease, or needing to carry a piano into the house. Make your deck or patio as accessible as possible by eliminating obstacles or providing an alternative to stairs. Gardens and outdoor living areas are especially suitable for gentle inclines and wide pathways. If your deck or patio design includes stairs, look at the possibility of adding a wheelchair ramp as a secondary access. By working such a ramp into your design now, you can pour footings or grade the site as you build your deck and then build the ramp itself sometime in the future. Strive for a curving, serpentine design rather than a zigzag, switchback configuration. (Think of you and your friends carrying that piano up the latter.)

The recommended minimum width of a wheelchair ramp is three feet, and the recommended slope is 1:12 (that is, 1 inch of rise for every 12 inches of horizontal run). A 2-foot change in level would require a ramp 24 feet long (as measured along the horizontal run, not along the inclined ramp). No run should be longer than 30 feet without a level resting place at least 5 feet long. You need to protect the downhill edge of the ramp with a continuous railing 32 inches high (36 inches for drop-offs greater than 30 inches). Contact your local county department of human services or a similar agency for updated recommendations.

Chapter 4

From Dreams to Plans

As you design your deck or patio, you need to make sketches, drawings, revisions, and more drawings. Many of these can be a few doodles on some scraps of paper, but sooner or later, you need to make accurate scale drawings. These detailed drawings are necessary for recording site information, visualizing possibilities, testing ideas, communicating about the project, getting a building permit, ordering materials, and guiding construction.

You don't need artistic talent or drafting experience to draw these plans. All you need are a few basic drawing tools, a little practice, and lots of patience. The patience comes in handy after you spend an hour drawing a complete site plan and you realize that the dimensions are off because you drew one of the property lines out of place. Or after you begin elevation drawings (side view) of a perfect deck design, only to discover that the deck covers an access opening to the home's crawlspace that you were hoping it would clear. (Back to the drawing board.) You can minimize such experiences by learning a few tricks of the trade, starting with the right tools.

Putting Ideas on Paper

Computers, cameras, copy machines, and similar equipment have revolutionized the world of design. You can easily find a place for these modern wonders, especially for complex or repetitive tasks, but your most versatile and user-friendly hardware is always a pencil. Together with your imagination and a few basic drawing tools (or a computer; see the accompanying sidebar "What about the computer?"), a pencil is really all the equipment you need — along with some of the items in the following list, of course, several of which you may already have (see Figure 4-1). The others are available at any art supply or full-service office supply store.

- ✔ **Drawing board.** Buy a drawing board large enough for 24-by-36-inch paper. You can make your own board by taping a vinyl sheet to a piece of plywood, but the light weight, flat surface, and smooth edges of a manufactured drawing board make it much easier to store, carry, and use.

- ✔ **Paper.** Ordinary plain paper is fine for sketches and preliminary drawings. Buy a few sheets of 24-by-36-inch drafting paper for a final site plan and for complex deck or patio working drawings. (18-by-24-inch paper is adequate for most decks and patios.)

- ✔ **Tape.** Use masking tape or drafting tape to hold the paper to the board. (Tools glide more easily over these types of tape.)

- ✔ **T-square or parallel rule.** Use an 18- or 24-inch T-square as a straight-edge for drawing horizontal lines or for holding a triangle against to draw vertical and diagonal lines. Hold the T-square firmly with its head flush against the edge of the drawing board. You don't need a T-square, however, if your drawing board has a parallel rule, which glides up and down the board on spring-loaded wires or guide hardware.

Figure 4-1:
You can draw your own plans by using these basic drawing tools.

What about the computer?

A computer is a powerful design tool that you can use in many ways, from making lists to generating complex drawings. Use your word-processing program to make a wish list, an inventory of site conditions, plant lists, a list of contractors, a breakdown of tasks to do, and so on. The computer enables you to easily revise and prioritize these lists.

If you have a spreadsheet program, use it for budgeting and estimating costs. You can also use it — or a scheduling program — to create a detailed construction timeline.

Another use of the computer is for research. CD-ROM programs, for example, can help you select plants, tour famous gardens, or learn about color. If you have access to the Internet, you can research such topics in databases or visit manufacturers' Web sites to find out about products, investigate building techniques, or chat with other gardeners and homeowners about specific questions you may have.

The most sophisticated use of a computer for design involves the use of programs that generate a complete landscape scheme with full working plans. Not only can you create a site plan and "test drive" different arrangements of plants and hardscape features, but you can also have the computer "grow" the plants to show how they may look in a few years. You can also plot the sun's path through the seasons to see where the yard is going to be sunny and shady or play with different combinations of color. More-specialized programs are available for designing specific structures, such as decks. After you finalize a design, the program calculates the materials that you need to build the structure.

The quality and price of this type of design software ranges widely, from 3-D CAD (Computer-Assisted Design) programs costing thousands of dollars and requiring powerful computer systems to relatively inexpensive 2-D programs with limited design flexibility, aimed at the home gardener. Design programs may be worth the cost if you have experience with CAD or graphics applications or you anticipate designing enough projects to justify the learning effort.

In spite of the speed, accuracy, and convenience that a computer can add to the design process, keep in mind that the final results depend on old-fashioned legwork. You have no real substitute for studying your site carefully and clarifying your own needs and capabilities. The more information you input into the program and use for evaluating suggestions, the better the design.

✔ **Architect's scale.** This triangular ruler enables you to draw and read dimensions in scale. Each edge of the ruler is marked in feet and inches according to different scales, such as $1/4$ inch = one foot or $3/8$ inch = one foot. Flat architect's scales double as a straightedge and are easier to read than triangular models but have fewer scales. (Notice that an architect's scale, based on sixteenths-of-an-inch increments, is different from an engineer's scale, which is based on tenths-of-an-inch increments.)

- ✔ **Triangles.** You quickly find yourself drawing most lines by using a triangle. If you have a 45-degree triangle and a 30-/60-degree triangle, you can use one or both to create 15-, 30-, 45-, 60-, 75-, 90-, 105-, 120-, 135-, and 150-degree angles.

- ✔ **Protractor.** Have one in case you need to read or draw any other angles.

- ✔ **Compass.** Use a compass to make circles and curves and to duplicate measurements.

- ✔ **Templates.** By using these plastic patterns, you can draw dozens of common shapes, such as circles, arcs, hexagons, and squares. Some are useful for making symbols to identify callouts. A French curve enables you to link arcs together in Classical proportions.

- ✔ **Pencils, erasers, brush.** Choose medium lead pencils for most work; you can vary the line weights by using different lead sizes. An art gum eraser minimizes smears. Sweep the board with a drafting brush.

- ✔ **Tracing paper.** This semitransparent paper saves teeth-gnashing. It enables you to experiment quickly with repetitive ideas without needing to redraw the entire plan each time . . . and without erasing what may turn out to be the best idea. Just tear off a piece, lay it over your first drawing, and sketch only the changes. Repeat with a fresh piece for each idea.

Growing a Plan

The development of a final site plan includes making drawings at the following stages. (See Chapter 1 for a description of the complete design process.) To develop your plan, follow these steps:

1. **Make a plot plan (see Figure 4-2).**

   Use 24-by-36-inch paper and, depending on the size of your property, draw the lot to $\frac{1}{8}$- or $\frac{1}{4}$-inch scale. This scale means that a property measuring 80 feet by 136 feet (approximately $\frac{1}{4}$ acre) would be 10 inches by 17 inches if drawn at $\frac{1}{8}$-inch scale or 20 inches by 34 inches if drawn at $\frac{1}{4}$-inch scale. Draw the property lines so that they have at least two inches of margin all around for notes and extraneous information. See Chapter 1 for a list of features to include in the plot plan.

2. **Experiment with various arrangements.**

   Lay tracing paper over your plot plan and draw goose eggs to represent the arrangement of activity areas in your yard. If the plot plan is too cumbersome, photocopy the parts of it that you're working on or use the sizing feature on the copy machine to reduce a copy to a manageable size. If the details and notes on your plot plan inhibit free thinking because they show through the tracing paper, make a clutter-free plot plan by tracing only the major features (property lines, house, and so on). To free up thinking, occasionally turn the paper around so that the farthest corner of your property is closest to you and vice versa.

3. Establish a preliminary site plan.

After you have a goose egg plan that you like, the next step is to give form and shape to the proposed features of your landscape scheme. Using the plot plan as a guide, make a scale drawing of only the existing site features that are to remain the same. Then, using tracing paper, experiment with shapes and sizes of the new lawns, flower beds, walks, and so on, including, of course, your new deck or patio. Do not "hard-line" these features into your site plan yet, unless you want to redraw the entire plan over and over as details change (or you're using a computer program).

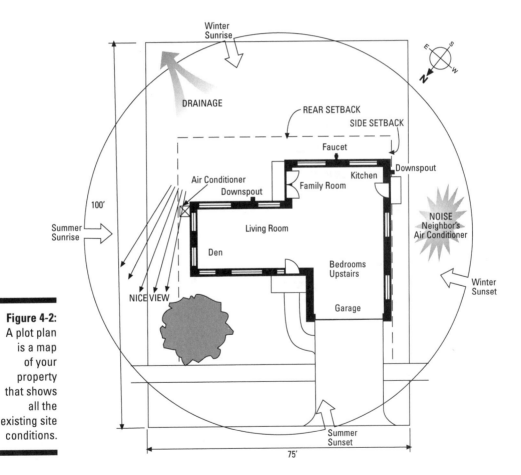

Figure 4-2:
A plot plan is a map of your property that shows all the existing site conditions.

TIP

Tips for avoiding common mistakes

As you make your scale drawings, you should be aware of some common pitfalls to avoid. Some of them seem insignificant, but they can accumulate into major errors or lead to serious design omissions. Observe these tips:

- Show the thickness of fences, house walls, railings, and similar slim features. Standard two-by-four stud walls are five to six inches thick, including siding and finish materials; omitting this dimension skews room sizes and the placement of intersecting walls.

- Show all windows and exterior doors on the main floor.

- Measure windows and doors from jamb to jamb; ignore the casings, or trim.

- Show door swings. Draw an arc showing the movement of the door from closed to fully open.

- In taking long field measurements on sloping ground, hold the tape measure as level as possible. Otherwise, your dimensions, as shown in plan view, are longer than the actual horizontal distances.

- Show features that you intend to remove, such as a tree, shed, or old patio, by using dashed lines.

- Show stairs accurately. Show the exact number of steps. Measure the width (depth) of each tread; don't guess.

- Be wary of "level" lots. Confirm drainage patterns and slope.

4. **Refine and revise the plan.**

At this stage, you focus on individual elements of the landscape, such as the deck or patio, by drawing, experimenting, and redrawing only that element until it "works" (without completely ignoring the rest of the site).

5. **Draw a final site plan (see Figure 4-3).**

After you have a satisfactory design for each element of the plan, you can put them all together into a final site plan drawn to scale. Although a plan view (aerial view) is usually all that's necessary at this point, you may want to draw an elevation (side view) or two to test the plan for any serious problems (such as missing stairs or a blocked view). For purposes of obtaining permits or construction bids, designate which features of the site are "existing," or original, and which are "proposed."

6. **Create construction drawings.**

Hardscape features that you intend to build, such as a deck or patio, require a full set of working drawings for obtaining permits, getting construction bids, ordering materials, and, of course, building them. These drawings typically include a site plan (which you have), plan view (overhead view of the finished structure), foundation plan, structural plan, elevation (side view of the finished structure, including the house, if attached), and whatever cross sections or exploded views are necessary to show all structural details. The site plan is typically in $^1/_8$-inch scale, the views and elevations in $^1/_4$-inch scale, and the details in $^1/_2$- or $^3/_4$-inch scale.

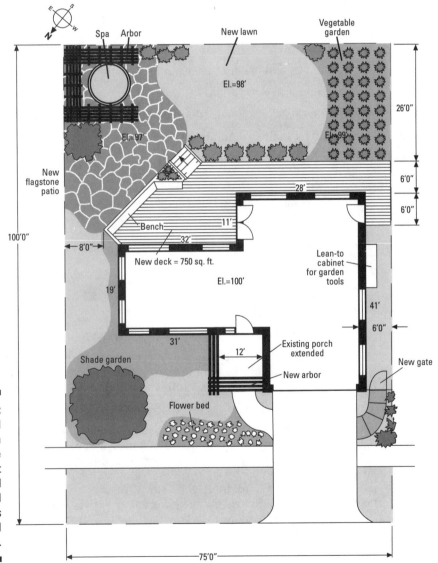

Figure 4-3: This final site plan includes the original plot plan with all proposed improvements and changes.

Is the Plan a Good Plan?

The final site plan launches you into the next step: making detailed construction drawings for your deck or patio (see Chapters 7 and 14). Before you take that step, do a final evaluation of your plan. First, see whether it includes the essential elements of a plot plan (listed in Chapter 1). The following checklist contains additional elements that you should include from your site evaluation and preliminary design work:

- North arrow
- Elevations and five-foot contour lines
- Setbacks and easements
- Alterations to the house (door, downspout, and so on)
- Retaining walls and grade changes
- New overhead or patio roof
- New spa
- Benches, planters, and other built-ins
- New paths, gates, stairs
- New fences, screens
- New electrical outlets
- New lights
- New water faucets
- New lawns, trees, shrubs, and planting beds
- Critical dimensions: length of property lines; dimensions of structures; distance of structures from property lines; clearance between close structures; width of paths; width and length of stairways; street or sidewalk easements

Finally, "test drive" the plan by laying out its various features in your yard using stakes, strings, hoses, boards, chalklines, and other markers. Set up furniture where you've marked a patio or deck. Simulate new trees with large umbrellas, stepladders, or helium balloons. Hang clotheslines where new fences are to go and drape sheets over them. Then walk around your fantasy landscape and imagine the different scenarios you've designed. Check views, clearances, access, privacy, shade, and so on. Then gather the family on your new "deck" or "patio" and relax with cool drinks.

Do Your Dreams Exceed Your Budget?

You can't get a firm estimate of costs for your design until you have a complete set of plans. On the other hand, you need to know what things cost so that you can design the landscape to fit within your budget. Faced with this chicken-and-egg dilemma, what can you do?

First, ignore the question until you complete your final site plan. That is, plan your ideal landscape with no restraints (except if you're tempted by an obvious budget-buster, such as a swimming pool). Let the site itself and your own dreams guide the design.

Next, assign an arbitrary cost, in round figures, to each element of your final plan (fences, lawn, flower beds, patio, deck, paths, raised planters, and so on). Try to be realistic about costs, but don't be afraid to guess. The important thing is to be thorough; make sure that you account for every major element of the plan, such as grading the site or removing a patio. Add up the total.

If your total estimate is wildly out of line, either your guesses are hopelessly unrealistic or your design is too ambitious. For a quick check, research costs of two or three of your items by asking neighbors or friends about the cost of comparable projects, by getting unit prices such as the square-foot cost of sod, or by consulting with a landscape contractor or landscape designer. Adjust your estimate to reflect this new information.

If you're comfortably close to budget, proceed with planning the highest-priority projects (usually fences, a deck or patio, trees, and walks). After you complete the working drawings and get firm estimates for each project, balance the estimate with its budget. If the estimate is below budget, assign the surplus to another budget. If the estimate is over budget, look for surplus money in other projects, downsize another project to create a surplus, or downsize the project itself. (For suggestions on how to save money on a deck or patio project, see Chapter 28.) You also can use all of your budget on two or three projects and defer others until later. If you do so, design low-cost, quick substitutes for the deferred projects so that your yard isn't an unfinished construction zone for several years.

A Plan Is More than Drawings

A deck or patio is more than a casual weekend project. Structurally, it must be as sound as the floor system in your home. It's also a major design element in the landscape, and it must withstand constant exposure to the weather. To build such an element successfully requires thorough planning, starting with a pleasing design. But having a set of plans on paper isn't enough. Planning also requires checklists and schedules. Use the following sample lists to start your own checklists of things that you must do before starting construction. Keep the lists handy so that you can add to them as you read about deck and patio construction in the next two parts of the book, while the ideas are fresh in your mind.

The following project checklist includes many of the tasks you must complete before and during construction:

- ✔ Complete a site plan.
- ✔ Complete working drawings of the deck or patio.
- ✔ Create a materials list.
- ✔ Create a spreadsheet of estimated costs.
- ✔ Make a list of contractors, if applicable.
- ✔ Interview contractors and obtain bids, if applicable.
- ✔ Evaluate bids and hire contractors, if applicable.
- ✔ Obtain a building permit.
- ✔ Order materials.
- ✔ Designate and clear storage area for materials.
- ✔ Round up tools.
- ✔ Plan how to collect and remove construction debris.
- ✔ Prepare the site (clear working area).
- ✔ Arrange for removal of excess soil.
- ✔ Do grading and excavating.
- ✔ Install underground utilities.
- ✔ Form and pour concrete footings, base.
- ✔ Build deck or patio.
- ✔ Build add-ons.
- ✔ Apply finishes.
- ✔ Install lighting, electrical, plumbing fixtures.

You need the following tools for a deck or patio project:

✔ **Tools for Layout**

- 25-foot tape measure
- 50-foot or 100-foot tape measure
- Nylon string or mason's twine
- Sledgehammer
- Builder's level or hydrolevel
- Carpenter's level
- Plumb bob

✔ **Tools for Excavation and Concrete Work**

- Square-nosed shovel
- Garden spade
- Post-hole digger or power auger for footing holes
- Wheelbarrow
- Rented backhoe or scoop loader, if needed
- Metal-cutting saw for rebar
- Buckets
- Hose and spray attachment

✔ **Tools for Building a Deck**

- Framing square
- Try, combination, or other small square
- Chalkline
- Handsaw
- Framing hammer (smooth face)
- Nail puller
- Nail set
- Wood chisels
- Rasping plane
- Power circular saw
- Power drill
- Power sander
- Power screwdriver
- Hammer drill, if needed
- GFCI-protected outlet
- Extension cords
- Socket wrenches
- Caulking gun
- Sawhorses
- Stepladder
- Brushes, sprayer, or paint roller, as needed
- Gloves
- Eye protection
- Dust mask
- Hard hat, for high decks
- First-aid kit

> ✔ **Tools for Building a Patio**
>
>   • Depends on whether you build it of brick, stone, or concrete; see Chapter 15.

Following is a sample materials list, without sizes and quantities, for a small deck:

> ✔ **Layout and Footings**
>
>   • Stakes
>
>   • Forming tubes or form lumber
>
>   • Gravel
>
>   • Rebar
>
>   • Concrete
>
> ✔ **Platform**
>
>   • Posts
>
>   • Beams
>
>   • Ledger board
>
>   • Joists
>
>   • Rim joist
>
>   • Blocking
>
>   • Decking lumber
>
>   • Fascia
>
> ✔ **Stairs**
>
>   • Stringers
>
>   • Treads

> ✔ **Railings**
>
>   • Posts
>
>   • Cap rail
>
>   • Top, bottom, and middle rails
>
>   • Spindles
>
> ✔ **Hardware**
>
>   • Post anchors
>
>   • Beam connectors
>
>   • Flashing for ledger
>
>   • Joist hangers
>
>   • Stair stringer brackets
>
>   • Tread brackets
>
>   • Lag screws for ledger
>
>   • Carriage bolts, nuts, washers for beams
>
>   • Duplex nails for forms and bracing
>
>   • Joist hanger nails
>
>   • Decking screws or fasteners
>
>   • Nails for railing
>
>   • Caulk
>
>   • Stain, sealer, or finish

Although these lists include building materials and tools that you commonly use for home improvement projects, you may not be familiar with all of them. For more information about deck-building tools and materials, see Chapters 5, 6, and 8. For information about patio-building tools and materials, see Chapters 14, 15, and 17 through 20.

Part II
Building a Deck

The 5th Wave — By Rich Tennant

In this part . . .

A deck is a fairly simple structure that almost anyone handy with a few tools can build. This type of project is excellent for practicing basic carpentry skills. You not only have the advantage of working outside, away from the living areas inside your house, but you also have the benefit of working in the fresh air. You are constructing something that you can actually *stand* on, building a relatively large structure in a relatively short time, and handling lots of beautiful wood.

A deck is also a substantial structure that you must treat seriously — it's not a birdhouse. These nine chapters give you the essential code information, building techniques, and safety tips that you need to complete your project successfully.

Chapter 5

Deck Specs: Sizing Up Your Deck

● ●

● ●

Decks must support heavy loads and resist swaying. Even if you don't host dance parties for sumo wrestlers, you must design your deck for the heaviest loads and most severe conditions you can reasonably expect, including earthquakes, high winds, and heavy snow. Your deck must also resist constant attacks from the ground, such as frost heaves, unstable soil, and the ravages of decay-causing organisms, and withstand constantly changing weather conditions. It must also be beautiful.

Designing a deck for such conditions may seem like a tall order, but a deck's structure is very logical and quite simple. It's just a well-organized stack of lumber — nothing too complicated to figure out. After you understand the basic components, you can adapt them to almost any configuration.

This chapter takes you through all the components of a deck, although not in the same order that you build one (from the ground up). Instead, I start with the easiest part of a deck to imagine — the platform — and then show you how to design a framework and foundation to support it and how to add other components to complete it. This sequence is the same one in which you want to design your deck — starting with the platform. Your site plan should already include its overall shape and dimensions (see Chapter 4).

Live loads and dead loads

How strong does your deck need to be? I base the tables in this chapter on a "live load" of 40 pounds per square foot *(psf)* and a "dead load" of 10 psf. *Live load* refers to the weight of furnishings, occupants, and temporary loads distributed over the entire platform, and *dead load* refers to the weight of the structure itself. This total design load of 50 psf is typical for most codes, but you should verify it with your building department; some local codes require support for 60 psf live loads or more.

If you anticipate any extraordinary loads on your deck, such as stacks of firewood, large planters, or a spa, consult with an architect or structural engineer for recommendations. (See Chapter 3 for more information.) Such loads require shorter spans, tighter spacings, and stouter lumber than these tables recommend.

Starting with the Platform

The platform for most decks consists of boards installed flat over a supporting framework (see Figure 5-1). The size, species, and grade of the decking boards and the alignment or pattern that they follow determine how you need to design that framework.

Lumber varies in strength according to species and grade (see Table 5-1). After you select the type of lumber for your decking, based on appearance, cost, availability, and similar factors (see Chapter 6), find out how much distance a board of that type of lumber can span between supports by consulting Tables 5-1 and 5-2 or the manufacturer's specifications.

Table 5-1	Strength Groupings of North American Softwoods*	
Group A	*Group B*	*Group C*
Cypress	Alpine white fir	Balsam fir
Douglas fir	Douglas fir (South)	Northern white cedar
Southern pine	Eastern mountain hemlock	Redwood (construction heart)
West Coast hemlock	Hem/fir	Southern white cedar

Group A	Group B	Group C
Western larch	Pine (except Southern)	
	Redwood (clear grades)	
	Spruce (Eastern, Englemann, Sitka)	
	Western red cedar	

Table assumes construction grade or #2 grade or better lumber.

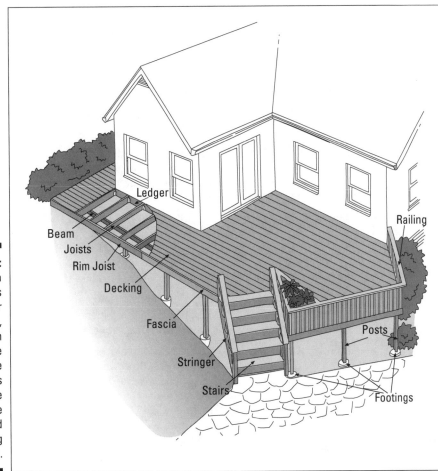

Figure 5-1:
Whether a deck is complex or fairly basic, as shown here, the same components make up the structure and finishing details.

Table 5-2	**Recommended Maximum Spans for Decking Boards, Based on Strength Groupings***		
Board Size	**Group A**	**Group B**	**Group C**
1-by boards**, laid flat	16"	14"	12"
$^5/_4$"-radius edge decking	24"	16"	16"
2x3s, laid flat	24"	24"	20"
2x4s, laid flat	24"	24"	20"
2x6s, laid flat	32"	24"	24"
2x3s, laid on edge	36"	32"	28"
2x4s, laid on edge	48"	42"	36"

*Table assumes construction grade or #2 grade or better lumber. Table assumes that loads are distributed over several boards and not concentrated on a single board.

**"1-by boards" refers to any board of nominal 1-inch thickness.

In using these charts, keep in mind the following points:

- ✔ You measure *spans* between support members; you measure *spacings* from center to center.

- ✔ The *nominal dimension* of lumber is different from the actual dimension. A board with a nominal dimension of 2x4, for example, measures $1^1/_2$" by $3^1/_2$". You do find one exception: $^5/_4$" lumber is actually that — $1^1/_4$" thick. These boards also are known as *radius-edged decking,* because the edges are rounded to a wider radius than are those of standard planed lumber.

- ✔ Preservative-treated lumber is typically #2 or better and falls within the same strength groupings as untreated lumber of the same species.

- ✔ If you install decking boards diagonally across supporting members, measure the span along the board's direction of travel and not straight across between the supporting members. This measurement exceeds the span values in Table 5-2. A board that you install at a 45-degree angle across two supports spaced 24" on center, for example, must be strong enough to span $33^1/_2$", not 24".

- ✔ If in doubt, use 2x6 decking lumber. It's thick enough to span 24" with a wide margin of safety, it's wide enough not to be springy, it's narrow enough not to warp easily, it's readily available, and it looks nice.

Figuring the Frame

Joists, ledger, beams, and posts are the main elements of a deck's framing system. Similar in function to a skeleton, they're the "bones" of the deck that hold it together and transfer the loads, or weight, to the foundation. And, as is true of "dem bones" from the old song, each element of the frame connects to the other in a logical sequence that descends from the platform to the ground. The size, length, and placement of each board depend on the maximum allowable span of the boards above it and, to some extent, the spacing of those below it. If you get bogged down in details while reading this section, follow the suggestions in the section "Feeling framed?" later in this chapter, to help you maintain perspective.

Joists

Joists are repetitive framing members, usually 2-by lumber set on edge, that support the decking boards, as shown in Figure 5-2. They can span fairly long distances because they're set on edge. The size of the joists, the species and grade of lumber, and the spacing between the joists determine exactly how far they can span. (*Spacing* here is the distance between joist *centers* and not the distance from inside to inside.)

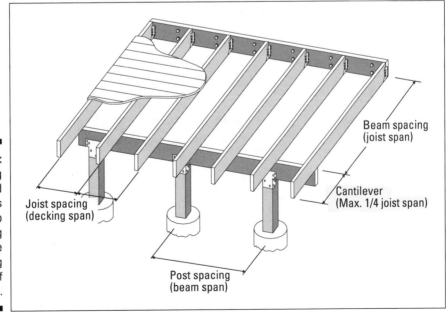

Figure 5-2: Understanding spans and spacings is essential to designing the supporting structure of a deck.

Beam spacing (joist span)

Cantilever (Max. 1/4 joist span)

Joist spacing (decking span)

Post spacing (beam span)

In determining the spacing between joists, use the maximum *span* (the distance between supports) of your decking boards as a guide for establishing joist spacing. For example, if you're planning a deck with Southern pine (Strength Group A in Table 5-1) and you're planning to use 2x6 lumber, you can see from Table 5-2 that your maximum span is 32". In general, start with a 24" spacing (unless the decking boards aren't of sufficient strength to span that far); you can always tighten up the joist spacing to 16" or 12" if the joists must span a longer distance than the 24" spacing allows.

In Table 5-3, you can see the maximum spans for various sizes of joists, given the spacing you choose. The joist itself may be longer, requiring support at several points. A common practice in deck construction, however, is to extend joists a few feet beyond the last beam, making the deck appear to float over the ground. (Refer back to Figure 5-3.) This extension is called a *cantilever* and must not exceed one-fourth the allowable span.

Table 5-3	Maximum Joist Spans, or Beam Spacing*		
Joist Size	*Group A*	*Group B*	*Group C*
12" Joist Spacing			
2x6	10' 4''	9' 2''	8' 10''
2x8	13' 8''	12' 1''	11' 8''
2x10	17' 5''	15' 4''	14' 10''
2x12	20' 0''	18' 8''	17' 9''
16" Joist Spacing			
2x6	9' 5''	8' 4''	8' 0''
2x8	12' 5''	10' 11''	10' 7''
2x10	15' 5''	14' 0''	13' 3''
2x12	17' 10''	16' 6''	15' 4''
24" Joist Spacing			
2x6	7' 10''	7' 3''	7' 0''
2x8	10' 2''	9' 6''	8' 10''
2x10	12' 7''	11' 7''	10' 10''
2x12	14' 7''	13' 6''	12' 7''

(continued)

Joist Size	Group A	Group B	Group C
		Table 5-3 *(continued)*	
	32" Joist Spacing		
2x6	6' 8''	6' 8''	6' 0''
2x8	9' 3''	8' 3''	7' 3''
2x10	11' 3''	10' 4''	8' 9''
2x12	12' 6''	11' 3''	10' 9''

*Lumber groups are based on the strength groups in Table 5-1. This table assumes construction grade or #2 grade or better lumber. Spacings are measured center-to-center. Spans are maximum distance between supports. Table assumes a live load of 40 psf and a dead load of 10 psf (see the sidebar "Live loads and dead loads," earlier in this chapter).

Ledger

Not all decks have a ledger — only those that you attach to a house. A *ledger* is a piece of 2-by lumber that you fasten horizontally to the side of the house where the deck connects. A ledger functions as a beam and supports any joists that you connect to it. Choose lumber that's one size larger than the joist lumber. (For example, if your joists are 2x8, use a 2x10 board for your ledger.) Decks that wrap around two sides of the house or that you tuck between intersecting house walls need a ledger on each wall. (One of the two may not support any joists because the joists run parallel with it.) For more information about ledgers, see Chapter 10.

Beams

Beams support the joists and carry substantial loads, as shown in Figure 5-3. Like joists, they are installed horizontally and on edge. The size of a beam depends on two variables: the spacing between beams and the spacing between the posts that support the beam (see Table 5-4). The spacing between beams (or between ledger and beam) shouldn't exceed the maximum allowable span for the joists they support, or the joists may break. If it does, you need to increase the joist size, space the joists closer together, or add another beam at midspan.

Figure 5-3:
The underside of this deck reveals how beams and joists support the decking boards.

After you determine the spacing between beams (or ledger and beam) and plot the beam locations, plan the beam sizes by consulting Table 5-4. Try to size each beam as large as possible to reduce the number of posts and footings (concrete supports placed in the ground); doing so keeps excavation and concrete work to a minimum and avoids a cluttered appearance. Each footing, however, is limited in how much deck load it can support, based on the bearing capacity of the soil, so you must make sure that you have enough footings to distribute the weight. (See the section "Getting Grounded," later in this chapter, for more information about planning the footings, or foundation.) If you're not comfortable doing calculations to figure out the minimum number of footings, a basic rule is to space them six to eight feet apart, based on the center of each footing — one footing for each 40 to 50 square feet of deck.

As you can with joists (see the section "Joists," a little earlier in this chapter), you can cantilever the ends of beams beyond the last posts to give the deck a floating effect. Limit the cantilever distance of beams, however, to one joist spacing (12 to 24 inches).

Beams can also support joists the same way that a ledger does: with *joist hangers* (metal U-shaped brackets for making connections where the end of one board butts into the side of another board). This arrangement makes the tops of the joists flush with the top of the beam, and is useful for low decks ("ground huggers"), where tight clearances restrict space for framing members. Joist hangers are also useful in multilevel decks where the same beam must support platforms of different heights. (The joists of the upper platform rest on top of the beam, and the joists of the lower platform are supported by joist hangers attached to the side of the beam so that the tops of the joists are flush with the top of the beam, creating a one-step difference in height between the two levels.)

The beam sizes that I list in Table 5-4 allow for both solid lumber and "built-up" beams of two or three pieces of 2-by lumber nailed together. The table assumes that all pieces of lumber in a built-up beam are full-length; none are spliced end-to-end. The table does *not* allow for *"sandwich" beams,* which are two 2-bys that sandwich, or are installed on both sides of, a post and are often used where a post extends up through the deck to double as a railing post. In such cases, choose a size of 2-by lumber that's at least one size larger than the specified beam to compensate for the fact that the two boards aren't fastened together for mutual reinforcement. For more information about beams, see Chapter 10.

Table 5-4		Maximum Beam Spans between Posts*								
Strength	Beam	Beam Spacing (Joist Span)								
Group	Size	4'	5'	6'	7'	8'	9'	10'	11'	12'
A	2x6 (2)	7'	6'							
	4x6	7'	7'	6'						
	2x8 (2)	9'	8'	7'	7'	6'	6'			
	4x8	10'	9'	8'	7'	7'	6'	6'	6'	
	2x10 (2)	11'	10'	9'	8'	8'	7'	7'	6'	6'
	6x8	12'	10'	9'	9'	8'	8'	7'	7'	6'
	2x8 (3)	12'	11'	10'	9'	8'	8'	7'	7'	7'
	4x10	12'	11'	10'	9'	8'	8'	7'	7'	7'
	2x12 (2)	13'	12'	10'	10'	9'	8'	8'	7'	7'
	4x12	14'	13'	11'	10'	10'	9'	9'	8'	8'
	2x10 (3)	15'	13'	12'	11'	10'	10'	9'	9'	8'
	6x10	15'	13'	12'	11'	10'	10'	9'	9'	8'
	2x12 (3)	16'	15'	14'	13'	12'	11'	11'	10'	10'
	6x12	16'	16'	15'	13'	12'	12'	11'	10'	10'
B	2x6 (2)	6'	6'							
	4x6	7'	6'	6'						
	2x8 (2)	8'	7'	6'	6'					
	4x8	9'	8'	7'	6'	6'	6'			
	2x10 (2)	10'	9'	8'	7'	7'	6'	6'		
	6x8	9'	8'	8'	7'	7'	6'	6'	6'	
	2x8 (3)	11'	10'	9'	8'	7'	7'	6'	6'	6'
	4x10	11'	10'	9'	8'	7'	7'	6'	6'	6'
	2x12 (2)	11'	10'	9'	8'	8'	7'	7'	6'	6'
	4x12	13'	11'	10'	9'	9'	8'	7'	7'	7'
	2x10 (3)	13'	12'	11'	10'	9'	8'	8'	8'	7'
	6x10	12'	11'	10'	9'	8'	8'	7'	7'	7'
	2x12 (3)	15'	14'	12'	11'	11'	10'	9'	9'	8'
	6x12	15'	13'	12'	11'	10'	10'	9'	9'	8'

Strength Group	Beam Size	Beam Spacing (Joist Span)								
		4'	5'	6'	7'	8'	9'	10'	11'	12'
C	2x6 (2)	6'								
	4x6	7'	6'							
	2x8 (2)	8'	7'	6'	6'					
	4x8	8'	7'	7'	6'	6'				
	2x10 (2)	9'	8'	8'	7'	6'	6'	6'		
	6x8	9'	8'	8'	7'	6'	6'	6'		
	2x8 (3)	10'	9'	8'	8'	7'	7'	6'	6'	
	4x10	10'	9'	8'	8'	7'	7'	6'	6'	6'
	2x12 (2)	11'	10'	9'	8'	7'	7'	7'	6'	6'
	4x12	12'	11'	10'	9'	8'	8'	7'	7'	6'
	2x10 (3)	13'	11'	10'	9'	8'	8'	7'	7'	7'
	6x10	12'	11'	10'	9'	8'	8'	7'	7'	7'
	2x12 (3)	15'	13'	12'	11'	10'	9'	9'	8'	8'
	6x12	15'	13'	12'	11'	10'	9'	9'	8'	8'

*Table assumes construction grade or #2 grade, or better. Beams are on edge. Spacings are measured center-to-center. Spans are maximum distances between supports. Table assumes a live load of 40 psf and a dead load of 10 psf (see the sidebar "Live loads and dead loads," earlier in this chapter).

Posts

After you figure out the post spacings, all you need to plan is what size lumber to use, which depends on the height of the post and the deck load it must support. For most decks, 4x4s are adequate, but if your deck is high or has very few posts, you should use a larger post size (see Table 5-5). To figure the deck load area, multiply the beam spacing by the post spacing to obtain the number of square feet. Look for the next highest number in the table and use it as the load area for sizing the post. Try to make the post sizes match the beam size for easier connections. For example, suppose that a deck is 6 feet off the ground and the posts are spaced 8 feet apart under beams that are spaced 10 feet apart. The load area is 80 square feet (8 x 10), so use the column with the next highest number: 84. In that column, the maximum heights for all post sizes are well above 6 feet, so you are safe to use a 4x4 post or any larger size. If the deck were 12 feet above the ground, you would have to use 6x6s for the posts, no matter what species of lumber.

Table 5-5		Recommended Maximum Heights for Deck Posts*									
		Load Area Supported by Post, in Square Feet									
Strength	**Post**										
Group	**Size**	**36**	**48**	**60**	**72**	**84**	**96**	**108**	**120**	**132**	**144**
A	4x4	10'	10'	10'	9'	9'	8'	8'	7'	7'	6'
	4x6	14'	14'	13'	12'	11'	10'	10'	9'	9'	8'
	6x6	17'	17'	17'	17'	17'	17'	17'	17'	16'	16'
B	4x4	10'	10'	10'	9'	9'	8'	8'	7'	7'	6'
	4x6	14'	14'	13'	12'	11'	11'	10'	9'	9'	9'
	6x6	17'	17'	17'	17'	17'	17'	17'	17'	16'	15'
C	4x4	10'	10'	9'	8'	7'	7'	6'	6'	5'	4'
	4x6	14'	13'	12'	11'	10'	9'	8'	8'	7'	7'
	6x6	17'	17'	17'	17'	17'	17'	17'	17'	16'	15'

Table assumes 40 psf live load plus 10 psf dead load (see the sidebar "Live loads and dead loads," earlier in this chapter). Lumber is #2 grade or better.

Although I've included taller posts in Table 5-5, decks with posts 8 feet tall and higher are a bit beyond the simple do-it-yourself project. Such decks must be braced and cross-braced to provide lateral support, especially in earthquake and high-wind areas. If you have such a deck in mind, I strongly recommend using an architect or a design engineer on the project.

Feeling framed?

All these numbers, tables, spans, spacings, lumber grades, load areas, and other variables may seem overwhelming. Even if you understand each variable perfectly, trying to account for all of them at once is a challenge, sort of like trying to get six frisky kittens to line up for a photo — if one moves, they all scatter. Don't despair. After you establish a few criteria, such as the overall dimensions of the platform, the type of decking lumber you want to use, or the preferred locations of your footings, you can design the rest of the structure around these fixed points. Change one of the criteria, and you can readjust all the components accordingly. This fluid process of going back and forth between the components to find the best possible solution makes designing a deck fun. Use the following tips to guide your planning:

✔ If you aren't starting with any known specifications, try the following "default" values: 2x6 decking boards, 2x8 joists on 24" spacings, 4x8 beams, and 4x4 posts. Check the tables to see whether these values work for your deck. Adjust any figures that you know don't work and make other adjustments accordingly.

✔ Strive for a balance between too few and too many supporting members. Avoid clutter, but spread the load over as many members as possible.

✔ Be wary of cantilever distances longer than two feet; they could make the deck too springy.

✔ Don't scrimp on joists. They're easy to lay out and install. Tighter spacing or a larger size than you may need makes the deck feel solid.

✔ Plan one post for every 40 to 50 square feet of deck. You can increase this area to 80 square feet if the footings cover at least 2 square feet of ground (17" square or a 19"-diameter circle). See the following section for more information.

Getting Grounded

The foundation for most decks is a system of isolated concrete footings with piers, pier blocks, or preservative-treated posts resting on them. If you attach a deck to a house, the house foundation also supports the deck. This foundation system has three functions: to support the weight of the deck, to anchor the deck against uplift and lateral movement caused by winds or earthquakes, and to keep vulnerable wood members from direct contact with the ground.

The most critical element of foundation design, which some overlook entirely, is the bearing capacity of the ground itself. Footings must rest on stable soil that's not susceptible to creeping down a hillside, buckling from cycles of freezing and thawing, or compressing from the weight of the structure. You must, therefore, dig footing holes below the frost line and below uncompacted or unstable surface soil. You must also design a deck to distribute its weight over enough footings (each of which must be broad enough) to prevent the concentrated loads from squishing into the ground. (See Chapter 9 for more information on preparing the site and about footings.)

Your building department can tell you what the minimum footing depth is for your area, based on the frost line and other local conditions. This depth can vary from a minimum of 12 inches below grade for flat sites in mild climates to 5 or 6 feet below grade in areas with severe winters. What's harder to find out is the bearing capacity of the soil itself, because conditions can vary widely within the same community.

Typically, most residential structures are built on soil with a bearing capacity of at least 2,000 pounds per square foot (psf), although in many areas the bearing capacity is only 1,000 psf. If you are not able to verify that the bearing capacity of your soil is 2,000 psf or more, you should assume that it is 1,000 psf. If you live on a steep hillside, your lot contains landfill, neighboring homes (or yours) have severe foundation problems, or your building department has designated your area as a special zone with unstable soils, you may have even weaker soil. If you face any of these conditions, you must enlarge the footing sizes or place the footings and posts closer together than specified in Table 5-5. Consult with a local architect or engineer qualified to design a footing system for your deck.

Assuming that the bearing capacity of your soil is 2,000 psf, you can calculate whether the footings for your deck bear that much weight. First, figure the deck area by multiplying length by width (for example, 30 x 24 = 720 square feet). Next, subtract from this total area the amount of deck that the house foundation supports, which is half the area between the ledger and first beam (for example, if the first beam is 10 feet from the house, multiply 5 (half of 10) by the length of the deck; 5 x 30 = 150 square feet, which you subtract from 720 sf: 720 - 150 = 570 sf). Multiply the remaining area of the deck by 50 psf (570 x 50 = 28,500 pounds) and divide this figure by the number of footings you planned (for example, 28,500 ÷ 15 footings = 1,900 pounds per footing). Assuming that each footing covers only one square foot, the answer should be less than 2,000 pounds. If each footing covers two square feet (approximately 17"x17"), the load for each footing could be as high as 4,000 pounds for soil with a bearing capacity of 2,000 psf.

Studying Stairs

Stairs (shown in Figure 5-4) are notorious safety hazards and are strictly regulated by building codes. These regulations make designing stairs fairly straightforward; the stairs almost design themselves (and they *are* safe). As with the rest of your deck, stairs present opportunities for creative design and decorative treatments, as long as they meet code. The following summary of stair requirements, based on typical code requirements, includes some specifications that are slightly more stringent than those of most codes; building outdoors gives you an opportunity to increase the margin of safety. Check with your local building department for other stair requirements.

✔ **Overall dimensions.** *Stairs* are defined as two or more *risers* (the vertical portion of each step). Stairs must be at least 36 inches wide (excluding handrails). The total rise of a flight of stairs, measured vertically from landing to landing, must not exceed 12 feet. For longer climbs, you must include at least one landing for every 12 vertical feet.

✔ **Riser and tread dimensions.** Risers should be no more than $7^1/_2$ inches high and treads no less than 11 inches deep. Riser heights and tread depths within a stair run should not deviate by more than $^3/_8$ inch.

✔ **Railings and handrails.** Platforms with a drop-off more than 30 inches high require a railing (see the section "Designing Railings," later in this chapter). Stairs with three or more risers require at least one handrail (one on each side if the stairs are open or are wider than three feet). Handrails must be *grippable* — that is, a continuous portion of the handrail must be $1^1/_4$ to 2 inches wide so that you can easily grip it, with at least $1^1/_2$ inches of clearance above and behind the rail and a maximum projection out from the wall of $3^1/_2$ inches.

The ends of a handrail must not be exposed (such ends are sleeve-catchers); handrails must terminate in a *newel post (end post)* or by a "return" into the wall. Handrails must be a uniform height above all stair treads: 34 to 38 inches as measured vertically from the stair nosings (front edges). Handrails for any stairs with a drop-off of more than 30 inches must include railings with protective screening along the side that consists of members spaced no more than four inches apart (see again the section "Designing Railings"), except where the "screening" comes down to the stair tread, where a six-inch opening is allowable.

✔ **Landings.** Landings must be at least as wide as the stairway and at least 36 inches deep. An exterior door must have a floor or landing on both sides, with the landing no more than one inch below the door's threshold. An exception is for doors that swing inward; the landing or platform can be up to eight inches below such a door.

Stringers, treads, and risers

The three main components of stairs are the *stringers* (main supports, resting at an angle), *treads* (the part you walk on), and *risers* (optional vertical boards behind each tread). See Figure 5-4. Stringers are usually 2x12s and can be *cutout* (notched for the treads) or *solid* (attached to treads by metal or wood cleats). Cutout stringers give stairs a more graceful appearance. Solid stringers create a strong diagonal line and are also less susceptible to rot. Two stringers are adequate for 36-inch-wide stairs; for wider stairs, provide a stringer every 32 to 36 inches. The stringers that terminate on the ground require a concrete landing or footings to support them (see Chapter 12).

Treads must be at least $1^1/_4$ inches thick. The front edge is called the "nosing" and should extend half to one inch beyond the riser or, if no riser, beyond the back edge of the tread below it. *Risers* (sometimes called kickers) add strength and minimize visual clutter but may become moisture traps. Open risers emphasize horizontal lines and make stairs seem less dominant but may contribute to feelings of vertigo.

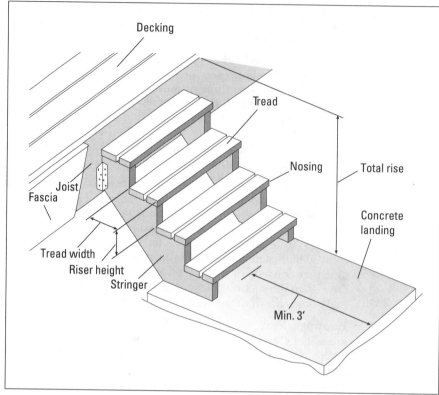

Figure 5-4:
The main
components
and
dimensions
that you use
for planning
stairs.

Labels in figure: Decking, Tread, Nosing, Total rise, Joist, Fascia, Concrete landing, Tread width, Riser height, Stringer, Min. 3′

Calculating stair dimensions

The overall stair dimensions, the number of steps, and the riser height and
tread depth for each step vary for each installation and hinge on a critical
relationship: the ratio between the riser height and the tread depth. Safety
and comfort require that steeper stairs have narrower treads; as you reduce
the riser height, you should increase the tread depth. A loose formula for
determining this ratio is that twice the riser height added to the tread depth
should equal 25 to 27 inches, as shown by the two examples in Figure 5-5.

This formula starts with the riser height. What number should you use? The
maximum is $7^1/_2$ inches, but for most outdoor stairs, you should aim for 6 to
7 inches — less if you're planning only a few very broad stairs that cascade
down from a deck platform. The riser height you choose should be a number that divides evenly into the total rise of your stairs, as measured from
top of landing to top of deck (or other landing). For example, if the deck is

54 inches above the landing, you would divide 7 inches into this measurement. The answer is seven and a fraction, so you must round the answer to the next highest whole number: eight. Next, using 8 as the number of steps, divide that number back into the total height, which is 54. The answer is $6^3/_4$ inches, which is the riser height.

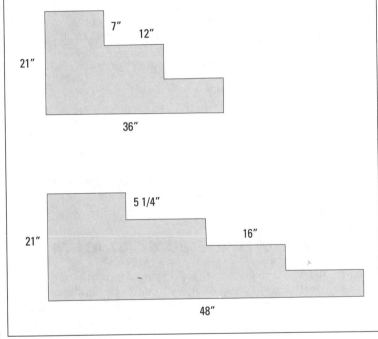

Figure 5-5:
The relationship between tread depth and riser height is critical for safety and comfort.

After you determine a comfortable riser height that divides evenly into the total rise, double this number and subtract it from 26. The answer gives you the appropriate tread depth for your riser height ($6^3/_4$ x 2 = $13^1/_2$. 26 - $13^1/_2$ = $12^1/_2$). Multiply this figure by the total number of steps to figure out the total run of the stairs (12.5 x 8 = 100 inches, or 8 feet, 4 inches). If they don't fit within the available space, reduce the tread depth by one inch. (**Remember:** The formula allows a total of 25 to 27 inches.) If the stair run is still too long, raise the riser height and recalculate again.

You can use the same formula to work backward. You may, for example, be planning a certain combination of lumber sizes to make the treads interesting and attractive — two 2x6s with a 2x2 between them ($12^1/_2$ inches) is very popular. This arrangement determines the tread depth. Subtract this number from 26 and divide the answer in half to obtain the riser height. Then adjust that number so that it divides evenly into the total rise.

Adding pizzazz

Your stairs don't need to look utilitarian. Add some style. One option is to blend them with the rest of the deck by repeating details. If the deck has a 2x4 *fascia* (a decorative trim piece), for example, trim the stair treads by using 2x4s, or repeat the same railing design.

Proportion and scale are important (see Chapter 3). Plan a generous width. The 36-inch requirement is only the minimum. A more comfortable width is four feet — five feet where people frequently pass each other. Plan short risers and deep treads where leisurely runs are appropriate. Stairs with 5-inch risers and 16-inch treads create a gentle transition, although the same stairs wouldn't be practical for long runs.

Stairs are often more attractive if they resemble a series of stacked platforms rather than a diagonal ramp. Horizontal lines are conducive to serenity and calm; a strong diagonal line disrupts this feeling. To disguise the diagonal stringers, attach 2x3 trim pieces to the front edges of the treads and continue the trim around the sides of the treads horizontally to cover part of the stringers. Another way to disguise diagonal stringers is to place planters or screening in front of them.

One-step or two-step changes in levels

Changes in levels add interest to a deck and are easy to build (see Chapter 12), but they're also easy to trip over if you don't design them carefully. One-step changes are especially hazardous because they're so subtle and difficult to see. To prevent pratfalls, make the step conspicuous: Change the pattern or direction of decking boards. Signal the transition with a planter at each end of the step. Install lighting under the step. Create a prominent shadowline by overlapping the top step by at least one inch.

Use the same techniques for two-step changes, which are platforms with an intermediate step between them. Design the intermediate step with the deepest tread possible; such a step is easier to see and negotiate and makes a nice sitting platform. Check with your local building department to see whether a handrail is necessary for an intermediate step.

Some final details

You can't plan stairs too carefully. They may seem like an afterthought that you work out during construction, but you should consider every detail possible in your plan. Besides safety considerations, which leave no margin for error, you must account for structural support and the surprising amount of space that stairs can take up. The following list includes details that are easy to overlook:

✔ For stairs that terminate on the ground, plan a concrete landing that extends at least three feet in front of the stairs. The landing also serves as a footing for the bottom of the stringers.

✔ If the stairs terminate on a sloped landing, such as an existing walk or patio, the bottom riser height must not vary more than three inches from one end of the riser to the other.

✔ If you plan more than one set of stairs for your deck, use the same riser height and tread depth throughout all the stairs, even if they aren't connected.

✔ As you count risers and treads to calculate total rise or total run of the stairs, remember that you always need one more riser than tread.

✔ Your plan should include such details as stringer attachments, footings, connections to landings, handrail design, and dimensions for rise and run. See Chapter 12 for more information.

✔ As you actually build the stairs, take site measurements to calculate the final riser height; don't rely only on drawings or plans.

Designing Railings

Railings (see Figure 5-6 and Chapter 12) are dominant design elements — often the only part of a deck that you really see because the platform has such a thin profile and, as a floor, tends to be overlooked. As do stairs, railings must adhere to very strict safety standards. Use the following list of typical code requirements as a planning guide. Consult with your building department to verify.

✔ **Where required.** Decks with a drop-off of more than 30 inches require protective railings. Planters and benches that you design to serve in lieu of railings must adhere to the same height and screening specifications as railings.

✔ **Height.** Railings must be 36 inches high (42 inches for some areas with very steep slopes).

✔ **Screening.** To protect infants, you must space railing members close enough together to prevent a four-inch sphere from passing through.

✔ **Lateral strength.** Railings must be strong enough to resist a lateral force of 200 pounds per square foot (psf).

The basic components of a railing are posts, rails, and *infill* (the balusters, wire screening, glass panels, or other material used to fill in the space between the top rail and the deck). You can attach posts to the perimeter of the deck platform, spacing them five to six feet apart, or you can design the deck so that the same posts support the deck beams and railings. Top the posts with a continuous cap rail to provide continuity and an attachment for certain infill designs. Other rails at the bottom and middle of the railing may provide further support, as necessary. The infill itself presents almost endless design possibilities. Consider the following factors in planning your railing design:

✔ **Style.** A simple design of vertical 2x2s spaced four inches apart serves for most railings. The repetitive pattern is pleasing, although so many vertical lines may clash with a deck's overall horizontal feeling. This design also makes a small deck feel like a crib. To minimize these effects, dress up the design by using prefabricated balusters instead of dimensioned lumber, decorate the posts with finials (decorative doodads, usually round, placed on posts or along the railing), or reduce the height of the vertical members by introducing a four-inch-wide horizontal space between the infill and cap rail. You can also exchange the vertical spindles for lattice panels, horizontal boards similar to the fencing around a horse corral, or more intricate designs; be aware, however, that such infills tend to obscure views more than vertical spindles. To minimize the effect of a railing altogether, match it to the house's siding or choose a see-through infill such as wire mesh, clear plastic, or horizontal cables spaced four inches apart.

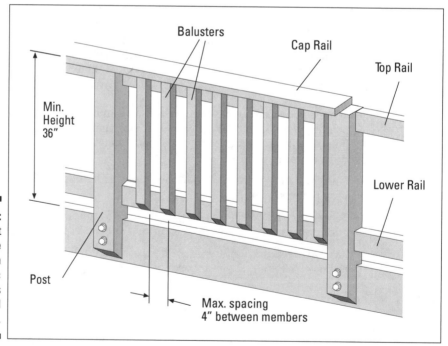

Figure 5-6:
Most railings are a variation of the basic components illustrated here.

✔ **Privacy and views.** Railings hinder views, which is good for privacy but bad for million-dollar vistas. Consider *all* views, including those from sitting positions on the deck, those from inside the house looking onto the deck, and those from the yard or neighborhood looking up to the deck. One railing design that satisfies most privacy and view requirements at the same time has screening only $30^1/_2$ inches high, a 4-inch-high horizontal space above it, and a 2x6 cap rail installed flat along the top.

✔ **Child protection.** In addition to observing the four-inch screening requirement, design the railing so that climbing it is difficult for youngsters. Avoid horizontal pieces; vertical balusters or spindles are more climb-proof. Make the cap rail difficult for small hands to grip. Use 2x6s laid flat or make the front edge of the cap rail flush with the support rail below it.

✔ **Cost.** Railings can be expensive. Most designs require a large number of 2x2s and other small-dimensioned lumber, which tend be the more expensive, knot-free grades. If you paint the railing, you can get by with a cheaper grade. Designs that include decorative balusters or prefabricated lattice can also cost a premium. A less-expensive infill material is vinyl-coated wire mesh that you staple to top and bottom rails. This mesh meets the screening requirement and gives you unobstructed views. Other relatively cheap materials are galvanized pipes and electrical conduit, which you can install horizontally, corral-style, if young buckaroos aren't using the deck.

For more information about railings, see Chapter 12.

Accounting for Add-Ons

As you plan the deck structure, consider any add-ons that your deck design includes, such as built-in benches, large planters, a spa, or an overhead. A spa is a concentrated load that exceeds the 50 psf design load that you use for calculating deck joists, beams, and posts. (See Tables 5-1 through 5-5, earlier in this chapter.) A spa requires additional reinforcement — both vertical and lateral — based on the specific design weight of the spa. For more information, see Chapter 3.

To integrate an overhead into the deck design, use the same posts to support both the deck and the overhead. Use 4x6s or 6x6s and increase the footing diameter by about 25 percent. You can also plan separate posts for the overhead that extend below the deck to their own footings. See Chapter 22 for more information.

For built-in benches and planters, see the construction information in Chapters 12 and 23. For many designs, you can simply build the bench or planter and attach it to the completed deck. Some planters, however, you must integrate into the deck structure. If you cantilever bench seats from the railing posts, for example, you need to space the railing posts three or four feet apart, instead of five or six feet, to give the bench seat enough support. If you plan large planters for a low deck, design them to extend through the decking to the ground so that bottoms aren't necessary and the soil doesn't add weight to the deck.

Planning the Finishing Touch

Deck finishes protect wood from the elements and, because they influence color, have a strong effect on the final design. Your choices for a deck finish are preservatives, sealers, stains, and paint. (See Chapters 6 and 13 for more information.) In planning the deck's color and appearance, you can choose natural wood tones, neutral gray tones, or paint schemes to match those of the house. Choose a finish while planning your deck, because your choice may influence which species and grade of lumber you want to use. If you stain the decking a dark color or use opaque stains, for example, they mask large knots and imperfections, enabling you to use cheaper lumber grades. If you want to retain the natural look of wood by using a clear sealer, you may not be able to use certain types of preservative-treated lumber.

Chapter 6

Choosing Materials for Your Deck

• •

In This Chapter

▶ Going with the grain

▶ Sizing up lumber

▶ Making connections

▶ Firming up footings

▶ Ordering specialties of the deck

▶ Finding a fine finish

• •

*B*uilding a deck is an excellent project for first-time builders because you have very few materials to learn about, and those same materials are basic to many other construction projects. But these materials can also be expensive. Knowing your options for materials helps you make decisions and tradeoffs that can reduce costs, maximize appearance, minimize maintenance, and extend the longevity of your deck. Wood is the dominant material and presents the greatest variety of choices (including simulated wood products that have appeared on the deck scene in recent years and are likely to multiply). Other materials with which you need to become familiar are fasteners, connectors, concrete, and finishes. You're not apt to find one store that offers all the choices that I present in this chapter, so shop around as much as possible. (For information about wiring, lighting, and plumbing materials, see Chapter 25.)

Going with the Grain

Some types of wood are suitable for deck construction; others aren't. The most important characteristic of wood for decks is durability: the capability to resist damage from moisture, insects, microorganisms (fungi and mildew), and ultraviolet rays. No wood is completely immune to these destructive agents, and over time, all wood completely decays. Some species of wood, however, have a natural resistance to some or all of these threats, and you can treat many other species of wood with preservatives, sealants, or paint to protect them for decades. Nonwood products also resist deterioration.

Wood also varies in strength, appearance, availability, and cost. If you design parts of your deck for certain strength groupings (see Chapter 5), you're going to choose lumber from that grouping or a higher one, of course. You must also consider appearance, especially in choosing decking. Knot size, grain pattern, ratio of sapwood to heartwood, edge treatment, natural color, and the capability of the wood to accept stain or paint affect your deck's overall appearance. Availability and cost also affect your choices, and these factors change constantly as forestry practices, conservation laws, distribution networks, retail trading patterns, expanding global markets, emerging technologies, consumer demand, and similar conditions change. Your local lumberyard may stock only a small fraction of the products available.

The following sections describe ten products that you commonly use on decks as the decking surface, the structural members, or both. The list includes the following products:

- Redwood
- Cedar
- Cypress
- Tropical hardwoods
- Preservative-treated pine
- Preservative-treated Douglas fir
- Other preservative-treated woods
- Nondurable lumber
- Nonwood alternatives
- Recycled lumber

The following sections acquaint you with the advantages and limitations of each choice.

Redwood

Many people visualize the classic deck surface to be clear (knot-free), all-heart (no sapwood) redwood with a natural finish, but only the premium grades fit this picture. Most grades have knots of various sizes and many also have a certain amount of sapwood. The heartwood has the deep reddish color and durability for which redwood is known; the sapwood is light yellow and vulnerable to rot and insect damage.

First-growth redwood is harvested from ancient forests, is increasingly hard to find, and typically has 20 or more growth rings per inch; second- and third-growth lumber, which dominate the redwood market today, typically have 10 or fewer growth rings and, therefore, aren't as strong or durable. Dense heartwood has natural immunities to insect and rot damage; the protective tannins can leach out of the wood, however, if you subject it to repeated cycles of wet and dry conditions without a protective coating.

Redwood weathers naturally to a dark gray color. To preserve its original fresh look (as shown in Figure 6-1), use a clear preservative and sealer, renewed periodically, or stain the wood a color as close to the original as possible. Finishes last longer on redwood than on most other woods.

If you intend to paint redwood or cover it with a heavy-bodied stain, consider less-expensive lumber; the benefits of heart redwood — its beauty and durability — aren't necessary under such coverage. Many products try to duplicate the look of redwood — indeed, in buying "redwood" make sure that you aren't buying just "red wood."

Although relatively strong for its light weight, redwood isn't used widely as structural lumber, except for posts and smaller beams close to the ground. It can be brittle and splits fairly easily. The absence of pitch, its beauty, and its stable dimensions make redwood a pleasure to work with. It resists warping and checking (which results from splits on the face of a board that cut across the grain) after you install it.

Figure 6-1:
Redwood's natural beauty makes for stunning decks.

Cedar

Cedar, shown in Figure 6-2, has a fine grain pattern and warm, rich colors; contains natural phenol preservatives; and resists moisture, making it ideal for outdoor building projects. It is, however, less termite-resistant than redwood. The color difference between heartwood and sapwood is less pronounced in cedar than in most woods. Cedar tends to have a rough surface, even if planed. It has no pitch or resins, making it easy to work with and resistant to warping. Cedar seasons quickly and accepts stains well. Although relatively strong for its light weight, it can be brittle and lacks high structural strength. Cedar weathers to a light silver-gray color unless you seal or stain it.

Figure 6-2:
Cedar decks, like this one, weather to a light silver-gray unless sealed or stained.

As with redwood, most cedar available on today's market is from second- and third-growth forests and is not as dense as old-growth cedar. Western red cedar is widely available in the western United States and Canada. Northern and southern white cedar, available in the East, and Port Orford cedar, a white cedar that's available on the West Coast, are not as strong. Alaskan yellow cedar, prized for use in boats and musical instruments, is harvested on a limited basis and is gaining popularity as a highly durable decking lumber.

Cypress

Logged in the southeastern United States, cypress is not widely distributed but is a regional favorite for decks. As are redwood and cedar, cypress is naturally rot-resistant. It has a distinctive reddish color and a pronounced grain pattern of contrasting dark and light colors. Cypress weathers to a light gray and is easy to work with. Although it's stronger than redwood and cedar, people use cypress primarily for decking and railings and not as structural members because of its relatively high cost.

Tropical hardwoods

The more familiar of these decking hardwoods such as mahogany, lauan, and teak have been joined by a host of exotic tropical woods with names such as bongossi, jarrah, ipe, kwila, bilinga, ekki, and angelim vermelho. These woods are generally stronger and more durable than redwood, cedar, or cypress and are often completely free of knots. Most tropical woods are dense and heavy, requiring you to predrill holes for screws or nails but making the wood naturally fire-resistant. Grown in regions with year-round growing conditions, these woods have a consistent grain pattern that accepts stains and sealers uniformly well. Left to weather naturally, they attain a smooth, silvery sheen. Sanding the surface restores it to its original brightness.

The cost of tropical hardwoods is often comparable to those of the premium grades of durable softwoods. Most exotic woods are not distributed widely beyond major importing centers. In investigating tropical hardwoods, inquire whether the lumber comes from well-managed, sustained-yield forests or from forests where clear-cutting and other questionable practices prevail. Many reputable dealers offer products certified by environmental organizations that encourage the responsible use of global resources.

Preservative-treated pine

Pine treated with a preservative that's injected into the wood under pressure makes a durable, handsome, and affordable deck material, as shown in Figure 6-3. Southern pine, which includes loblolly, longleaf, shortleaf, and slash pine, is especially desirable because it's very strong, produces an attractive grain pattern, and retains a tough surface. The preservative that most treated lumber uses is chromated copper arsenate (CCA), an inert inorganic compound that bonds with the wood fibers and doesn't leach out easily if the wood gets wet. The wood has two levels of treatment: heavy, for ground contact, and lighter, for above-ground exposure. The copper tints the wood a green color, which weathers to a natural gray. Many manufacturers mask the green color with tan, golden, or reddish stains that resemble natural cedar or redwood.

Figure 6-3:
Pressure-treated pine is a popular choice for decks, even intricate decks such as this one.

Pine is prone to warping, cracks, splinters, and pitch pockets, whether treated or not. It's also tougher to saw and nail than are redwood or cedar. Because the treatment raises the moisture content of the wood, you need to let it dry before you build with it, or the wood may shrink and crack excessively. In buying the lumber, specify air-dried-after-treatment (ADAT) or kiln-dried-after-treatment (KDAT) to ensure low moisture content, or you can air-dry it yourself for at least two months by stacking it carefully, placing sticks spaced every two feet between each layer of boards, and keeping the stack protected from rain. The preservative treatment is intended to deter damage from mold, mildew, fungus, and insects, but it doesn't resist moisture; you need to apply paint, stain, or a sealer to preservative-treated wood after it seasons for a few weeks. Some manufacturers add a water-repellent sealer to the preservative, which may account for the higher cost of some products if you're comparing prices.

The preservative treatment penetrates only sapwood and not heartwood, requiring you to use grades of lumber with at least $2^1/_2$ inches of sapwood and no more than half an inch of heartwood. With Southern pine, these lesser grades are nevertheless strong enough for structural use, which makes this product one of the few woods that you can use economically for all parts of a deck. Other species of treated pine, such as ponderosa and white pine, are not as strong as Southern pine.

Preservative-treated Douglas fir

Like yellow pine, Douglas fir is exceptionally strong. It's abundant in the Northwestern U.S. and in western Canada. Unlike pine, however, Douglas fir requires *incisement*, or punctures, to enable preservatives to penetrate deep enough for long-term protection. As a result, the wood is not suitable for decking, railings, and other exposed applications where the incisement marks would be objectionable. It does, however, make excellent lumber for posts, beams, ledgers, and other framing members that remain hidden under the deck.

Wood with a high level of preservatives, which is intended for ground contact and rated as .40 pounds of chemical per cubic foot of wood (pcf), is dark green or almost black in color. Wood treated for above-ground use, with a rating of .25 pcf, has a light-green or tan color. As with most preservative-treated lumber, you should paint, stain, or seal this wood as soon as possible to protect it from moisture and ultraviolet rays from the sun.

Other preservative-treated woods

Pine and Douglas fir are the most common and the strongest woods available with pressure treatment, but you may find spruce, hemlock (often referred to as hem/fir), or other species in your area. Pressure-treating lumber is an accepted method of conserving wood by utilizing lesser grades of lumber and increasing the longevity of wooden structures, so most manufacturers offer preservative-treated lumber in whatever species is feasible.

Make sure that the species and grade match the strength grouping you choose (see Chapter 5), that the preservative has a rating of at least .25 pcf, and that the preservative penetrates 85 percent of the sapwood as viewed in cross section. As with any preservative-treated wood, observe all manufacturers' recommendations.

Nondurable lumber

Some decks contain untreated lumber for certain structural members, such as beams or joists, because the required size or grade is not available in a durable wood or the structural members are heavily protected by paint or site-applied preservatives. Nondurable wood, even if protected by paint, stain, or a sealer, may deteriorate rapidly if moisture gets trapped under the coating. If you choose nondurable lumber merely to save money, consider that the cost of preservative-treated lumber is only nominally higher in the overall deck budget (and probably cheaper in the long run).

Nonwood alternatives

In the last few years, the wood-products industry has undergone a revolution. "Engineered" wood that doesn't look like wood but performs better than solid wood is gaining wide acceptance as a preferred alternative to traditional "dimensioned" lumber. Many of these new products are manufactured from pulp logs and recycled materials. Most are not suitable for outdoor use, but a few have been engineered for decks and other backyard structures and have entered mainstream building practices. One, a wood-polymer composite consisting of recycled plastic products and waste wood, resembles 2x6 or $^5/_4$x6 decking boards. It's not intended for structural use. It requires no sealers or finishes, although you can paint or stain it if you want, and it weathers to a light-gray color.

Other alternatives to wood include decking and railing members made out of vinyl or polyvinyl chloride (PVC) and steel joists manufactured for interior use in commercial buildings which, because they're galvanized, are also suitable for outdoor applications.

Recycled lumber

Don't overlook recycled lumber from an old deck or outdoor structure. If you can find someone who's demolishing a deck, you may have access to redwood or cedar decking that's still in good condition. Remove the decking boards and nails, turn the boards over, and run a router with a rounding bit along the edges to give them a clean, uniform look. Install the boards and give them a light touchup with a floor sander before staining or sealing them.

Sizing Up Lumber

After you decide on the type of wood you're going to use, you still must become familiar with some other characteristics of lumber, including size, defects, and terminology.

What's a "2x4"?

In lumberland, an inch isn't always an inch. Boards that you call 2x4s and 2x8s because they're supposed to measure two inches by four inches or two inches by eight inches . . . really don't (measure out to those dimensions, that is). These terms refer to the board's *nominal* size, which is the approximate size of the board before someone dries and planes, or *dresses,* it to a smaller, uniform size. You use the nominal size in referring to span charts, plans, retail purchasing, and general communication about your project, but you should also be familiar with the finished, or actual, size as you're estimating deck coverage and measuring boards for cutting and fitting (see Figure 6-4).

Table 6-1 shows typical finished sizes for lumber, although these dimensions may vary. Keep in mind that lumber that's not surfaced, or planed, is referred to as *rough* lumber. Although closer to its nominal size than surfaced lumber, it's not uniform in size, and so you shouldn't use it where sizes must be accurate and consistent. Rough lumber isn't suitable for joists that must be of uniform thickness and depth, for example, but it makes a good ledger board because only one edge (the top) needs to be flush with other boards.

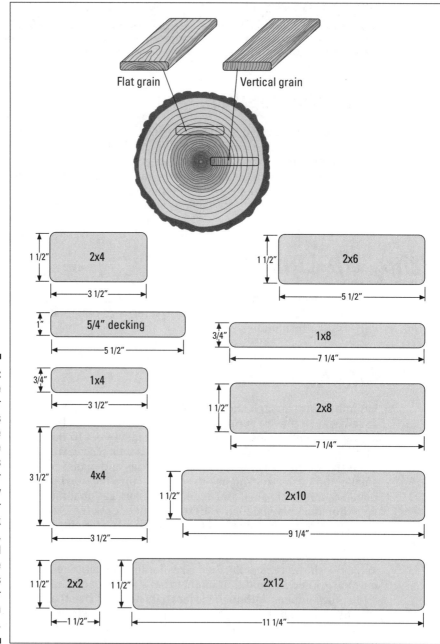

Figure 6-4:
These
lumber
profiles
illustrate
the relative
actual sizes
of lumber
typically
used for
deck
construction,
as well
as the
differences
in their
grain
patterns.

Table 6-1	Nominal and Actual Sizes of Softwood Lumber
Nominal Size	*Actual (Surfaced) Size**
1x2	$^3/_4$'' x $1^1/_2$''
1x3	$^3/_4$'' x $2^1/_2$''
1x4	$^3/_4$'' x $3^1/_2$''
1x6	$^3/_4$'' x $5^1/_2$''
1x8	$^3/_4$'' x $7^1/_4$''
1x10	$^3/_4$'' x $9^1/_4$''
1x12	$^3/_4$'' x $11^1/_4$''
$^5/_4$x4	1 to $1^1/_4$'' x $3^1/_2$ to 4''
$^5/_4$x6	1 to $1^1/_4$'' x $5^1/_2$ to 6''
2x2	$1^1/_2$'' x $1^1/_2$''
2x3	$1^1/_2$'' x $2^1/_2$''
2x4	$1^1/_2$'' x $3^1/_2$''
2x6	$1^1/_2$'' x $5^1/_2$''
2x8	$1^1/_2$'' x $7^1/_4$''
2x10	$1^1/_2$'' x $9^1/_4$''
2x12	$1^1/_2$'' x $11^1/_4$''
4x4	$3^1/_2$'' x $3^1/_2$''
4x6	$3^1/_2$'' x $5^1/_2$''
4x8	$3^1/_2$'' x $7^1/_4$''
4x10	$3^1/_2$'' x $9^1/_4$''
4x12	$3^1/_2$'' x $11^1/_4$''
6x6	$5^1/_2$'' x $5^1/_2$''
6x8	$5^1/_2$'' x $7^1/_4$''
8x8	$7^1/_4$'' x $7^1/_4$''

*Sizes vary depending on such factors as moisture content. Always check.

Board lengths are much easier to understand. Most lumber is sold in 2-foot increments, from 6 to 20 feet long. A few items, such as manufactured non-wood products, may be available in limited sizes, and some lumber, such as tropical hardwoods, may come in random lengths.

Finding faults

Wood is alive; it moves and, of course, comes from living trees, so it's not always stable. The sophisticated manufacturing techniques and quality control that people use to produce lumber ensure a generally uniform, but not perfect, product. Whenever you buy lumber, you must assume a certain number of defects; the following list includes the most common board boo-boos that you can expect to find:

- ✔ **Bow.** The board, lying flat, looks like a long ski with uplifted ends. You can correct this problem by nailing the board in place or, if necessary, cutting off a severely bowed end.

- ✔ **Check.** The board has a split near the end that doesn't go all the way through the board. Cut off the bad end.

- ✔ **Crook.** The board, lying flat, curves; turned on edge, the board has a crown, or hump, in the center. If you install the board on edge, point the crown up; if you install it flat, straighten the board as you fasten it.

- ✔ **Cup.** The long edges of the board curl upward (or downward), creating a trough. Turn the board over so that it dries evenly or cut out the affected part.

- ✔ **Knot or knothole.** Tight knots are okay. Loose knots, which have a dark ring around them, eventually fall out and may leave holes in the deck surface.

- ✔ **Shake.** The board develops a long crack where growth rings separate from each other. Also called *shelling*. Install the board "bark side up" (see Chapter 11) so that the grain exposed on the surface of the board tightens rather than opens up.

- ✔ **Split.** The board is cracked all the way through, usually at an end. Cut off the split end.

- ✔ **Twist.** The board corkscrews from one end to the other. Cut off the worst end and nail the board securely.

- ✔ **Wane.** The edge of the board is missing some wood (usually bark). Turn the board over or trim off the bad edge.

Learning lumber lingo

As you browse through lumberyards and home centers, you may come across strange terms that everyone else seems to know. The following list of timber terms can help you decipher the lingo:

✔ **ADAT (air-dried after treatment):** Lumber that's preservative-treated and left to dry for a certain time before being shipped. *See* KDAT.

✔ **BD FT or BF (board feet):** A measurement by which lumber is often sold; one board foot measures 1 inch by 1 foot by 1 foot; a 2x4 that's 12 feet long is 8 BF; a 2x6 that's 12 feet long is 12 BF.

✔ **BTR (better):** A higher grade than the stated grade; for example, at least half of the boards in a unit of "No. 2 and BTR" are higher graded than No. 2 and would be excellent for deck construction.

✔ **CLR (clear):** No knots.

✔ **CLR HRT (clear heartwood):** No knots, no sapwood; a premium grade of wood.

✔ **CON HRT (construction heart):** A grade of redwood with no sapwood, a minimal number of tight knots, and suitable strength for structural purposes.

✔ **DF (Douglas fir):** Lumber made from any Douglas fir.

✔ **DF/L (Douglas fir/larch):** A type of Douglas fir with different strength ratings from Douglas fir grown in other regions.

✔ **FG (flat grain):** A board with a wavy and irregular grain pattern on the face and straight, parallel grain on the edges. *See* VG.

✔ **GRN (green):** Lumber that hasn't had time to dry, or *season,* and is prone to shrinking.

✔ **KD (kiln-dried):** Lumber that's dried in a kiln to a very low moisture content.

✔ **KDAT (kiln-dried after treatment):** Preservative-treated lumber that is low in moisture content and not prone to shrinking or splitting.

✔ **LBR (lumber):** That about says it all.

✔ **LF (lineal feet):** Measurement by the actual length of the board, regardless of its nominal size. A 1x6 that's 10 feet long is 10 LF.

✔ **MBF (thousand [*mille*] board feet):** *See* BD FT.

✔ **PT (preservative-treated or pressure-treated):** Lumber treated with a preservative that's injected into the wood under pressure at an EPA-approved facility.

✔ **RED (radius-edged decking):** Lumber that's $^5/_4$ inches thick with rounded edges, specifically developed for use in deck surfaces.

✔ **RL (random lengths):** Lumber sold at a certain price with no choice of lengths.

✔ **RGH (rough):** Lumber that isn't surfaced; close to nominal size in dimension.

- **S-DRY (surfaced dry):** Lumber that's both surfaced and air-dried; suitable for decks.

- **S-GRN (surfaced green):** Lumber that's surfaced only but not dried; prone to shrinking and splitting.

- **S1S2E (surfaced 1 side, 2 edges):** All but one face of a board bearing this grading is planed; you can install the board with the smooth side out or the rough side out, depending on the desired appearance; sometimes called *fascia grade*.

- **S2E (surfaced 2 edges):** Only the two edges are planed; both faces are rough.

- **S2S (surfaced 2 sides):** The two sides, but not the edges, are planed.

- **S4S (surfaced 4 sides):** All sides and edges are planed; the most common format.

- **SEL (select):** In some grading systems, the highest grade of lumber, based on appearance.

- **STR (structural):** In some grading systems, a grade of lumber high in strength and suitable for critical load-bearing members.

- **SYP (Southern yellow pine):** Lumber made from Southern yellow pine.

- **VG (vertical grain):** A board with a parallel and fairly straight grain pattern on the face of the board and a wavy pattern on the edges; also called *edge-grained* or *riff sawn. See* FG.

- **WRC (western red cedar):** Lumber made from western red cedar.

Making Connections

You need more than gravity to hold a deck together. The secret to building long-lasting outdoor structures is to nail, screw, strap, glue, and connect the heck out of 'em. Starting from the ground up, the following list reviews the various fasteners that you should use to connect your deck. (See Figure 6-5 for an illustration of typical fasteners.) Your local building code may require certain connectors — for example, approved post anchors for the footings. Make sure that you follow the manufacturer's specifications in nailing or bolting framing connectors. Always choose corrosion-resistant connectors, such as those with a hot-dipped galvanized coating or those made from stainless steel.

- **Post anchors.** Use these brackets to tie the deck posts securely to the footings. Embed the lower part of the bracket in wet concrete and bolt the post to the upper part. You can buy *post anchors* to fit either surfaced or rough lumber. Some anchors are adjustable, enabling you to move the post up to one inch in any direction. Most brackets are galvanized sheet metal. Heavy-duty welded brackets, which are called _column bases_ and which you must paint, offer more decorative options.

✔ **Post caps.** Use these brackets, made from galvanized sheet metal or welded steel, to connect posts to beams. They also connect beams together where they join end-to-end over posts. Use a smaller _end post cap_ for connecting a post to the end of a beam. Alternatives to post caps are _T-straps,_ triangular plywood _gussets_ (use preservative-treated or marine plywood), and custom-welded brackets.

✔ **Joist hangers.** _Joist hangers,_ which provide a strong connection between joists and ledgers or beams, are made for various sizes of joists. Some are skewed 45 degrees to the right or left, making them handy for decks with angles, such as an octagon deck or a deck that fits around a bay window. You can also use joist hangers to support the upper end of stair stringers. In buying hangers, look for _16d galvanized joist hanger nails_ (16d stands for 16 penny; see the last entry in this list); these nails are stout enough to hold the weight but short enough not to penetrate through the joist lumber.

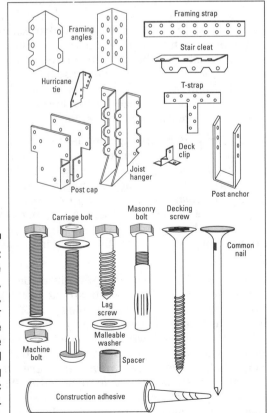

Figure 6-5: The brackets, connectors, and other hardware shown here are typical for building a basic deck.

✔ **Other framing connectors.** *Beam hangers,* which come in various depths for different size beams, are a variation of joist hangers. They also come in different widths: 3-inch for doubled 2-by lumber, $3^1/_2$-inch for standard 4-by lumber, and 4-inch for rough 4-by lumber. Another connector that's useful for deck construction is the *hurricane tie,* or *rafter tie,* which is designed for roof construction, but you can use it on decks to secure joists to the tops of beams. Two simple connectors for reinforcing joints are the *framing strap* ($1^1/_2$ inches wide by 12 or 24 inches long) and the *framing angle* (a 90-degree angle bracket for inside corners). If you build stairs with solid stringers, use *stair brackets* to support the treads.

✔ **Bolts and lag screws.** Use galvanized bolts and lag screws to connect brackets to major structural members or to connect deck components to each other — such as railing posts to joists — or to the house. *Machine bolts* have a hexagonal (hex) head and require a nut and washers. Use $3/_8$-inch diameter bolts for attaching connectors to posts and beams, and $1/_2$-inch diameter bolts for connecting components together. Use *carriage bolts,* which have a rounded head that's more attractive than the crude hex head of a machine bolt, wherever appearance is important. Use a *lag screw,* which is a large screw with a hex head, in lieu of a bolt where you have no access for attaching a nut. If you're connecting wood to masonry, such as a ledger to the house foundation, use a *masonry bolt* or *expansion bolt,* which has expanding devices built into the bolt. Both require drilling a hole into the wall before inserting and tightening the bolt. Wherever you bolt a major structural member to another deck component, use *malleable washers (massively thick)* rather than the more familiar *cut washers.* Malleable washers, which are available in galvanized or black (rust-prone) finish, grip the wood without compressing and weakening it.

✔ **Spacers and flashing for ledger.** Although neither item is a connector, as such, add one or both items to your materials list for connecting the ledger to the house. Insert *spacers* (waferlike devices with holes for bolts, made for this purpose from plastic or metal) behind the ledger to provide a gap for air to circulate and prevent rot from forming between the ledger board and house siding, or tuck a long strip of *metal flashing* under the siding and over the top of the ledger to prevent moisture from seeping into the joint. (See Chapter 10 for more information about installing a ledger.)

✔ **Deck fasteners.** Although nails (usually 10d galvanized common nails) are the traditional method of fastening deck boards to joists, *galvanized deck screws* and other fasteners are quickly gaining ground. Screws have more holding power and enable you to easily adjust or replace boards. Because both nails and screws have visible heads that may mar the deck surface, however, manufacturers have developed alternative fasteners that remain hidden. One is *construction adhesive,* which is applied by using a caulking gun and bonds extremely well. It's difficult to use with anything but perfectly straight boards, however, and, after you install it, makes the removal of boards impossible without damaging them. *Decking clips* and metal *fastening strips* are hidden devices that grip the decking boards from below.

✔ **Nails.** Building a deck requires an assortment of nails, which come in various lengths designated by the letter *d* (but referred to as *penny*). For temporary forms and bracing use *8d* and *16d duplex* nails, which have a double head for easy removal. All other nails should be corrosion resistant, either *hot-dip galvanized (HDG)* or *stainless steel*. Redwood and cedar have tannins that corrode some galvanized nails but don't affect stainless steel nails. Use *16d twist,* or *spiral shank,* nails for fastening 2-by lumber to thicker members and *12d common* nails for attaching 2-by lumber to other 2-by lumber or for installing decking. Use *8d, 7d,* or *6d box* nails for attaching 1-by fascia, railing members, and other small-dimensioned lumber. Finally, have a few *6d* and *4d finishing* nails on hand for repairing splits or attaching small trim pieces.

Table 6-2 enables you to estimate how many pounds of nails you may need if you have an idea of how many connections you need to make. The main point, of course, is that you need many pounds of larger nails and very few pounds of smaller sizes.

Table 6-2	Sizes, Lengths, and Quantity of Selected Nails			
		Number of Nails Per Pound		
Nail Size	*Length*	*Common*	*Box*	*Finishing*
2d	1''	875	1,000	1,350
3d	1¼''	565	635	800
4d	1½''	315	475	585
6d	2''	180	235	310
8d	2½''	105	145	190
10d	3''	70	95	120
12d	3¼''	62	90	115
16d	3½''	50	70	90
20d	4''	30	51	63

Firming Up Footings

Except for sprawling decks with dozens of footings or decks in cold country where deep footings are necessary, most decks involve a relatively small amount of concrete. For very small amounts — three or four footings of two or three cubic feet each — you can buy sacks of concrete mix. For decks with a dozen or so moderate-sized footings, you can mix your own from bulk ingredients or order a delivery of ready-mixed concrete. For any project involving more than a yard of concrete, order ready-mix (see Chapter 17).

The basic ingredients of concrete are sand, gravel, cement, and water, mixed in a correct ratio. If you order bulk ingredients and mix them yourself, order 1,310 pounds of sand, 1,730 pounds of gravel, and six 90-pound sacks of cement for each cubic yard (27 cubic feet) of concrete. (*Note:* A sack of *cement,* which is pure portland cement without sand or gravel, is different from a sack of *concrete mix,* which has cement, sand, and gravel.)

You also need reinforcing steel for your concrete footings and piers. Use No.4 (half-inch diameter) *rebar* (or *reinforcing bar*), which is sold in 20-foot lengths but can be cut at the lumberyard for easier transportation. A typical 18-inch-square deck footing with a 3-foot pier requires about 10 feet of rebar (see Chapter 9). You also need *tie wire* to tie rebar together and *dobies,* which are small cubes of concrete with wires embedded in them that you use to hold rebar off the ground.

If you don't form and cast your own piers, you can buy prefabricated concrete pier blocks to set into the fresh concrete of the footings. Some have a small block of wood attached to them with a few nails; others have post anchors cast into them. Buy the type with post anchors.

Ordering Specialties of the Deck

Some manufacturers offer specialty items intended for decks, such as balusters and finials for railings, molded handrails for stairs, modular corner pieces for curved railings, and prefabricated stair parts. Most of these items are embellishments that suit ornate designs, reminiscent of Victorian garden architecture, and you can order them through magazine advertisements, catalogs, or customer-service counters at large home centers. Make sure that you include them in your materials list.

Finding a Fine Finish

The options for finishing your deck, besides leaving the wood to weather naturally, are wood preservatives, sealers, semitransparent stains, solid stains, and paints. Many manufacturers combine two or more finishes into one product, such as a stain that contains a sealer, preservatives, and ultraviolet-ray absorbers. The most effective finishes are those that penetrate the wood, such as water repellents, water-repellent preservatives,

Estimating concrete

One of the most important techniques for working with concrete is knowing how to estimate the quantity you need. You don't want extra concrete to dispose of, and you certainly don't want to run short just as you're finishing a pour. Use the following guidelines for making an accurate estimate:

✔ The basic measuring units for estimating and ordering concrete are cubic feet and cubic yards.

✔ You can make a preliminary estimate of how much concrete you need based on your plans, but wait until *after* you dig the footing holes and build forms before you make a final estimate.

✔ If the footing hole or pier is square or rectangular, calculate volume by multiplying *width* x *length* x *depth* (to which the concrete is to be poured). If the hole is round, use the formula πr^2 x *height*, where π is 3.1416, *r* is the *radius* of the hole's cross section (don't forget to multiply this number by itself), and *height* is the depth of the hole or the total height of the finished concrete pier, whichever is greater. Add an extra foot or two of concrete if the bottom of the pier hole is flared.

✔ *Important:* Take all measurements in inches or feet and fractions of feet. Do not mix feet and inches. You could calculate a hole 18 inches square and 30 inches deep, for example, as 18 x 18 x 30 *inches* or as 1.5 x 1.5 x 2.5 *feet*. If you use inches, convert your answer to cubic feet by dividing by 1,728 (the number of cubic inches in one cubic foot).

✔ To calculate the volume of a complex shape, such as a round pier connected to a square footing, separate the shape into simple forms, calculate the volume of each form, and add them together for a total (in cubic feet).

✔ Add the volume of all footings and piers together (in cubic feet).

✔ Estimate how many sacks of concrete mix you need by dividing the volume of one sack into the total cubic feet (80-pound sacks are .67, or $\frac{2}{3}$, cubic foot; 60-pound sacks are .45 cubic foot). If, for example, the total concrete that you need is 16 cubic feet, you need 24 80-pound sacks or 36 60-pound sacks of concrete mix.

✔ For large quantities, convert cubic feet to cubic yards by dividing by 27 (the number of cubic feet in one cubic yard). A total of 42 cubic feet of concrete, for example, is 1.6 cubic yards.

✔ Add an extra 10 percent to your total to compensate for irregular excavations and to ensure that you don't run short.

and semitransparent stains. Those that form a film on the surface aren't as durable. Varnish, for one, is completely unsuitable for decks. Paint and solid-color stains are better in some situations. Begin your investigation early by buying small samples and testing them on various types of wood that you're considering for your deck.

The following list includes the benefits and disadvantages of each type of finish:

- **Preservatives.** Wood preservatives are essentially mildewcides, insecticides, and fungicides that protect the wood from attack. Preservative-treated lumber, which already contains preservatives, is more effective than wood coated with a preservative on the job site. Treated wood should be stained, sealed, or painted.

- **Sealers.** Sealers are water-repellent compounds that soak into the wood and prevent it from absorbing water, which could cause cracking, splitting, and warping. They also retard the loss of *lignin,* a natural substance in the wood that, if lost, causes the wood to weather and turn gray. Sealers containing ultraviolet (UV) inhibitors slow this process even more. Use a clear sealer to prolong the natural, fresh look of the wood. Avoid clear sealers that leave a hard finish, such as varnish or plastic floor finishes; they're not true sealers, can be slippery, and eventually crack and blister.

- **Semitransparent stains.** Most semitransparent, or light-bodied, stains penetrate into the wood and blend with its natural color to give it a new soft color and enhance the grain pattern (but also, unfortunately, any defects in the wood). You must renew the stain periodically, although the light color makes wear and tear less noticeable than do paint or darker stains. Some stains are formulated for use over preservative-treated lumber. Choose stains specified for decks. Avoid latex semi-transparent stains, which form a fine film on the wood that peels and wears off easily.

- **Solid stains.** Solid stains have much more pigment than do semitransparent stains and, as a result, don't penetrate into the wood as much. They almost mask the wood completely, as paint does, but allow some of the grain and texture of the wood to show through. Many solid-color stains, especially oil- and latex-based stains, are more suitable for siding than decks. Choose a nonchalking type of stain and plan to renew it every year. You can use a solid stain over weathered or previously stained wood.

- **Paints.** Paint offers the most color options and dresses up lower grades of wood better than other finishes by hiding knots and imperfections. It's expensive and requires applying a primer and one or more top coats. Paint is not a preservative, however, so the wood is still subject to decay if not treated beforehand with a preservative. Choose a paint formulated for exterior decks and use a compatible primer. To make a painted surface less slippery, mix in some silicone sand with the fresh paint. Renew the paint as cracks and wear begin to develop. After you paint a deck, you must continue to repaint it; none of the other finishes is an option, although you can change paint colors.

Note: For information about wiring, lighting, and plumbing materials, see Chapter 25.

Chapter 7

Drawing the Final Deck Plan

*Y*our final deck plan should include all features, great and small. Drawing a complete set of working plans may seem a tedious task, but the advantages more than justify the effort. Not only do clear drawings enable you to make an accurate materials list and obtain a building permit, but they also help you think through each step of the building process. Draw the plans as if someone else must build the deck while you're out of town and can't be reached by telephone; don't assume that you can work out the details later.

If needed, review the guidelines in Chapter 4 for making a scale drawing. Using your site plan and the deck specs that I provide in Chapter 5, start your drawings with an overhead view, called a *plan view,* of the finished deck (see Figure 7-1). Then use this drawing as a guide for drawing the *framing and foundation plan, elevations,* and *details.* You also need to become familiar with the construction information that I give you in Chapters 8 through 13.

Figure 7-1:
A plan view
represents
the general
layout of
the deck as
it appears
from above,
with
dimensions
included.

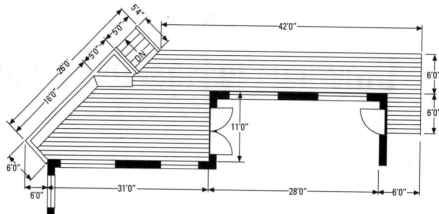

Plan View

Draw a plan view of the complete deck in ¼-inch scale. (A deck measuring 28 x 40 feet would require 7 x 10 inches of paper in this scale.) Observe the following guidelines:

- ✔ If the deck is attached to the house, show the house walls, doors, and windows.

- ✔ Draw the individual deck boards to scale. Make each board slightly wider than the actual size to account for a ³/₁₆-inch gap between boards.

- ✔ Check the length of boards and make adjustments, if necessary. If the decking boards are 16'4", for example, you may want to change them to exactly 16 feet to prevent waste, because lumber comes in 2-foot increments.

- ✔ Include railings (top view), stairs, built-in planters, and overheads.

- ✔ Indicate dimensions by using lines and arrows off to the side, showing precisely where measurements start and end.

- ✔ Use an arrow and the word *up* or *down* to indicate the direction of stairs, starting at the deck platform.

Framing and Foundation Plan

After you complete the plan view, you need to draw a framing and foundation plan (see Figure 7-2). Think of this plan in layers, beginning with decking boards on top and progressing downward through the joists, beams, posts, and footings. The following guidelines can help you avoid common mistakes and omissions:

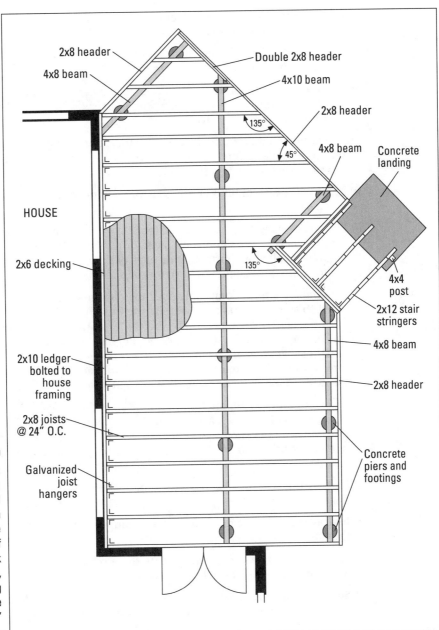

2x8 header

Double 2x8 header

4x8 beam

4x10 beam

2x8 header

135°

45°

4x8 beam

Concrete landing

HOUSE

2x6 decking

135°

4x4 post

2x12 stair stringers

4x8 beam

2x8 header

2x10 ledger bolted to house framing

2x8 joists @ 24" O.C.

Concrete piers and footings

Figure 7-2: A framing and foundation plan is like an X-ray of the deck from above, showing all the "bones."

Galvanized joist hangers

✔ Include all joists, beams, ledgers, headers, blocking, stair stringers, and — where visible — posts.

✔ Show all footing locations; if you represent footings as circles (drawn with a compass), they're easier to see.

✔ Draw a small area of decking boards in a "quiet" part of the drawing (with no beams or footings below them) to show how the decking pattern runs in relation to the joist layout.

✔ Be careful where boards cross each other; don't draw lines through boards and make sure that the correct board appears on top where two boards intersect.

✔ Identify the size of lumber you use for each member (2x6, 4x8, and so on).

✔ Show the *on-center* (O.C.) dimensions for joist and beam spacings. Clarify whether the dimension lines for outside (first and last) joists and beams align with the outside *edge* of the board or the *center*. (To avoid confusion, delineate both measurements.)

On-center is a term commonly used in construction to indicate how far apart to space boards at repeated intervals. You take the measurement from the center of one board to the center of the adjacent board and so on. You need to understand that the dimension remains constant whether you measure from center-to-center or from edge-to-edge (as long as you measure from the same edge of each board — for example, left edge to left edge or right edge to right edge).

✔ Be aware that discrepancies are bound to occur between the overall dimensions of the deck *framing* and the overall dimensions of the finished *deck* (as shown in your plan view) if the edge of the decking overhangs the joists or the outer edge of the deck has a fascia (a trim board).

✔ Identify the size of all angles other than 90 degrees by using an arc and degree notation.

✔ In drawing stairs, remember that the number of treads is one less than the number of risers.

✔ Show joist hangers. You can indicate them by drawing a small L-shaped angle on each side of the joist where it intersects the ledger or beam.

✔ Show blocking between joists. If drawing each board muddles the plan, indicate the line of blocking by using a dashed line.

Elevations

Show the deck in *elevation,* or side view, from at least one side (see Figure 7-3). The elevation view(s) enables you to see posts, railings, edge details, benches, stairs, an overhead, the slope of the ground, the height of the deck, and the size of the deck in relation to the house. It doesn't show interior portions of the deck; it includes only the components that you can see from that side. Choose the side that shows stairs or changes in deck levels most clearly. Render the profile of the ground, or grade, as accurately as possible so that you can establish the height of the deck above the ground.

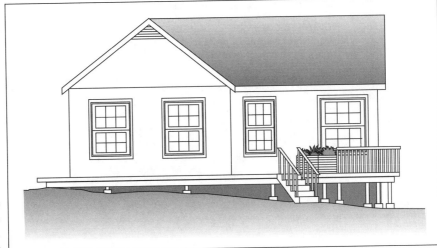

Figure 7-3: An elevation view shows how the deck looks from the side.

Sections and Details

Sections and details clarify how you're going to build the deck. For simple decks, one section drawing should be enough to show all structural connections and details. Larger or more complex decks may require more than one section and possibly separate detail drawings for critical components. Although you draw sections in the same scale as the framing plan or elevation (normally $1/4"$), you draw details in a different scale ($1/2"$ or $3/4"$), as shown in Figure 7-4. The following construction elements should be apparent in the framing plan, sections, or details. (For more information, see Chapters 9 through 12.)

- ✔ **Lumber sizes:** Indicate the size you're using for each component.

- ✔ **Footings:** Show the typical depth, width, height above ground, and rebar location for footings. Specify any footings that deviate from the typical footing, such as a stair landing or post footings to support a privacy screen not supported by the deck.

✔ **Posts:** Show the typical connection to footings and beams.

✔ **Ledger:** Show how it connects to the framing in the house wall and how the connection is weatherproofed.

✔ **Beams:** Show connections to joists.

✔ **Stair stringers:** Show connection to deck framing and footing; show riser and tread dimensions.

✔ **Railings:** Show how posts connect to the deck framing and how rails, balusters, cap, and other details are assembled.

✔ **Bolts and hardware:** Specify the location, diameter, and length of all bolts and lag screws and the location and size of all connecting hardware (except nails and deck fasteners).

✔ **Decorative cuts:** Show the cutting angles and depths for any decorative cuts, such as angled balusters or chamfered post edges.

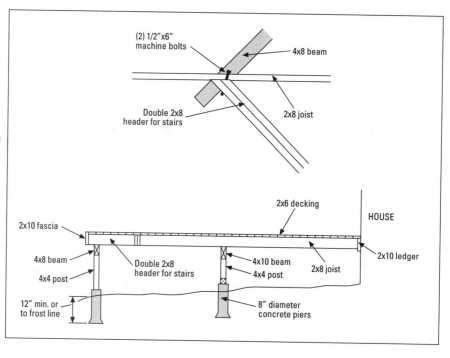

Figure 7-4:
Draw sections in the same scale (¹/₄") as the framing plan and elevations. Draw details in ¹/₂" or ³/₄" scale.

(2) 1/2"x6" machine bolts
4x8 beam
2x8 joist
Double 2x8 header for stairs

2x6 decking
HOUSE
2x10 fascia
2x10 ledger
4x8 beam
Double 2x8 header for stairs
4x10 beam
4x4 post
2x8 joist
4x4 post
12" min. or to frost line
8" diameter concrete piers

Chapter 8

Before You Build

*G*etting ready to build may take a few days or a few weeks, depending how complex your deck is and how much experience you have in construction. If you start building your deck without planning and preparing correctly, your project may become an endless ordeal of setbacks and frustrations. Many of the final arrangements that I discuss in this chapter depend on complete working drawings, but you can begin the preliminary tasks ahead of time, even as you read this book. (See Chapter 4 for more information on plans.) Successful construction is at least 50 percent planning, before building even begins.

Finalizing Your Materials List

Using your materials list as a guide (see Chapter 4 for a sample) and your working drawings for reference, make an itemized list of all the materials you need. Divide the materials into categories: lumber, concrete, hardware, finishes, and so on. Make sure that you include such add-ons as a lighting system, a spa, awnings, or built-in furniture.

If you have a computer with a spreadsheet, build your materials list on the spreadsheet so that you can budget the job more easily. By using cross-referencing techniques, you can categorize materials by deck component (for example, all the materials that you need for framing) as well as by type of material (say, all 2x6s). You can use the list of components as a guide for building the deck.

Confirming Costs

With complete drawings and a materials list, you have the basis for an accurate cost estimate. The first and most obvious cost to consider is that of materials. You can estimate this cost quite accurately in one of three ways. If you hire a contractor, the final bid that you accept includes this cost and, therefore, defines your budget. If you're building the deck yourself, you can have suppliers bid on your project. Many suppliers offer discounts for large orders. Some suppliers may not stock all the items on your list, so dividing your list into costs for lumber, concrete, and so on is often convenient. Just make sure that, as you compare bottom-line prices, all the prices quoted include the same items. The third method for verifying the cost of materials is to obtain prices for each item separately and total them yourself.

Another cost to consider is labor. A contractor's bid, of course, includes that cost. But if you hire workers on an hourly basis, you need to estimate how many hours you expect to employ them. By some inexplicable magic, that cost is very often about the same as the total materials cost, so you simply double it. You can also estimate labor costs by setting up a project schedule and assigning a labor estimate to each phase of construction — for example, one day to excavate footing holes or two days to fasten the decking.

The third budget category to account for is hidden costs. Building a deck requires many incidental items that you can easily overlook. Many of these items aren't even part of the deck. Altogether, they can add up to a significant surprise.

Following are some possible hidden and incidental costs you may face in building a deck:

- Fees for duplicating plans and drawings
- Permit fees
- Dump fees for debris or excavated soil
- Tool rentals
- Tool purchases
- Blade sharpening or replacement

- ✔ Extension cords
- ✔ Employer overhead for hiring labor
- ✔ Safety gear: gloves, glasses, dust masks
- ✔ Ramps, scaffolds, platforms
- ✔ Vehicle wear and tear
- ✔ Delivery charges
- ✔ Plastic sheeting to cover supplies or site
- ✔ Lumber for stakes, forms, braces
- ✔ Forming tube for circular piers
- ✔ Tie wire for securing rebar
- ✔ Weed-control products
- ✔ Repair of trampled landscaping
- ✔ Repair of trampled lawn sprinklers
- ✔ Repair of damaged fences
- ✔ Replacing gutters or downspouts
- ✔ Patching siding
- ✔ Repairing or repainting back of house
- ✔ Brushes, rollers, tarps for applying finish
- ✔ Electrical outlet for new wiring or lighting
- ✔ Extending plumbing for a new faucet
- ✔ Mistackes (oops . . . *mistakes!*)

Scheduling the Project

Perhaps you've seen television shows where a deck materializes in a half-hour program and so you figure that yours may take a weekend. Don't count on it. The nice thing about a deck is that scheduling isn't nearly as critical as with other projects. The deck is outside and so doesn't disrupt your house; life can go on. But you still should make a quick estimate of the time you expect to take building the deck by listing the tasks you need to complete and estimating when you think that you can finish each one. No doubt, nobody wants the deck completed faster than you do so that you can enjoy it, but you're even more motivated if you hold yourself to a schedule. The best way to take advantage of enthusiasm and momentum is to devote a full week or two to building your deck.

Hiring Help

If you plan to hire a contractor to build your deck, you must clarify the scope of the work. You can have the contractor take responsibility for the entire project or for a certain part, such as the footings and framing. Whichever arrangement you set up, observe the following guidelines to ensure a smooth and successful relationship:

✔ Unless you want the contractor to design the deck for you, have copies of your finished working drawings available before you begin talking with contractors.

✔ Obtain bids from several contractors. Clarify what the bids include and exclude — for example, who's responsible for getting the permit or removing debris?

✔ Check references, including customers, banks, and licensing boards.

✔ Verify that the contractor is licensed, has all required bonds, and has proof of insurance for property loss or damage and for workers' compensation.

✔ Read the contract carefully. It should contain the total cost of the job, dates to start and complete work, method of payment, and reference to the working drawings and materials specifications to be used.

✔ Whenever you discuss changes to the plans, get a written change order from the contractor that specifies the changes and their costs.

✔ Do not make final payment until you obtain "lien releases" from any subcontractors or materials suppliers engaged by the contractor. These are parties who, if the contractor doesn't pay them, could force you to pay them by placing a lien on your property. The lien release is verification that they've been paid and waives their right to lien your property.

✔ Above everything else, keep channels of communication open. Discuss concerns as they arise. Go over such details as parking, access to your yard, liability for tools left on the job, storage areas, use of the telephone and bathroom, starting and quitting times, pets, radios, and pampered plants.

Getting a Permit

Contact your building department early in the planning process to find out what deck projects require a permit. As soon as you complete your plans and verify your budget, apply for any necessary permits. Your contractor may also make this application for you.

The application for a simple deck may take only a day or two to process, but some building departments, especially during busy times of the year, may require several weeks to review plans for a large project. The permit should indicate when inspections must take place. For a deck, the only inspections normally required are for the footing holes prior to pouring concrete and the final inspection.

Hauling In and Hauling Out

Take a few minutes to figure out where you can store materials and how you intend to get them there. Choose areas at least 6 feet (ideally 10 feet) from the deck site and access paths to store the following materials:

- ✔ Stack lumber on a flat, dry, shaded surface, such as a patio or garage floor, to keep it from warping. Don't store boards upright against a wall.
- ✔ Cover expensive decking lumber to protect it from dust and rain, and store sacks of cement or concrete mix under cover.
- ✔ Store preservatives, stains, paint, and similar toxic materials in a locked cabinet or shed.
- ✔ Set aside a few empty shelves for storing nails, bolts, brackets, screws, and similar hardware; these items have a way of cluttering the ground or floor.
- ✔ Set up a tool bin and a parking area for wheelbarrows.

The few minutes that you spend organizing these areas before construction can save you hours of futile searching later and go a long way toward ensuring a safe worksite.

You should also think about the debris that you're going to need to haul *away* from the job site. You're sure to have soil from the footing excavations, scrap lumber, demolition scraps (from an existing back porch, for example), excess paint or preservatives, and lots of bent nails. Set up areas where you can toss these materials; keep clean fill, toxins, trash, and reusable scraps all separated from each other to make disposal easier. Decide whether you're going to haul things away yourself or hire a disposal service.

Lining Up Tools

Referring to the list of tools that you need for the project (see Chapter 4), round up your tools to see which ones you already have and which ones you need to buy, rent, or borrow. The tools that you use for deck building are basic to most construction projects, so you may just want to buy as many as you can for future projects.

Invest in the highest quality tools that you can afford. Replacing inexpensive tools usually ends up being more costly in the long run, and losing time because of a broken or ineffective tool is as exasperating as it is costly.

Prepping Yourself

Are you ready to build? This book gives you the information you need, but you must supply the attitude and fortitude. Assess yourself. If you're out of shape, be aware that your first task is the most strenuous: digging holes and pouring concrete. Do some workouts ahead of time and ease into the heavy work slowly or arrange for help. If you plan to have family and friends help with construction, treat the project seriously. Avoid turning it into a party. Stress safety and encourage lots of communication.

Before starting construction, review the following safety guidelines and make sure that everyone on the job site is familiar with them:

- ✔ Wear comfortable clothing. Keep long sleeves buttoned or rolled up and don't wear jewelry that may catch on tools or boards. Wear heavy shoes or boots during excavation and framing.

- ✔ Have safety glasses, dust masks, gloves, ear protection, and hard hats handy and use them as necessary.

- ✔ Lift with your legs, not your back, and avoid lifting and twisting at the same time.

- ✔ Use sturdy ladders and set them on a stable footing.

- ✔ Keep the worksite floor clear of scraps, idle tools, and other tripping hazards.

- ✔ Remove protruding nails from scrap lumber or bend the nails over.

- ✔ Reconnoiter the job site before you leave each day to make sure that you left no uncovered footing holes, unmarked tripping hazards, loose beams, or other hazards that could harm wandering children. If necessary, rope off the area and post signs.

- ✔ Make sure that extension cords and power tools are plugged into outlets with *GFCI* (ground-fault circuit interrupter) protection. Your garage or bathroom may have such outlets, or you can buy a portable GFCI outlet.

- ✔ Operate power tools with caution; observe the manufacturer's safety recommendations. Unplug tools if you need to change blades or bits.

- ✔ Use common sense. Don't work if you're fatigued or your mind is on other things. Warn other workers about unsafe conditions. Keep asking yourself, "What would happen if . . .?"

Chapter 9

Site Prep, Footings, and Piers

• •

In This Chapter

▶ Preparing the site

▶ Laying out the deck

▶ Excavating and forming footings

▶ Pouring concrete

• •

Construction begins! Time to swing into action with some tools and start building your deck. The first phase of the project is the *foundation*. Although the footings and piers are the most obvious part of the foundation, the site itself — the grade and the ground below it — are just as important. You must prepare the site correctly to prevent erosion and moisture problems and excavate carefully for the footings to give them a stable base. Layout is also a critical step in building the foundation. *Layout* establishes the footing locations and an accurate reference for constructing the rest of the deck. This chapter gives as much emphasis to both these operations (site preparation and layout) as to the concrete work that most people associate with building a foundation.

Preparing the Site

The first step is to mark off the approximate area where you intend to locate the deck by using stakes and string or chalklines on the ground. You don't need to make an accurate layout (see the section "Laying Out the Deck," later in this chapter), but you should have a reasonably close guess in case you need to account for setbacks, easements, underground utilities, obstructions, or other factors. Preparing the site involves one or more of the following tasks: altering the house, demolishing an existing patio, grading the soil, establishing correct drainage, and controlling weeds.

Demolition derby

If you're attaching the deck to your house and plan to alter or repair any exterior areas of the house, especially where the deck is to cover them, perform this work first. Such alterations may include removing a back porch or stairs, repairing damaged siding, repainting, moving foundation vents that the deck's ledger board may cover, moving a crawlspace access that the ledger may cover, relocating downspouts, and extending downspouts to carry water beyond the deck area.

If you're installing a new door or window, wait until after you build the deck to do so. The deck provides a convenient platform for completing the exterior part of the installation.

If your deck is going to cover an existing patio that slopes away from the house by at least a quarter inch per foot, leave the patio in place and break holes through it where the footings for the deck go. The patio enhances drainage, inhibits weeds, provides a convenient storage platform, and keeps the area under the deck clear. If the patio doesn't slope away from the house, break it up and remove the concrete. Otherwise, because of the shade from the deck, puddles may accumulate against the house foundation.

Be your own bulldozer

Clear the deck site of weeds and other plants and grade the soil so that it slopes away from the house at a rate of at least a quarter inch per foot. (See Chapter 16 for information on grading techniques.) Tamp the soil so that it's firm and retains the correct slope. If you bring in soil to fill low areas, make sure that you excavate footing holes below the new soil. Remember that the footing holes themselves yield a substantial amount of soil that you can use as fill.

The water's got to go

The area under a deck should not give water the opportunity to accumulate and saturate the soil. The moisture from wet ground or standing water accelerates wood decay. Lingering puddles encourage mosquitoes and other insects, and water that doesn't drain away from the house seeps toward the foundation, leading to moisture problems in the basement or possibly foundation settlement.

If your yard slopes away from the deck site after you grade it, you should have no trouble with drainage. Surface water simply runs into other, safer areas of the yard. If grading your deck site lowers it below the surrounding grade, surface water has no place to run and backs up under the deck. To solve this problem, you need to install subsurface drainage. Follow these steps:

1. **First, look for a low point in your yard where you can run an underground drain pipe out to "daylight."**

   The pipe should be four inches in diameter and slope away from the deck site at a rate of $1/8$ inch per foot. The outlet of this pipe must disperse the water into *your* yard, not your neighbors'. If your property lacks such a low point, you can run the pipe to the street gutter in front of your home or to a municipal storm sewer. If that isn't possible, terminate the drain pipe in an underground *dry well,* an excavation approximately eight feet deep and three to four feet wide that you fill with stones and rubble and cover with top soil. The dry well enables water to percolate into the soil more quickly than from the surface.

2. **After you identify where the drain pipe is to terminate, excavate a trench from that point to the deck site and another trench along the deck perimeter, 14 to 16 inches deep.**

   Slope the ditches toward the termination point at a rate of $1/8$ inch per foot.

3. **Place two inches of one-inch *drain rock* (one-inch rock with no sand) in the bottom of the perimeter trench and lay four-inch diameter plastic (PVC or ABS) perforated drain pipe on the rock.**

   Continue this pipe to the termination point or connect it to four-inch-diameter unperforated plastic pipe that goes to the drain site.

4. **Backfill the trenches with eight inches more of drain rock, cover the rock with filter fabric or newspapers, and fill the trenches with top soil.**

No more weeds

Weeds and plants under a deck not only look unruly, but they also emit moisture that can encourage the decay of deck members. Low decks inhibit most weed growth, but high decks admit enough sunlight for them to thrive. After clearing the deck site of all vegetation and grading the site, you can treat the soil with a pre-emergent weed killer or place a layer of weed-control fabric over the area and, after installing the footings and posts, cover the fabric with a few inches of sand, decorative gravel, or mulch.

Laying Out the Deck

Layout is the process of setting up string lines to guide the placement of footings, posts, and deck framing (see Figure 9-1). You can do your layout before or after you attach the ledger board to the house (for attached decks; see Chapter 10 for more information about attaching ledgers). If you install the ledger first, the ledger makes a convenient and accurate point of reference for laying out the deck. The advantage of attaching the ledger later is that you have something to do while the concrete sets.

Off the wall

To begin the layout, follow these steps:

1. **Mark on the house wall where the two deck corners connect to the house.**

   If the ledger is in place, its ends indicate the corners. If the ledger isn't up yet, mark the house wall above or below the ledger location so that string lines don't interfere with installing the ledger.

2. **Cut two pieces of 2x4 24 to 30 inches long to nail to the house at each mark.**

   These pieces are called *cleats*. For information about 2x4s and nails, see Chapter 6.

3. **Nail these temporary cleats to the house by using 16d duplex nails driven through the siding into the wall framing.**

   The cleats should be level and centered under the marks. Tack a 6d box nail into the top of each cleat at the mark for a string line.

Build better batterboards

Next, build *batterboards* for the remaining two corners of the deck. Batterboards are simple frames to which you attach string lines and which enable you to adjust the string lines easily. Build them four to six feet behind the deck corners in both directions — far enough back not to interfere with deck construction. To build the batterboards, follow these steps:

1. **Drive a pair of sharpened 2x4s into the ground for each batterboard, approximately three feet apart.**

2. **Using a water level, builder's level, or long straightedge and level, mark all the stakes at the same level as the top of the cleats that you nailed to the house.**

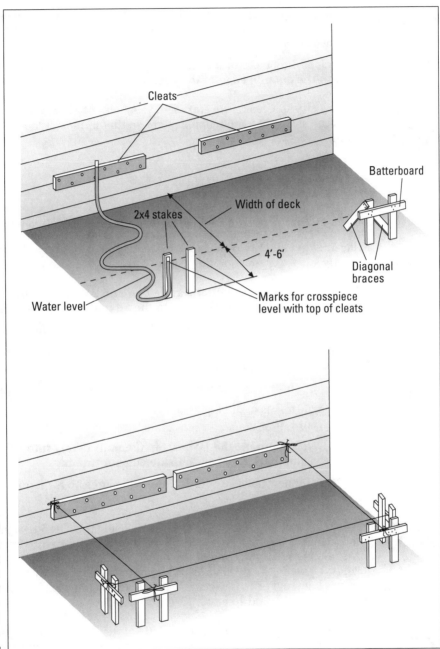

Cleats

Batterboard

2x4 stakes

Width of deck

4'-6'

Diagonal braces

Water level

Marks for crosspiece level with top of cleats

Figure 9-1:
Lay out the deck location by using batterboards and string lines.

3. **Nail a 2x4 crosspiece to each pair of stakes on the side facing away from the deck site; align the top of the crosspiece with the level mark that you made on each stake.**

4. **Tack 6d box nails into each crosspiece at the point where it aligns with the outside edge of the deck framing.**

In nailing crosspieces to the stakes, have a helper hold a sledgehammer behind the stake that you're nailing into so that it doesn't loosen from the ground.

Getting strung out

With batterboards and cleats in place, you can stretch string lines between them to create an outline of your deck. You may need to adjust the nails and string lines several times to get accurate distances between the corners and perfectly square corners. Follow these steps:

1. **Tie nylon string, sometimes called *mason's twine,* to the 6d nails on the house cleats and stretch it to the 6d nails on the batterboards.**

2. **Tie another string line between the two outside batterboards.**

   These three string lines, together with the house wall, should form a rectangle that represents the outside edge of the deck framing.

3. **Measure both diagonals to see whether the corners are square.**

   If the diagonals aren't equal, adjust the position of the nails and string lines until they are.

4. **After you complete the layout, tap the nails firmly into the cross-pieces and mark them as "outside edge of framing."**

   (You add new nails later to set the string lines up for footing locations.)

Another method for checking corners is by using the "3-4-5 triangle." Mark a point on one string that's three feet from the corner; measure from the corner along the other string or the house wall and mark it at four feet. The distance between the two marks (the hypotenuse) is exactly five feet if the corner is square. For more accurate checking, use multiples of 3, 4, and 5 feet, such as 9, 12, and 15 or 12, 16, and 20 feet.

If one side of the deck aligns with the side of the house and the corner of the house is not perfectly square, fudge the layout slightly to bring the side of the deck in line with the side of the house. Otherwise, even though your deck is perfectly square, it may look crooked.

Yours may be exceptional

The layout that I describe in the preceding section is for a simple rectangular deck that you build at the level of the ground floor. Many decks don't fit this description and require different layout techniques. Use the techniques that I describe for those special situations:

- ✔ **If your deck isn't attached to the house:** Start the layout by driving temporary stakes at the four corner locations. Then build batter boards (see the section "Build better batter boards," a little earlier in this chapter) behind the two corners of the longest side and string a line between these batter boards over the corner stakes. Take measurements between the string line and any fence or yard features with which you want the deck to be parallel and make adjustments as necessary. Then build batter boards behind the other two corners, stretch the other three string lines, and check them all for square.

- ✔ **If your deck is large or complex:** Many decks are large, are L shaped, consist of a series of separate platforms, or have curved sides. For large decks, set up batter boards and additional string lines between the perimeter's string lines wherever interior beams or rows of footings line up. For complex shapes, such as a series of platforms or an L-shaped deck, set up batter boards and string lines for each component of the deck. For curved corners, run string lines as if the sides intersected in a square corner. Then, using a rope tied to a stick as a compass, scribe an arc on the ground where the curved corner belongs, starting and ending the arc beneath the string lines.

- ✔ **If your deck is on a steep site or is a second-story deck:** Batterboards for most decks are about three feet high, but if your site slopes away from the house the batter boards for the downhill edge of the deck may need to be several feet higher to be level with the ledger. Rather than build tall batter boards that require stepladders to reach (which is done for home construction), simply build short batterboards and stretch the string line downhill at an angle. Although the string lines don't guide you in establishing the correct level for the deck framing, you can easily take measurements from the floor of the house or another reference point as you install the framing members.

Excavating and Forming Footings

Deck footings and posts seldom align with the perimeter of the deck framing, so you must move the string line(s) in to line up over the centers of the footing locations. If, for example, your plan has footings centered 24 inches from the outside edge of the deck, move the string line in accordingly. Then, starting at one end of this string, measure to the center of the first footing location and, by holding a plumb bob against the string at this point, mark the center of the footing on the ground by using a stake, chalk, flour, or spray paint. Do the same for the other footings. Then mark the outline of each footing by centering a cardboard template over the mark and sprinkling chalk all around its edge.

Designer shoes

Footing design must accomplish two goals: provide a stable base for the weight of the deck and elevate all wooden members at least 12 inches above the ground (see Chapter 5). The minimum size for the base of each footing is normally 18 inches square (20 inches if round) and at least 12 inches high. Each footing supports a pier that extends above the ground at least 8 inches (measured from the high side, if the ground slopes). The pier can be a precast pier with a metal post anchor, a concrete pier formed and poured along with the footing, or a preservative-treated post specified for ground contact and embedded a few inches into the concrete footing. You then backfill the hole for this post with compacted gravel or alternating layers of compacted soil and compacted gravel. Whichever design you use, observe the following reminders:

- The base of each footing must be level and have square, not rounded, edges to prevent rocking.
- The base of the footing must extend below the frost line.
- Each pier must be level and plumb in both directions.
- Each pier must have a metal bracket that elevates the post above the concrete. (An exception would be posts that are completely buried.)
- If you use precast piers, choose those with a metal bracket. Avoid piers that have only a wood block or a center pin for connecting them to the post.
- If the deck is a ground-hugger that requires placing beams directly on the piers, the piers must all be level with each other and the pier brackets must be aligned perfectly.

Dig this

Before excavating for the footings, verify all dimensions, including the depth that your local building code requires. Then follow these steps:

1. **If you installed weed control fabric or you're building over a patio, cut or break through the material to expose the ground beneath.**

- **2. Using a posthole digger, hand auger, or power auger, dig the footing holes, as shown in Figure 9-2.**

   Keep the sides straight and the bottom level. Don't overdig, or you end up wasting concrete.

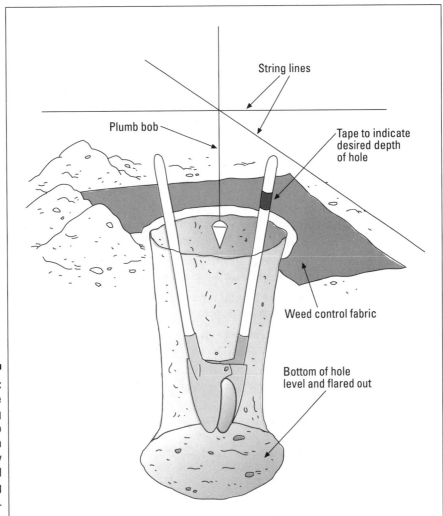

String lines

Plumb bob

Tape to indicate desired depth of hole

Weed control fabric

Bottom of hole level and flared out

Figure 9-2: Excavate footing holes to the depth required by your local building code.

3. Flare the bottom of the hole outward a bit to broaden the footing base.

You can do so by using a thin shovel called a trenching shovel or by carefully working a square-nosed shovel around the bottom of the hole. The bottom of the hole should be undisturbed soil, not loose soil.

True to form

After digging footing holes, your next task is to build forms for the concrete. Before building the forms, place a three- to four-inch layer of gravel in the bottom of the hole for deep footings in areas with frost conditions.

For shallow footings, place a grid of reinforcing bars *(rebar)* in the bottom of the hole, as shown in Figure 9-3. To make the grid, cut six pieces of rebar six inches shorter than the width of the footing. Using tie wire, tie them together in a crisscross pattern. Place the grid on concrete *dobies* (three-inch cubes of concrete); you should have three inches of clearance all around the grid. Follow these steps to build the forms:

1. **Buy a length of 8- or 12-inch diameter forming tube and, using a circular power saw, cut a section for each pier that's four inches shorter than the depth of the footing hole.**

2. **Center the tube under the string lines and suspend it so that the top extends eight inches above the grade.**

3. **Using deck screws and a power screwdriver, secure the tube to a pair of 2x4s that you lay across the hole.**

4. **Drive a stake next to each end of the 2x4s and, after you have the tube centered and plumb, screw the 2x4s to the stakes.**

5. **For additional bracing, run 1x4s diagonally from the stakes to the upper part of the tube; secure them by using deck screws.**

6. **Cut a length of rebar for each pier the same length as the tube and set it aside for the concrete pour.**

If you prefer, you can make four-sided rectangular forms out of scrap lumber or plywood instead of using prefabricated forming tubes. Wrap wire around the forms to reinforce them. For a decorative effect, nail triangular strips of wood around the top inside edges and along the inside corners of the form; the pier now has beveled edges. You can also line the forms with bubble wrap or other textured material to give the concrete an interesting surface.

Another decorative forming technique is to roll strips of roll roofing into tubes, with the mineral surface facing in. Tie string or wire around them and suspend them in the footing hole as forming tubes. The roofing leaves a nice texture on the surface of the concrete.

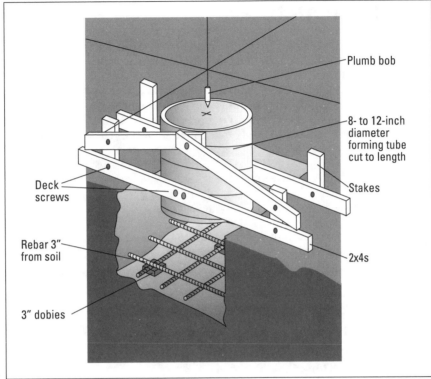

Plumb bob

8- to 12-inch diameter forming tube cut to length

Stakes

Deck screws

Rebar 3" from soil

2x4s

3" dobies

Figure 9-3:
This footing hole is ready for concrete.

If your deck includes a concrete landing or footing for stairs, excavate and form it at this time. After you complete all the forms, call for an inspection. (Check your building permit for procedures.) Meanwhile, calculate the exact volume of concrete you need for the pour. (See Chapter 6 for more information.)

DANGER

Safety on site

Contact with wet (unhardened) concrete, mortar, cement, or cement mixtures can cause skin irritation, severe chemical burns, or serious eye damage. The Portland Cement Association recommends that you wear waterproof gloves, a long-sleeved shirt, full-length trousers, and eye protection when working with these materials. If you have to stand in wet concrete, use waterproof boots that are high enough to keep concrete from flowing into them. Wash wet concrete, mortar, cement, or cement mixtures from your skin immediately. If the mixtures make contact with your eyes, flush your eyes with clean water immediately. Indirect contact through clothing can be as serious as direct contact, so promptly rinse out wet concrete mortar, cement, or cement mixtures from clothing. Seek immediate medical attention if you have persistent or severe discomfort.

Placing Concrete

After the building inspector okays your forms and footing holes, you can fill them with concrete. You can estimate the amount of concrete you need by measuring the footing holes and pier forms and then calculating their volume in cubic feet. If you need less than half a yard (14 cubic feet) of concrete, mix sacks of concrete mix in a wheelbarrow. For larger amounts, mix bulk ingredients in a concrete mixer (available from a rental agency) or order a delivery of ready-mix concrete. If the truck can't back up to your deck site, order a concrete pumping service along with the ready mix.

After you have the concrete, whether you ordered a ready-mix delivery or mixed it yourself, you must place it in the footing holes and pier forms as quickly as possible. Follow these steps:

1. **Place enough concrete in the bottom of each footing hole to fill it slightly above the bottom of the pier form.**

2. **Using a piece of rebar or similar rod, settle the concrete by jabbing it several times.**

3. **Fill the form, jabbing the concrete to settle it.**

4. **Tap the sides of the form with a hammer to release air pockets.**

5. **Using a scrap of wood, strike off the concrete so that it's level with the top of the pier form.**

6. **Take the rebar and, after the concrete sets for a few minutes, push it vertically into the center of the pier and footing until it's buried one to three inches below the concrete surface.**

7. **Measure along the string to find the midpoint of the post or footing.**

8. **Holding a plumb bob against the string at that point, force the post anchor into the fresh concrete and center the anchor under the bob.**

   Align the brackets of all the post anchors in the same direction.

9. **Using a torpedo level or other small level, adjust each bracket so that it's plumb and level and recheck to see that it's centered under the string lines (see Figure 9-4).**

   (If you're using an adjustable style of post anchor, embed the bolt in the concrete now and, after the concrete hardens, secure the two-piece adjustable bracket to the bolt.)

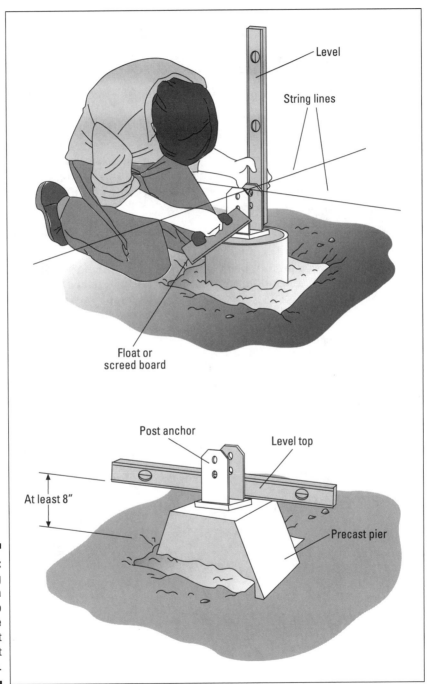

Level

String lines

Float or
screed board

Post anchor

Level top

At least 8"

Precast pier

Figure 9-4:
Use string
lines and a
plumb bob
to guide the
placement
of post
anchors.

Making a batch from scratch

Although you can measure bulk ingredients by the shovelful, you achieve a stronger, better-proportioned concrete mix by using the following method: You need four five-gallon plastic pails and a bathroom scale. To make each cubic foot of concrete, place 22 pounds of cement in one bucket, 50 pounds of sand in the second bucket, 65 pounds of gravel in the third bucket, and 11 pounds of water in the fourth bucket. Clearly mark how high each ingredient fills its bucket. Mix the dry ingredients together in a cement mixer, slowly add the water, and mix for three minutes. While the concrete is mixing, refill the buckets to the marks for the next batch. You may need to alter the amount of water, depending on the dampness of the sand.

If you're using precast piers, soak them in water before placing them in fresh concrete. Fill the footing hole with concrete and *screed* (drag a board across) it level by using a wooden float or scrap of wood. Centering the pier under the string lines, place it in the concrete, then push it down an inch or so and level it; the top should be at least eight inches above the grade (the adjacent ground).

The deck site is now a safety hazard, with forms, post anchors, and stakes cluttering the ground. Place wooden boxes or plastic pails over the metal post anchors, which may be sharp, or fence off the site to keep children from wandering in.

To give the concrete time to cure sufficiently, don't remove the cardboard forming tubes or wooden forms for at least five days. The concrete, however, is strong enough for you to proceed with deck building after the first day.

Get a load of this

Most ready-mix concrete trucks hold nine or more yards of concrete, but you can order much smaller amounts. If you order a delivery, you're charged a per-yard fee for whatever quantity of concrete you order (whether you use it or not). In addition, you may have a short-load charge for ordering any quantity less than a specified amount (usually four yards) and a stand-by charge for any additional time that the truck must remain at your site beyond a basic per-yard time limit (usually five minutes per yard). If you order a pumping service, make sure that the two companies coordinate their time schedules. The pumper should arrive first and be set up as the concrete arrives.

Not all concrete is the same. Mixes vary in cement content, aggregate size (the maximum size of rocks in the sand/gravel mix), water-to-cement ratio, slump (or consistency, from soupy to stiff), and additives. In ordering, clarify that the concrete is for deck footings and whether you plan to use a pumping service. If you're asked for additional information, specify the following:

Cement content: 600 pounds (often referred to as a *six-sack mix,* becuase cement comes in 94-pound sacks).

Aggregate size: Maximum ³/₄ inch; ³/₈ inch if the concrete is pumped through a three-inch hose instead of a four-inch hose.

Water/cement ratio: Specify a ratio of 1:2 (.5) or ask for a recommendation.

Slump: Four inches (the number of inches that fresh concrete in a 12-inch-high cylinder slumps after you remove the cylinder).

Additives: None (unless very unusual conditions require an accelerator for cold weather, a retardant for hot weather, or a plasticizer for low water:cement ratio; consult with the delivery company).

Chapter 10

Framing the Deck

Time to attack that pile of lumber? (I hope that the boards you need for framing are on top.) While the concrete for the piers and footings hardens, you can begin framing the deck by installing the ledger board. Then, after the concrete sets for a day or two, you can install the posts and beams.

These framing members are critical components of your deck. Be fussy. Verify all the dimensions in your plans, measure twice before cutting boards, and use your level often to keep the members plumb and level. After you install the ledger and beams, your deck finally begins to take shape as you install the joists and blocking.

Installing the Ledger

A *ledger,* or *ledger board,* is a 2-by piece of lumber that you attach to the side of the house and to which you attach deck joists. Installing a ledger involves a bit more than just bolting it to the side of the house. The "bit more" is key. Many decks fail because the ledger board decays, the ledger board wasn't securely fastened to the house framing, or the framing members inside the wall weren't strong enough for the extra load. Attaching a ledger also disrupts the external "skin" of the house, making it vulnerable to moisture penetration unless precautions are taken. The following techniques, which vary depending on the type of wall surface and house construction you have, are somewhat involved but ensure a high level of protection.

Before attaching a ledger, check the affected section of the house carefully. You don't want to cut or nail into a water line, electrical line, heating and air conditioning duct, or the like.

Get the wall ready

The first step in safely attaching a ledger is to prepare the wall. Follow these steps:

1. **Scribe a level line along the wall for the top of the ledger ($2^1/2$ inches below floor level if the decking boards are 2-by lumber; $1^1/2$ inches for $^5/_4$-inch decking boards).**

   You can mark a long level line in any of the following three ways:

   • Using a helper, hold a long straightedge with a level on it against the house and scribe the line.

   • Link a series of marks that you make by using a long level.

   • Using a hydrolevel or a builder's level, make two end marks that are level with each other and then snap a chalkline between them.

   If the siding is stucco, plywood, or board siding that makes full contact with the *sheathing* (plywood or similar panels between the studs and siding) behind it, you're done with the wall; proceed with preparing the ledger. (In other words, skip ahead to the section "Get the board ready," a little later in this chapter.) *Note:* Some walls don't have sheathing.

   If the siding is vinyl, aluminum, shingles, or wooden lap siding that doesn't make full contact with the sheathing behind it, proceed to the next step.

2. **Remove a section where you intend to install the ledger, as shown in Figure 10-1.**

3. **Cover the exposed sheathing with a piece of metal *flashing* (aluminum or galvanized sheet metal, which you can buy in strips of various widths and lengths) or any rubber-vinyl membrane specified for use as an ice and water shield.**

4. **Tuck the flashing under the siding above it, smooth the flashing flat against the sheathing, and bend the bottom to lap over the siding below it.**

5. **Bend and lap the ends over the adjacent siding an inch or so, seal the joint with caulking, and nail it tight.**

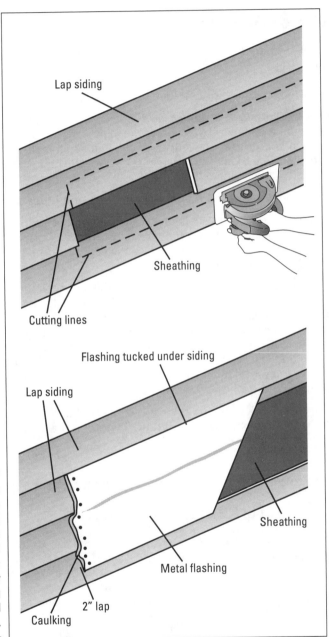

Lap siding

Sheathing

Cutting lines

Flashing tucked under siding

Lap siding

Sheathing

Metal flashing

2" lap

Caulking

Figure 10-1:
Remove the siding and protect the house wall from moisture by installing metal flashing.

Get the board ready

With the wall prepared, you can turn your attention to the ledger itself. Follow these steps:

1. **Cut the ledger board to length.**

   If you don't intend to install a *fascia* (a decorative trim board) along the sides of the deck, thereby covering the joint between the ledger and outside joists, shorten the ledger by one and a half inches at each end to provide room to lap the outside joists over the ends of the ledger for a more attractive connection.

2. **Mark the locations on the board for drilling bolt holes.**

   Bolts need to be four to six inches from each end of the board, one and a half inches from the top, and two inches from the bottom. Space the remaining bolts every 16 to 24 inches staggered top and bottom or every 24 to 32 inches in pairs.

   Don't use this spacing if you're attaching the ledger to the house above or below floor level. Instead, align the bolt holes with the wall studs behind the siding. To do so, probe the siding or sheathing for nail patterns that reveal the wall studs behind; hold the ledger in place and mark where it aligns with the studs. Drill the bolt holes $1/16$-inch larger than the bolt size. (If you're attaching the ledger to brick, concrete, or other masonry, drill holes in the board *after* you drill them into the masonry. See the following section.)

3. **Do a quick check of the hole locations to see if any may interfere with the joist layout (see the section "Installing the Joists," later in this chapter, for layout instructions).**

What lurks behind the wall?

Most decks that you attach to a house are at floor level, so the framing member to which you're likely to bolt or screw the ledger is a floor joist — probably the *band joist* (also called a *rim joist*) — nailed to the ends of the main joists. (See the accompanying figure.) If the house wasn't framed correctly, this band joist may be secured only by 16d nails driven into the ends of joists. This connection is barely strong enough for normal house loads; a heavily loaded deck may rip the joist away from the house. Correct house framing requires nailing 16d nails every 16 inches down through the wall plate and floor sheathing into this joist. If you suspect that shortcuts were taken, reinforce the band joist by *toenailing* (driving at an angle) 16d nails every eight inches up through the sheathing and band joist into the floor sheathing and wall plate above it. Also toenail opposing nails into the foundation sill or wall plate below the joist.

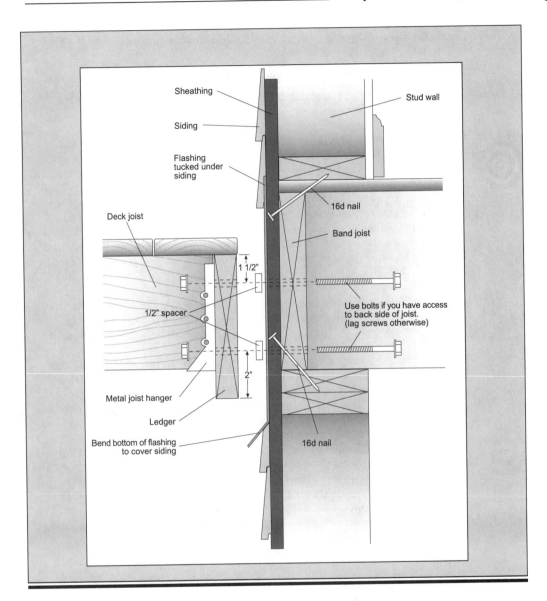

Sheathing

Siding

Flashing
tucked under
siding

Deck joist

Stud wall

16d nail

Band joist

1 1/2"

1/2" spacer

Use bolts if you have access
to back side of joist.
(lag screws otherwise)

2"

Metal joist hanger

Ledger

Bend bottom of flashing
to cover siding

16d nail

Board meets wall

Attach the ledger to the wall by following these steps:

1. **Position the ledger against the wall, keeping the top aligned with
   your guideline.**

2. **Tack the ledger in place by using 16d duplex nails or prop it up by using temporary braces.**

3. **Using the ledger as a template, mark the hole locations on the wall.**

4. **Take down the ledger and drill pilot holes into the house for the bolts or lag screws.**

If you use bolts — which you should if you have access to the back side of the joist from the basement or crawlspace — drill holes of the same diameter as the ledger holes all the way through the siding, sheathing, and joist. If you drill pilot holes for lag screws, use a quarter-inch bit for $3/8$-inch lag screws or a $5/16$-inch bit for half-inch screws. Drill to a depth that enables $3/8$-inch screws to penetrate one and a half inches and $1/2$-inch screws to penetrate two inches into the *framing* (not just the sheathing). The lag screw or bolt should be four to six inches long — long enough to go through the ledger, a half-inch spacer, the siding and/or sheathing, and one and a half inches of framing.

If you need to drill through metal flashing and the flashing is aluminum, use a hole saw. If the flashing is galvanized steel, use a metal-cutting bit lubricated with a few drops of oil that you release from a drinking straw as you drill.

Before lifting the ledger back in place, prop it into an upright position and push all the bolts and washers through the holes. Use malleable washers. After inserting the bolts, slide a spacer onto each bolt on the back side of the ledger board. Use plastic or aluminum spacers specifically designed for this function or group five or six cut washers onto each bolt.

Inject caulking into each of the holes drilled into the house wall and spread a small amount around the edge of each hole. With a helper, carefully lift the ledger into place and start the bolt or lag screws in their holes. Slowly tighten them with a socket wrench until the ledger is snug and level. The spacers create a one-half- to three-quarter-inch gap behind the ledger that prevents moisture from getting trapped, which would eventually cause the ledger board or siding to decay.

Installing the Posts

After you install the ledger and the concrete has set, you can install the posts. Follow these steps:

1. **First, rough-cut each post 6 to 12 inches longer than you need.**

2. **Install one of the end posts first, setting it into the bracket of the post anchor and temporarily staking it in place so that it's perfectly plumb.**

3. Using a hydrolevel, builder's level, or long straightedge and carpenter's level, mark the post at the same level as the top of the ledger board.

4. Measure down from this mark the depth of the joist material (2x8, 2x10, or whatever) plus the depth of the beam and then mark this point.

5. Using a square, scribe a line around the post at the mark.

6. Remove the post, cut it off at the line (unless it's a long post intended to support the railing), and dip the cut end in clear preservative.

7. Place the post back in the same position and secure it to the bracket by using nails or bolts.

   Hold the post plumb by using temporary bracing.

8. Erect the opposite end post in the same manner.

9. String a tight line between the tops of the two posts and use the line to mark the intermediate posts for cutting.

10. Cut and install the other posts.

11. After installing all the posts, brace each one with temporary diagonal braces if the tops move.

You can also mark and trim the posts after installing them, as shown in Figure 10-2, instead of taking them down for cutting. This procedure, however, can be very dangerous. Attempt it only if you're experienced in making horizontal cuts.

Installing the Beams

Beams, which rest on the posts, are critical framing members. They must be level and firmly connected to the posts. With the posts in position, attach a beam bracket (also called a *post cap*) to the top of each post for the first beam, as shown in Figure 10-3, using 16d galvanized common nails or carriage bolts. Beams can be solid lumber, such as a 4x10 or a 6x8, or built up from two or three thicknesses of 2-by lumber. (See Table 5-4 in Chapter 5 for details.) Solid beams take less time to install and don't have cracks between boards for moisture to collect in. They're more expensive than built-up beams, however, and may not be available in certain lengths.

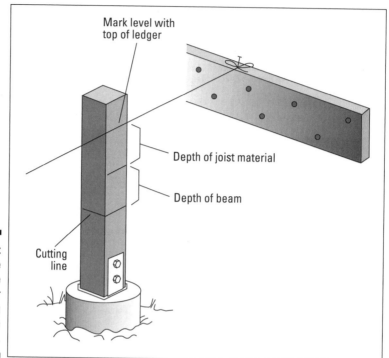

Mark level with top of ledger

Depth of joist material

Depth of beam

Cutting line

Figure 10-2: Mark the tops of the posts for trimming after they're in position.

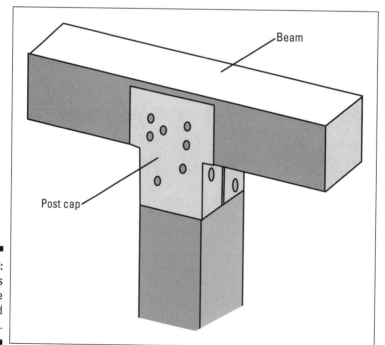

Beam

Post cap

Figure 10-3: Post caps help secure beams and posts.

Board + board = beam

To make a built-up beam, stagger the splices at least four feet apart. Plan the splices on the outside members of three-member beams so that they align over a post or reinforce them by using metal straps. Use preservative-treated lumber and treat the cut ends. Align the *crowns*, or natural curvature of the boards, in the same direction. If the beam has two members, each one and a half inches thick, it's only three inches thick; to widen it to three and a half inches to conform to the width of a 4x4 post, place a short half-inch plywood spacer (preservative-treated) between the boards every 16 inches. To keep water from collecting on the tops of the spacers, cut the tops at an angle. The water then flows through the spaces between the boards. Nail the members together with 12d galvanized common nails one and a half inches from the edges. Reinforce the connections by using carriage bolts every four feet, especially for beams with plywood spacers sandwiched between the boards.

Beam me up

After your beam is ready, follow these steps to install it:

1. **Cut the beam to length and apply clear preservative to the cut end.**

   Cut it to the length specified in your plans. If you're joining beams end-to-end for a long run, cut the lengths so that splices occur over posts.

2. **Raise the beam(s) into place, using as many helpers as you can find.**

   Make sure that the crown side of the beam faces up. (Sight along the length of the beam to check.) Otherwise, it may sag. If the posts are tall, place sturdy stepladders next to them to rest the beam on before the final lift.

3. **Before securing the beam to the brackets, measure to make sure that the post centers are the same distance apart at the tops of the posts as they are at the bases.**

   Make adjustments by knocking the posts right or left with a sledgehammer instead of trying to slide the beam. (The ends of the beam should align with the original string line placements that represent the outside edge of the deck framing).

   To give the ends of the beam a decorative (and safe) touch, cut off the bottom corners at a 45-degree angle or round them and sand them smooth.

4. **Secure the beams with bolts, screws, or nails.**

   If you're bolting several boards together and the bolt doesn't go through the holes because they aren't aligned perfectly, remove the bolt and bend it slightly by whacking it with a sledgehammer; then drive it through the holes with the hammer.

Making a post sandwich

If your deck design has 2-by stringers attached to the sides of the posts (a post sandwich) in lieu of beams resting on top of the posts, these stringers require a different type of attachment. The customary method is simply to bolt these stringers to the sides of the posts, but this connection is weak and often fails. Instead, notch the sides of the posts to "let in" the stringers (if you're using a minimum of 6x6 posts). Follow these steps:

1. **Cut the notches to a depth equal to the thickness of the stringer lumber.**

2. **After notching all the posts, set the stringers in place and drill bolt holes through** the connection at each post (two holes at each post).

3. **Remove the stringers and apply preservative to the notches and bolt holes.**

4. **Install the stringers, using malleable washers on both sides of the bolts.**

5. **If the posts don't extend through the deck to support the railing or an overhead but terminate under the deck, protect the top of the post with a galvanized sheet metal cap or cut the top of the post to a pyramid shape to repel water.**

A bracing experience

Decks with posts higher than five feet or decks not attached to the house require permanent diagonal bracing — local codes may vary — to prevent lateral sway. Although you can install the braces at any time during construction, doing so is easiest before you put the joists in place. Use 2x4 braces if they're shorter than eight feet and 2x6s for longer braces. Follow these steps:

1. **Cut the ends at an angle so that they align vertically after you install the brace to repel moisture.**

2. **Run braces from the bottom of one post to the top of the adjacent post in a zigzag pattern along the beam, or install pairs of braces in an X shape in alternating post bays (the spaces between posts).**

   See Figure 10-4. If you don't have much room underneath the deck, use Y-bracing, also shown in Figure 10-4.

3. **Bolt the braces to the posts with two carriage or machine bolts at each connection.**

   Avoid butting two braces together, which requires four bolts. Instead, place the braces on opposite sides of the post and use the same two bolts for both braces. For X-bracing, bolt a 4x4 block between the braces where they intersect.

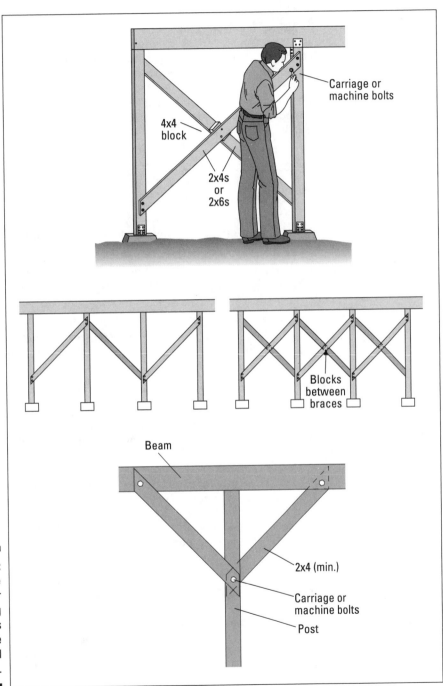

Figure 10-4:
Brace the posts after installing the beams to give the deck lateral stability.

Installing the Joists

The joists complete the basic framework for your deck platform. Follow these steps to *lay out,* or *mark,* the joist locations:

1. **Starting at either end of the ledger board, scribe a pair of vertical lines one and a half inches apart, using a try square or combination square to keep the lines accurate.**

   (A shortcut is to scribe only one line and mark an X on whichever side the joist goes.) Make the first joist flush with the end of the ledger, unless you cut the ledger one and a half inches short to attach the joist to its end. (See the section "Installing the Ledger," earlier in this chapter, for more information.)

2. **Lay out the rest of the joists by using the spacing specified in your plans (typically 16 or 24 inches).**

   This spacing is specified *on-center,* but measuring from left edge to left edge or right edge to right edge of each joist produces the same spacing.

   Once you reach the opposite end of the ledger, you will probably find that the spacing doesn't come out even for the end joist. That's okay; the last spacing can be less than, but not more than, the specified distance.

3. **Next, lay out joist locations on the beam.**

   Make sure that you start the layout from the same end of the beam that you started the ledger layout — getting turned around and inadvertently reversing the layout is all too easy, resulting in jumbled joists. See Figure 10-5.

If your deck is too wide for single joists to span, you must splice the joists over one of the beams. You can do so by lapping the joists or butting them end-to-end and nailing metal straps or short lengths of joist lumber to each side of the splice. If you lap joists, remember to offset the joist layout one and a half inches on the subsequent beam.

How would you like that sliced?

You may need to cut some joists to length before installing them. If the joists don't require splicing and are cantilevered out beyond the beam, wait until you install all the joists before trimming the ends. If joists require splicing, cut the first joist to length before installing it. Measure from the ledger to the midpoint of the beam and cut the joist a quarter inch shorter than the measurement. Measure for each joist in case the beam and ledger aren't perfectly parallel.

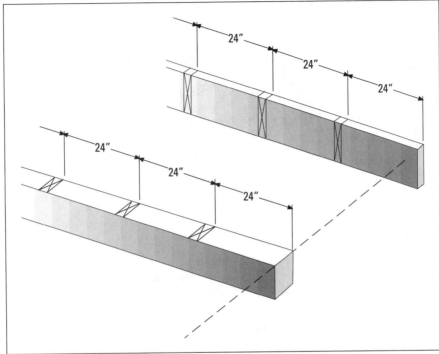

Figure 10-5:
Lay out the
joist pattern
on the
ledger and
beams.

Getting into the rhythm

Installing joists is a repetitive operation. Follow these steps and refer to Figure 10-6:

1. **Attach the joist hangers to the ledger board.**

   Using a scrap of joist lumber as a gauge, set the joist hangers so that the tops of the joists are flush with the top of the ledger. Nail only one side of the joist hanger to the ledger, aligning it with the layout line. Use 16d galvanized joist hanger nails.

2. **Begin installing each joist by resting one end on the beam and sliding the other end into the joist hanger.**

   Do not butt the joist into the ledger; leave an eighth to a quarter inch of clearance.

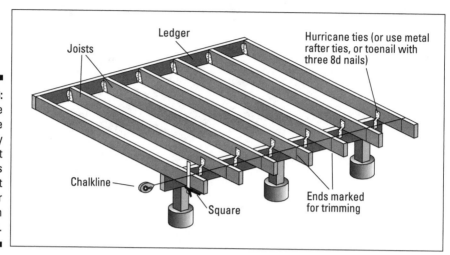

Figure 10-6:
Attach the joists to the ledger by using joist hangers and support the other ends on beams.

3. **Squeeze the joist hanger closed and nail the loose side to the ledger and then nail the hanger to the joist on both sides.**

   Use 16d galvanized joist hanger nails. To keep the nails from splitting the end of the joist, hold a sledgehammer against the opposite side of the joist that you're nailing.

4. **Secure the joist to the beam by toenailing it with three 8d galvanized common nails or attaching a metal rafter tie or *hurricane tie* (another type of bracket used for attaching boards set on edge to beams below them).**

5. **Secure both ends of each joist before installing the next joist.**

If you're lapping the outside joists over the ends of the ledger board (as I describe in the section "Installing the Ledger," earlier in this chapter), drill three pilot holes in the end of each joist and nail the joists to the ledger by using 16d galvanized spiral-shank nails. Then reinforce the joint with a metal corner bracket (not a joist hanger) on the inside corner.

Head 'em up

The free ends of the joists are vulnerable to severe warping if you don't attach the *header* — a single piece that attaches to all the joists, also called a *rim joist* or *band joist* — to them the same day that you install the joists (see Figure 10-7). To trim the joists and attach the header, follow these steps:

1. **Measure out from the ledger and mark the same distance on both outside joists.**

2. **Snap a chalkline between the two marks.**

3. **Using a combination square, mark a cutting line on the side of each joist where the chalk line crosses it.**

4. **Trim off the end of each joist at this mark.**

5. **Measure and cut a header out of joist lumber.**

6. **Mark the joist layout on the back side of the header.**

7. **Working from one end to the other, attach the header to the ends of the joists with 16d galvanized spiral-shank nails or three-inch deck screws.**

   Drill pilot holes for the screws or nails at the ends. As you attach the header to each joist, straighten the joist by using a crowbar, if necessary, to align it with the layout mark.

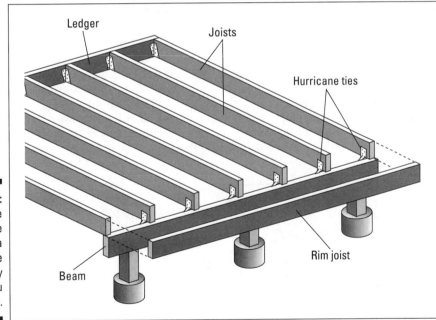

Figure 10-7:
Secure the ends of the joists to a header the same day that you install them.

Ledger

Joists

Hurricane ties

Rim joist

Beam

Installing Blocking

Most codes require a row of *blocking* — short lengths of joist material — between the joists wherever they cross over a beam and at the midpoint of spans exceeding a certain length, depending on the joist size and spacing. Typically, joists 2x8 or larger should have blocking every eight feet; check your local code. To install blocking, follow these steps:

1. **Snap a chalkline across the tops of the joists along the inside edge of the beam.**

2. **Mark a vertical line along the side of each joist at the chalk mark.**

3. **Cut blocking from the joist lumber.**

   Measure between joists and cut each piece to that length as you work your way along the beam instead of cutting all the blocks at once.

4. **Install the first block and nail it from both ends with three 16d galvanized spiral shank nails.**

5. **Nail the next piece with 16d nails at both ends.**

   You may need to stagger the blocking on both sides of the chalk line to make nailing easier as shown in Figure 10-8.

As you work your away along the row of blocking, notice that nailing in one direction tightens the joints, and nailing in the other direction loosens them. To prevent loosening the joints, have a helper hold a sledgehammer against the opposite end of the line of blocking as you nail toward it. If any of the blocks pushes a joist out of alignment, cut the next block shorter or longer to re-establish the joist layout.

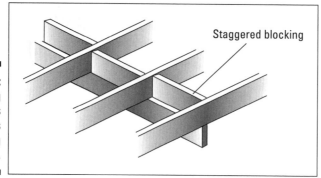

Figure 10-8:
Blocking prevents the joists from turning over.

Staggered blocking

Pickled board feet

To prevent rot and decay, always apply preservative to the ends of boards that you cut for framing members, even if you intend to apply preservative, stain, or sealer to the deck later. The most effective treatment is to soak the end of the board by dipping it in a container of preservative instead of brushing the preservative on the board. Set up a dipping station by laying plastic sheeting on the ground next to a wall or fence and placing a partially filled container of preservative on the sheeting. Set a scrap of plywood or lumber next to the container where you can stand each board for a few minutes after you remove it from the preservative.

Chapter 11

Decking Your Deck

. . . .

In This Chapter

▶ Racking the boards

▶ Fastening the boards

▶ Notching for obstacles

▶ Trimming the ends

▶ Adding a fascia

. . . .

*T*he moment that you drive that last joist nail, you probably want to pounce on the big pile of decking boards and install a few. But don't set any boards on the joists until you first coat the joists with water-repellent sealer, especially the tops. (Use a combination sealer and preservative if the joist lumber isn't preservative-treated.) The tops are extremely vulnerable to rot because most deck fasteners penetrate them and the deck boards trap water on them. Some builders lay strips of 30-pound roofing felt or old vinyl flooring along the tops of the joists to protect them even more.

You should also apply a coat of finish to the decking boards before you install them if you have sufficient room to lay them out in a shaded, well-ventilated area (see Chapter 13). If you don't have the luxury of space, you need to use the deck platform itself. This project is a good one for some helpers to take care of while you're framing the deck.

Installing the decking boards is a satisfying and relatively easy process — a nice payoff for all that head-scratching and board-nudging that getting the deck framed required. You still have details to work out, and you must keep your mind on safety, but this phase of the project is fairly relaxing. Just keep in mind that you're only at the halfway point. Don't send out the party invitations yet.

Racking the Boards

Imagine building a deck and, after you finish, realizing that the board right in front of the expensive French doors has a huge knot in it and that the boards hidden away from view have the prettiest grain patterns. To prevent this nightmare from occurring, sort through the stack of decking lumber and set aside a few of the best and worst boards. If one side of a board is not acceptable, but the other side is, make sure that the acceptable side is "bark side up." (The grain pattern, as viewed in cross section, looks like a rainbow.)

Starting along the house wall, *rack,* or lay out, the decking boards over the joists. Space them loosely, with a few inches of space after every four boards or so. Place the best boards in front of doorways, picture windows, and stairs; in prominent traffic areas; and along the outside edge of the deck. Place the clinkers close to the house and where furniture covers them.

Be careful walking on boards as you approach the ends. If the end of a board doesn't rest on a joist, it can't support your weight. Wear shoes with light-colored soles to avoid scuffing the boards.

If the boards are unfinished, flip them all over and roll or spray a coat of finish onto the bottom side. For a thorough job, set them on edge and treat the exposed edge; repeat the process for the other edge. Be careful not to get dribbles on the top faces of the boards. Protect the area below the deck by using plastic sheeting or drop cloths.

If the deck is too long for one board to span, butt boards together. Plan the joints to align over joists. Stagger the joints so that they alternate over different joists, separated from each other by at least two joist bays (spaces between joists), as shown in Figure 11-1. If you need to cut boards, cut them slightly long and trim them later (except where a board butts between two others).

Fancy decking patterns

Although herringbone designs and other intricate patterns may add interest to a deck, they often look too busy. Some variations in the normal decking pattern, however, can serve as very effective design features — for example, a border of one or two boards around the edge of the deck or a change in the direction of decking at different deck levels. If your deck plan includes pattern changes, keep the following tips in mind:

✔ Decking placed diagonally over the joists requires tighter joist spacings (see Chapter 5).

✔ Where a border runs parallel with the joists, you want to nail blocking every 24 inches, on-center, between the last two joists to support the border boards.

✔ Where boards butt end to end, even at an angle, you must support the joint with a joist or blocking.

✔ Where decking boards change direction and create a long joint, double the joist under the joint to create a solid nailing surface and to support any intermediate joists that tie into it.

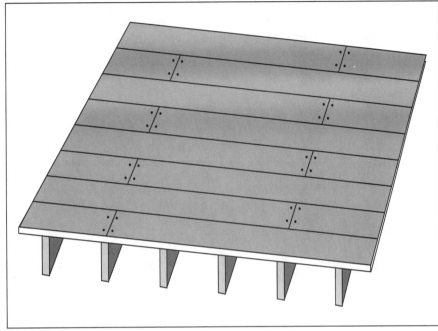

Figure 11-1:
Stagger end
joints at
least two
joists apart.

Fastening the Boards

Start the decking installation along the house wall or on the prominent side of a stand-alone deck. Leave at least a quarter inch of clearance along the wall. Then follow these steps:

1. **Snap a chalkline across the tops of the joists to align the outside, or nearest, edge of the board.**

2. **Start fastening the board at one end (either flush with the edge of the joist or overhanging it, if you prefer), making sure that it has enough overhang, and as you work your way along the board, straighten it as necessary.**

   To straighten a bowed board, drive a chisel into the top of the joist nearest the deflection and, using the chisel as a lever, force the board into alignment.

As you fasten each board to the joists, maintain a gap between boards — $1/16$ to $3/16$ inch, depending on how wet the lumber is. To keep this gap uniform, make spacers from scrap plywood or use 10d nails driven through a scrap of wood. (Blunt the ends of the nails and don't leave the spacers lying about.)

Do a quick calculation to see how close the edge of the last board comes to the edge of the header joist. As you install the decking, take frequent measurements between the installed boards and the edge of the deck to see whether you need to adjust the gaps between boards to gain or straighten the layout.

Fasteners

The traditional decking fasteners are nails, which are still effective but are rapidly giving way to deck screws and hidden clips as the fasteners of choice. (See Chapter 6 for tips on choosing materials such as nails.) Wherever you install boards that you may need to remove, such as over a crawlspace access, pipes, or other utilities, use screws.

If you use nails, choose hot-dip galvanized or stainless steel. Use 16d common nails for 2-by lumber and 10d for $5/4$-inch boards. Use two nails per joint. Drive the nails in opposite directions into the decking at a 30-degree angle, $3/4$ inch from the edges of the board, as shown in Figure 11-2. To keep the rows of nails straight, hold a framing square along the nail heads in the previous two boards to align each new nail. Drill pilot holes for nails at the ends of boards. Drive nails into the soft part of the grain to minimize splitting. Set the heads slightly below the surface. If you dent a board, moisten the depression with warm water to swell it back to normal.

Galvanized deck screws, driven with a power drill or power screwdriver, have the advantage of greater holding power, tapered heads that embed in the wood, and easy removability. They're more expensive than galvanized nails. Unlike nails, you can drive them straight into the board. Use the same techniques for spacing and aligning the screws as you would for nails. If you don't have a power screwdriver, consider renting a heavy-duty model with an automatic screw-feeding clip.

For other fasteners, such as hidden clips or construction adhesive, follow the manufacturer's directions. Some decking clips require tipping the board on edge, fastening all the clips, and snugging the board into place by toenailing the opposite edge. Another fastening system requires attaching strips to the joists from below the deck and driving screws up through the strips into the decking boards.

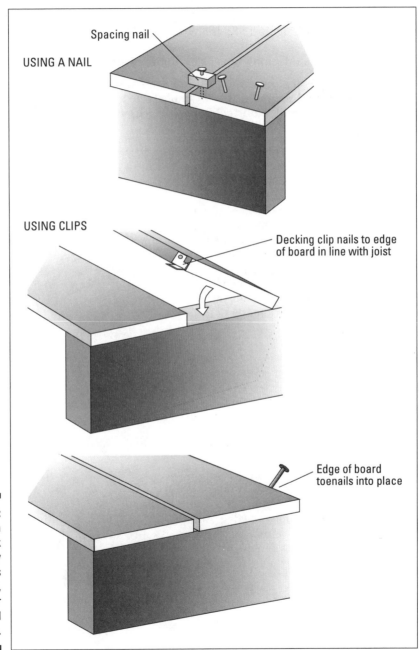

USING A NAIL

Spacing nail

USING CLIPS

Decking clip nails to edge
of board in line with joist

Edge of board
toenails into place

Figure 11-2:
You can
fasten deck
boards by
using nails
(as shown),
screws, or
specialized
fasteners.

Notching for obstacles

To fit decking boards around railing posts, chimneys, downspouts, or other obstacles (see Figure 11-3), follow these steps:

1. **Install all decking boards up to the obstacle.**

2. **Lay the next board in position against the protrusion and mark the board where the sides of the obstacle intersect it (leaving a $^3/_8$-inch gap around the obstacle for air circulation).**

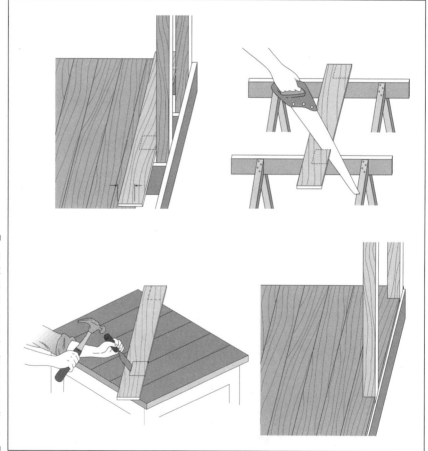

Figure 11-3:
To fit boards around obstacles, mark each board for cutting by holding it in place and measuring the depth of the notch.

The patio at right blends into its lavish surroundings with understated pavement, delicate furniture, and potted plants that echo the soft lines of the slope.

If you're trying to take advantage of a spectacular view such as the one at left, a minimal railing and few plantings avoid obstructing the view, while the angle of the deck's floorboards directs the eye outward.

The focus of the yard at right is the deck itself, with strong, thick lines that unify the many levels and roles of this deck.

The patio at right practically melts into the surrounding garden. Meandering paths; seating areas and overgrown, ragged paving stones; and multilevel installments among the multi-leveled plantings leave the visitor wondering which came first: the patio or the garden.

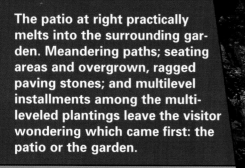

At left, serene, stylized wooden decking continues the "Great Outdoors" theme of the boulders and carefully selected plants to unify the decorative and practical areas of this yard into a coherent design.

In the example at right, the yard becomes an extension of the deck itself because of a consistent, planar scheme among all the elements — patio, lawn, stairs, pergola, and benches — and the repetition of identical benches throughout the entire plan.

A clever or subtle treatment of ordinary deck or patio elements can turn them into standout features. The conversation area above becomes a secret oasis if hidden in a jungle of plants and separated from the house.

The cooking area above seamlessly blends into the house, adding function without obstruction. A whirlpool getaway (left) is much more dramatic left glowing in the surrounding darkness rather than lit up with glaring floodlights.

Be aware of how your outdoor living spaces interact with their surroundings. The striking, architectural deck at right, set on the edge of an otherwise unassuming landscape, both adds drama to the yard itself and directs the eye outward to the view beyond.

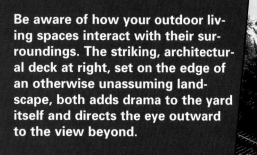

If you have your heart set on a patio as attention grabbing as this mint-julep-drinking, hoop-skirt-wearing example at left, make sure that you can convincingly integrate the effect with your home's existing lines and features.

The relaxed conversation area at right literally extends the interior living area by becoming a room in itself, with "carpeting" of warm brick, "walls" of ivy, and carefully arranged container plants.

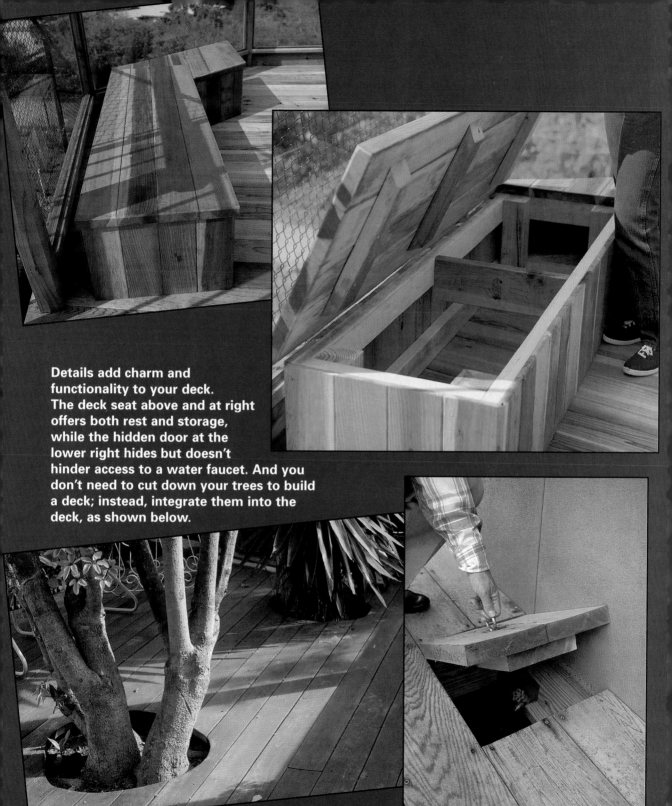

Details add charm and functionality to your deck. The deck seat above and at right offers both rest and storage, while the hidden door at the lower right hides but doesn't hinder access to a water faucet. And you don't need to cut down your trees to build a deck; instead, integrate them into the deck, as shown below.

Similar basic building techniques can serve completely opposite purposes. The lattice screen in the example above right separates and conceals an unattractive view, while the lattice pergola at the right protects the deck (and its occupants!) from sun and wind, yet still provides peek-a-boo views of the surrounding area. Consider, too, how the clean lines of the railing above would change with potted ivy or wisteria draped over the side.

Know your ultimate goal in choosing paving materials, whether it's aesthetics or practical use. The natural, "stepping-stone" effect of the patio at top is lovely, but how well would it accommodate heavy traffic? Kids? Pets? Furniture? An automobile? High heels? Consider how the atmosphere and practicality of the above patio (and your own plan) would change with other materials. Commonly used materials include (from left to right, second row) flagstone, brick and concrete, exposed aggregate, stamped concrete, and concrete pavers.

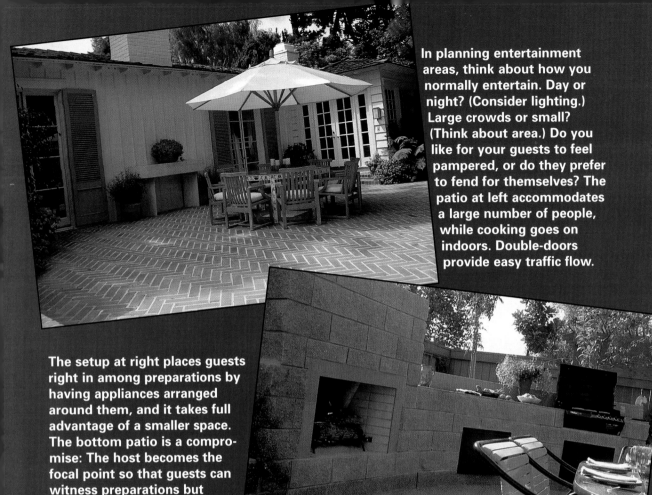

In planning entertainment areas, think about how you normally entertain. Day or night? (Consider lighting.) Large crowds or small? (Think about area.) Do you like for your guests to feel pampered, or do they prefer to fend for themselves? The patio at left accommodates a large number of people, while cooking goes on indoors. Double-doors provide easy traffic flow.

The setup at right places guests right in among preparations by having appliances arranged around them, and it takes full advantage of a smaller space. The bottom patio is a compromise: The host becomes the focal point so that guests can witness preparations but remain separate from the work.

Consider also the atmospheres that the different building materials convey: Large stone blocks give the middle patio an earthy, casual feel, while the tiles at left dramatically increase the festiveness of preparations.

3. **With the board pushed tightly against the obstacle, measure the distance between the edge of the board and the exposed edge of the decking board under it.**

4. **Subtract this distance from the width of the decking to calculate how deep the notch must be.**

   Be sure to add ³/₈ of an inch for clearance.

5. **Cut along the marks to notch the board.**

To fit a board around a round or irregularly shaped object, install full decking boards as close to the object as possible. Measure the shortest gap between the obstacle and the closest installed decking board and set a compass to this measurement (subtracting ³/₈ of an inch for clearance). Lay the next board on top of the installed boards, snugging it against the object. Holding the compass upright, scribe the profile of the obstacle onto the board by tracing along it with the compass.

Trimming the Ends

To mark the ends of the boards for trimming, snap a chalkline along the edge of the deck. If you're installing a fascia board or trim that's flush with the surface of the decking (for a nice, clean look), trim the boards flush with the side of the outside joist. If you prefer to leave the edge of the decking exposed, allow it to overlap the joist by half an inch for a clean shadowline. Trim all of the boards at once, using a circular saw. For a perfectly straight cut, tack a straightedge on the decking to guide the saw. Clean up the edges of the cut boards with a sander or rasping plane.

Adding a Fascia

To trim the deck with a decorative fascia board (see Figure 11-4), select long, straight, clear pieces of lumber. Use 2-by lumber, one size larger than the joist size, if the fascia is to be flush with the top of the decking. If the fascia fits below the decking, choose 1-by boards the same depth as the joist lumber or 2x4s to create an interesting stepped effect. Some suppliers offer "fascia-grade" lumber that's surfaced on one side and rough on the other, which gives you a choice of textures.

If your deck has stairs, install the stringers first and cover the connections with fascia (see Chapter 12). Everywhere else, install the fascia after completing the decking and before installing the railing.

The most critical aspect of installing fascia is to apply preservative and sealer liberally where the joist and fascia board make contact. This connection is vulnerable to water that can seep between the two boards and get trapped.

Cut fascia boards by using 45-degree bevel cuts (adjusting the saw blade to 45 degrees). This angle enables you to make miter joints at the corners and overlapping joints where you must join two fascia boards for a long edge. To keep from marring the surface of the fascia with nail or screw heads, attach it by driving galvanized deck screws through the joist or header into the fascia board from behind. Space screws 6 to 8 inches apart along the top edge and 12 to 16 inches apart along the bottom.

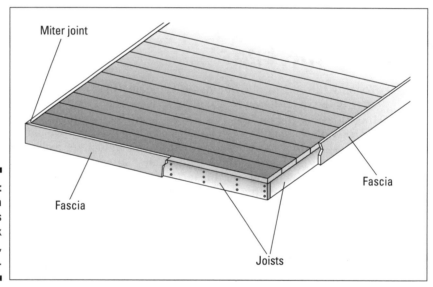

Figure 11-4:
A fascia board gives the deck a clean, trim look.

Chapter 12

Building Stairs, Railings, and Benches

*A*fter completing the deck platform, you can turn to building stairs, railings, and benches. Schedule plenty of time to build the stairs and railing so that you don't need to leave the deck in an unfinished condition for long periods of time. A deck with an inviting platform but uncompleted railings or stairs is a safety hazard. If necessary, rope off portions of the deck that have an unprotected drop-off.

Installing Stair Stringers

The first step in building stairs is to calculate the exact dimensions of the riser and tread. (See Chapter 5 for information on deck specs and stair dimensions.) First, measure the vertical distance between the stair landing and the top of the deck platform. To do so, place one end of a long straight-edge on the deck platform and hold it out level over the stair landing. (You need someone to help you and possibly a stepladder as well.) Measure down from the bottom of the straightedge to the landing. This distance is the total rise of the stairway.

Compare this distance with the total rise dimension you used for your preliminary calculations. If the numbers are identical, use the riser and tread dimensions in your plans. If the total rise doesn't match your design estimate, recalculate the stairs by using the same technique that I describe in Chapter 5: Divide a desirable riser height, such as seven inches, into the total rise; then round the answer up to the next whole number and divide that number into the total rise. The answer is the new riser height. To determine the tread width, double the riser height and subtract the sum from 26. Remember that the riser heights or tread depths cannot vary from each other more than $^3/_8$ inch over the entire run of stairs.

Laying out the first stringer

Stringers are the main diagonal stair members that support the treads. For stringer stock, choose a straight 2x12 that's four feet longer than the total run of the stairs. (The *run* is the horizontal distance.) Select a piece that's completely free of knots along the bottom edge (as held with the crown up). Lay this board on sawhorses with the bottom edge close to you.

A quick way to verify the length of the stringer is by using a framing square: Find the dimension on each leg (in inches) that corresponds to the total rise and total run, respectively (in feet), of the stairs. Measure the distance between these two marks and convert it into feet. Add two feet, and you have the length of the stringer stock.

After you have stringer stock that's the correct length, you need to lay out (or mark) the stock to fit the planned staircase. Follow these steps:

1. **Place a framing square along the top edge of the stringer, near one end, with the *tongue* of the square (the shorter leg) facing that end and the two legs of the square pointing away from you. (See Figure 12-1.)**

2. **Carefully position the square so that the outer edge of the tongue intersects the top edge of the board at exactly the riser height dimension you chose and the outer edge of the *blade* (the longer leg) intersects the top edge at exactly the tread width.**

3. **Using a sharp pencil or knife, trace along the outer edge of the square to mark a cutting line for the notch.**

   Mark the stringer carefully by using a sharp pencil, knife, or scribe. Sloppy marks and measurements accumulate as you move down the stringer, causing a significant deviation over the length of the stringer.

4. **Slide the square "down" the stairs and repeat this operation, aligning the riser height on the tongue with the end of the tread mark you just made.**

To speed up layout and reduce the risk of misreading a measurement, clamp a straight scrap of wood onto the bottom of the square, snugly against the stringer, while holding the square in position. This cleat stops the square at the correct readings on the tongue and blade. You can also buy miniature clamps that you tighten onto the two blades of the square (called *stair gauges* or *stair buttons*) that do the same thing. And notch the back of the top riser if you're using joist hangers.

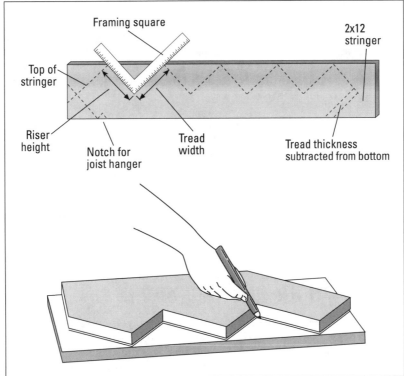

Framing square

2x12
stringer

Top of
stringer

Riser
height

Notch for
joist hanger

Tread
width

Tread thickness
subtracted from bottom

Figure 12-1:
Use a
framing
square to
lay out
a stair
stringer for
cutting.

Cutting the stringers

After you finish marking all the notches (counting the treads and risers
carefully), mark a line for cutting off the bottom of the stringer parallel with
the treads. Before you cut out the stringer, adjust this line to compensate for
the thickness of the tread material; otherwise, the bottom step ends up too
high. Making this adjustment is called _dropping the stringer_. If your stair
stringers rest on a level landing, drop the stringer (move the cutting up) a
distance equal to the thickness of the tread stock. If the stringer rests on a
footing that's separate from the landing or on a raised cleat, or the landing
slopes from side to side, take these factors into account in adjusting the
cutting line.

Cutting out the notches requires accurate, straight cuts. If you use a circular
power saw, keep the blade on the inside of the cutting marks. (Because you
cut on alternating sides of the lines, you can easily get confused.) Don't
overcut by running the blade beyond the inside corner of the notch (which
you must do for some cuts to compensate for the curvature of the blade);
stop each cut at the corner and complete the cuts with a handsaw.

After cutting the first stringer, test it by setting it in place. The stringer should fit; the treads should be level and the risers plumb. Place tread stock on the bottom riser and measure the distance down to the landing; this distance should be the same as the riser height. Do the same on the top tread; the distance from tread stock to the deck surface should also be the same as the riser height. Double-check all the other riser heights. (You don't need to place tread stock on them.)

If the stringer fits perfectly, use it as a pattern for cutting out the second stringer (and others, if required). If the stringer isn't satisfactory, use it as a guide for laying out a new stringer pattern, making whatever adjustments you need. After cutting out a new stringer and testing it, use this new stringer as a pattern for other stringers.

After cutting out all the stringers, treat the cut edges with a combination preservative and sealer to prevent trapped moisture from causing the wood to decay.

Installing the stringers

If the stringers rest on a concrete landing, you must either treat them with a preservative or use a durable species of lumber. Treat the cut ends with additional preservative. Before installing the stringers, attach a pair of preservative-treated 2x4 cleats (short pieces of lumber) to the landing to align with the inside edges of the stringers by using one of the following methods of attachment:

- Install J-bolts in the fresh concrete (which requires accurate placement before you have final stair dimensions).
- Drill holes in the concrete and install expansion or masonry bolts (the easiest method).
- Rent a powder-actuated fastener and shoot nails through the cleats into the concrete. (This tool uses 22-caliber loads to fire nails into concrete; for safe use, follow the rental agency's instructions carefully.)

Attach the top of the stringers to a double header, double joist, or beam, using a joist hanger for each stringer. (Notch or slot the stringer for the bottom flange of the hanger.) Follow these steps:

1. **Attach a hanger to each stringer.**

2. **Set the stringers in place and clamp them to the cleats on the landing.**

3. **Place a level across the stringers at several treads to make sure that they're level.**

4. **Check all measurements, make final adjustments, and nail the joist hangers to the deck.**

5. **Attach the bottoms of the stringers to the cleats by using deck screws or lag screws.**

Your stringers should now be securely attached to both deck and footing (see Figure 12-2).

Laying out a solid stringer

Lay out a solid stringer the same way as you do a cutout stringer, using the same riser and tread dimensions (see the preceding section). Cut only the bottom and, if necessary, the top. After testing the first stringer, lay out a matching stringer in the opposite direction and trim the end(s).

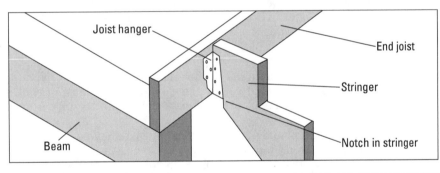

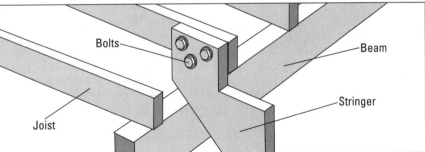

Figure 12-2: Attach stringers securely to the deck and footing.

Attach stair angles, which are metal L-shaped brackets, to the inside of each stringer. Align the top of each angle along the tread line that you scribed on the stringer. Attach the cleat with one-and-a-half-inch galvanized lag screws (no washers). Be very careful: The brackets have sharp corners. Install the stringers the same way as you do cutout stringers (see the preceding section).

If you want to conceal the stair angles, install them *upside down* against the stringers. The treads butt against the flanges of the brackets and conceal them.

Installing Treads and Handrails

Before installing the treads, treat the bottoms and edges with preservative and sealer. For solid stringers, cut the treads half an inch short to allow a quarter-inch clearance at each end. Install the treads, starting at the bottom. Overhang the front of the stringer cutouts (or stair brackets, for solid stringers) one to one and a half inches. Leave a $^3/_{16}$- to $^1/_4$-inch gap between boards for water to drain through. Attach the treads to cutout stringers by using deck screws. Attach treads to solid stringers with one-and-a-quarter-inch lag screws driven up through the brackets from below the stairs.

Before installing handrails, review the requirements for handrails in Chapter 5. In addition to a grippable handrail, you must provide screening along the exposed edge of the stairs if the drop-off is greater than 30 inches.

For the handrail and screening, begin by installing posts at the top and bottom and every four to six feet in between. Attach the top posts by bolting them to the edge of the deck or by one of the other methods that I describe for deck railing posts. (See the section "Installing Railing Posts," a little later in this chapter.) The posts must be high enough for the 36-inch deck railing. Attach the bottom and intermediate posts to the stringer(s) with two half-inch carriage bolts. Cut the posts long and trim them after you install them. For a decorative touch, cut the bottom of the intermediate posts at a 30- or 45-degree angle. For a more secure bottom post, install a post anchor as you pour the concrete landing or set a preservative-treated post specified for ground contact in the concrete, embedding it in a hole at least 18 inches deep.

After installing the posts, attach a string from the bottom post to the top post that's parallel with the stair stringer and at a uniformly consistent height of 34 to 38 inches above all the tread *nosings* (the front edges). Mark where the string intersects each post. You want to attach the handrail at this point.

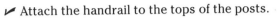

For the handrail itself, you have the following options:

- ✔ Attach the handrail to the tops of the posts.

- ✔ Hang the handrail on the sides. Hanging it on the side enables you to finish the top of the railing the same way as the rest of the deck and makes the handrail less conspicuous. There must be at least one and a half inches of clearance between the handrail and other railing members.

- ✔ The handgrip portion of a handrail should be between an inch and a quarter and two inches in cross-sectional dimension.

If you use a wooden handrail, choose a tropical hardwood, if available, because hardwood doesn't splinter as readily as soft woods do. Finish it with a sealer and attach it by using brackets available for this purpose from hardware stores or home improvement centers. Use curved pieces at the ends of the handrail, if necessary, to terminate it in the posts. Another handrail option is one-and-a-half-inch galvanized or copper pipe. Copper pipe is especially attractive, and you can solder tees and curved fittings to straight lengths for smooth transitions.

To add the screening and complete the stair railings, follow the same techniques as for the deck railings. (See the section "Adding Rails and Screening," a little later in this chapter.)

Building Steps and Stepped Platforms

Some decks are low enough that the ground is only a step or two away. Other decks may have multiple levels separated by only a step or two. These changes in levels are too small for complete stairs with stringers, treads, and handrails. Instead, you can build a single step by using one of the following techniques. You must still observe the basic riser and tread ratio (two risers plus tread equals 25–27 inches).

For a change in platform levels, utilize the convenient dimensions of 2x6s. Set 2x6 cleats on edge and attach 2x6 tread stock to the tops. The combined height of the two components is exactly 7 inches ($5^1/_2$ inches + $1^1/_2$ inches), an ideal riser height. If the platforms are separated far enough to require two steps, build an intermediate step at the midpoint. If the platforms are 13 inches apart, for example, build the step by ripping 2x6 stock to 5 inches (using a table saw or circular saw with a ripping guide) and making cleats out of it to set on edge. Screw or toenail them to the lower deck surface and attach 2-by lumber to the tops for the tread. The combined height of the two components is $6^1/_2$ inches, exactly half the 13-inch total rise.

If you need an intermediate step to step down from the deck, you can provide a stepping stone by using a native stone or casting one out of concrete, or you can suspend a step from the deck framing. To do the latter, suspend 2x6 supports from the bottom of the deck joists with joist hangers, extending them out past the edge of the deck 15 inches or so. Attach tread stock to the top of the extended portion of the supports for a step.

Installing Railing Posts

If you support the deck on perimeter posts that extend up through the decking, use these posts for the railing posts. Simply trim the tops at $34^1/_2$ inches above the deck surface to accommodate a 2-by cap rail.

If you need to attach posts, here's the easiest method:

1. **Bolt the posts to the outside of the joists and header(s).**

   Use 4x4s and space them evenly, four to six feet apart, along each side of the deck.

2. **Cut an inch-and-a-half-wide notch out of the bottom of each post so that it laps over the deck surface, leaving a two-inch-thick "tail" to bolt to the joists.**

   Without the notches, mounting posts on the deck corners that align with the rest of the posts would be impossible.

   To notch the corner posts, don't cut the inch-and-a-half-wide notch all the way through the post. Stop it one and a half inches short of one side to create an L-shaped notch that wraps around the deck corner.

For a decorative touch, bevel the bottoms of the post "tails" 30 or 45 degrees. After cutting and notching the bottoms, trim the tops of the posts so that they rise $34^1/_2$ inches above the deck surface. Secure each post with two half-inch carriage bolts (see Figure 12-3).

If you don't want to attach posts to the outside of the deck, install the posts inside the deck perimeter by bolting them to the joists before installing the decking boards. Set the posts three or four inches in from the edge of the deck and then notch and fit the decking boards around them. Attach cleats or blocking to the deck framing, as needed, to support the ends of decking boards that butt into the railing posts. This method gives the edge of the deck a clean, uncluttered look.

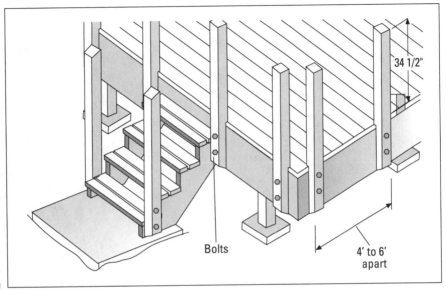

Figure 12-3:
You can attach railing posts to the perimeter of the deck or set them in for a cleaner appearance.

34 1/2"

Bolts

4' to 6' apart

Adding Rails and Screening

You can install a variety of different railings, based on your particular design (see Figure 12-4).

Unless your railing design has continuous rails attached to the outside face of the railing posts, install top and bottom rails between the posts to support the balusters or other screening material. To install the rails, follow these steps:

1. **Mark and cut 2x4 rails to fit between the posts.**

   Mark all the posts four inches above the deck surface. For each bay, measure the distance between the posts at the marks and at the tops of the posts. Cut 2x4s to these dimensions.

2. **Set the bottom rail in place, on edge, with the inside face flush with the inside faces of the posts (unless you use vinyl-coated wire for the screening, which requires the rails to be flush with the posts on the outside face).**

3. **Attach the rail to the posts by driving two three-inch galvanized deck screws at an angle through the face of each post and into the rail.**

   If the wood is brittle, drill pilot holes through the posts first.

4. **Drive additional nails at an angle up through each end of the rail and into the post and then down through each end of the rail and into the post.**

5. **Install the top rails the same way.**

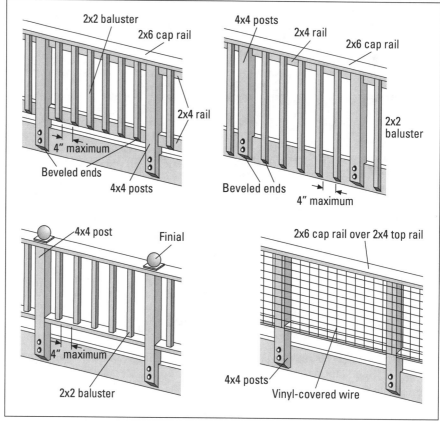

Figure 12-4:
You can install several different types of railings by using standard-dimensioned lumber or specialized railing pieces.

Cap rail

Install the cap rail using 2x6 lumber of the same or better grade as the decking boards. Start on one of the sides connected to the house. Follow these steps:

1. **Cut one end of a board square and set it on the posts, butted against the house wall.**

2. **Mark a 45-degree angle on the board, centering the mark exactly over the corner post.**

3. **Cut along this mark and attach the cap rail by driving four three-inch deck screws down through it into each post or by driving the screws up at an angle through the posts and into the cap rail.**

4. **Install the cap rail for the opposite side of the deck the same way.**

5. **Prepare the cap rail for the third side.**

   Lay the rail in place so that the ends overlap the two rails you already installed. Position the cap rail precisely and, from below, scribe a cutting line on each end by tracing a pencil along the cut edges of the two installed boards.

6. **Cut along these marks and attach the rail for the third side by using deck screws.**

If you're installing a curved railing, use prefabricated railing pieces or cut curved sections out of 2x12 stock and join them together into a continuous curve with dowel joints, using a waterproof adhesive to do so.

Screening

After you install the top, bottom, and cap rails, you can attach the screening to the top and bottom rails. If the screening is vinyl-coated wire, secure it to the outside of the rails and posts by using galvanized wire staples, stretching the screening as you attach it. If the screening is prefabricated lattice panels, attach them to the outside faces of the top and bottom rails by using two-inch deck screws or 6d galvanized box nails. Make the bottom edge flush with the bottom of the lower rail. After installing the lattice, attach 1x4 trim along the lower outside edge of the lattice by using galvanized deck screws or 8d galvanized box nails.

If you install balusters, space them no farther than four inches apart. Attach each 2x2 baluster or round spindle to the top and bottom rails by using 8d galvanized box nails or three-inch deck screws. Drill pilot holes first. An alternative railing design, using the same balusters or spindles, is to eliminate the bottom rail, attach the top rail so that the outside face is flush with the outside face of the deck platform, and cut the balusters long enough to butt into the bottom of the cap rail and overlap the deck platform by six inches. For a decorative touch, cut the bottoms of the balusters or spindles at an angle.

To speed up installation of the balusters, cut a scrap of wood just shorter than four inches and use it as a spacer for positioning each new baluster as you attach it.

Building Simple Benches

A built-in bench is like a magnet, making a deck instantly inviting. Benches help to define areas of the deck and add focal points to large expanses of decking. You can design a very simple bench with no back or blend a bench into a railing or planter design to incorporate those elements into a back. (See Figure 12-5 for a simple bench design.)

For basic dimensions, the seat should be 15 to 18 inches high and at least 15 inches deep. If you add a back, it should be at least 12 inches high and lean back at an angle of 20 to 30 degrees from vertical. If the bench is part of a railing, extend the back 36 inches above the *seat* (not just the deck) and observe the screening requirement, including the area below the bench seat.

An elegant low bench

A classic design for a deck bench of any length is to make the seat out of 2x2s, 2x4s, or 2x6s (or a combination) running lengthwise and trim the edge with a fascia of 1x4s or 2x4s. To prevent nail heads or screw heads from showing on the top surface, construct the bench seat face-down by laying out the long boards and attaching 2x4 cleats to them every three to four feet. Leave a quarter-inch gap between the seat boards. Taper the bottom edges of the cleats at each end so that the ends are 2 inches deep, instead of $3^1/2$ inches, to conceal them behind the fascia. First, drill pilot holes $1^3/4$ inches into the cleats (to countersink the screws) and then attach the cleats by using three-inch deck screws driven down through them into the seat boards.

After assembling the seat, attach legs or supports to the cleats. Cut them out of 2x8 or 2x10 lumber, 14 to 16 inches long, or cut pairs of 4x4s to the same length. Attach the legs to the cleats by using $3^1/2$-inch carriage bolts and use a framing square to align the legs. Turn the bench over, set it in place, and attach it to the decking by driving deck screws through the legs into the deck boards or by using angle brackets that you screw to the deck and then into the legs. To conceal angle brackets, screw all of them down to the deck first and then set the bench in place with the legs on top of the lower flanges.

To complete the bench, install 1x4 or 2x4 fascia boards around the seat. Cut the corners at 45 degrees to make miter joints and attach them by driving screws into them from the back, not from the face. Smooth all the edges by using a rasping plane and sandpaper.

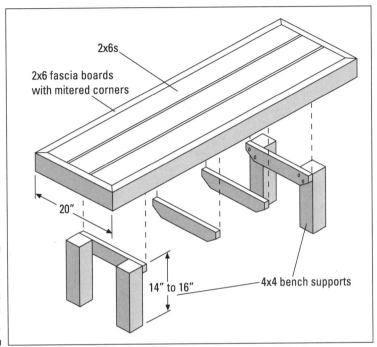

2x6s

2x6 fascia boards
with mitered corners

20"

14" to 16"

4x4 bench supports

Figure 12-5:
This bench
design is
easy to
build.

Variations on the basic bench

Using the basic bench design that I describe in the preceding section, you
can adapt the bench for different effects in several ways. Here are just a few:

- ✔ To give the bench a more substantial look, replace the legs with simple
  boxes measuring 12 inches square. Attach them to the decking and
  cleats by using deck screws.

- ✔ To give the bench more delicate details, don't attach a fascia to the
  edge of the seat boards. Instead, use a router with a roundover bit and
  go around the top edge of the seat boards to give them a more refined
  profile.

- ✔ Add a decorative edge to 1x4 stock and attach it below the seat boards
  rather than to the edges, as you do with a fascia. You need to add some
  cleats and blocking to which you attach the decorative trim.

- ✔ Finally, you can dress up the cleats and legs by cutting them into
  decorative shapes with S curves or similar classic profiles.

Chapter 13

Finishes and Maintenance

● ●

In This Chapter

▶ Reviewing your finish options

▶ Preparing the deck for finishing

▶ Applying a deck finish

▶ Maintaining your deck

● ●

As you and your family stand back to admire your brand-new deck, insects and microorganisms inhabiting your property are equally impressed. ("Oh boy, free food!") These insects and microorganisms, however, aren't the only enemies lurking around your deck. Ironically, the two most devastating threats are the same elements that trees require to manufacture wood in the first place: sunlight and water. As strong, beautiful, and durable as a new deck may appear, it begins an inevitable slide into decay the moment you install the first boards — unless you protect the wood from its natural enemies. Unfortunately, no protection lasts indefinitely. You must renew the finish and maintain your deck to keep it looking new. In a sense, you never finish the finish.

Applying finish to a deck is not difficult, but if you have experience finishing wooden furniture or painting a house, you're likely to find finishing a deck to be somewhat different. For one thing, the large surface and outdoor exposure can be formidable. And the demanding conditions (a horizontal surface subjected to constant sunlight, rain, and use) require specialized products that must meet multiple challenges.

Reviewing Your Finish Options

The first rule of deck finishing is to use a product specifically designed for horizontal deck surfaces. Finishes intended only for siding or fences or "all-purpose" coatings designed for concrete and masonry as well as wood don't stand up to the abrasion, direct sunlight, and moisture conditions to which deck surfaces are exposed. Avoid paint and film-forming solid stains on the deck platform. Use the following guidelines, based on the type of wood you used to build your deck, to make a final decision about finishes. (See Chapter 6 for more information about finishes.) You may want to use different finishes on different deck components, such as a clear sealer for redwood decking and paint for the railing.

- ✓ **Preservative-treated wood.** The easiest finish to apply on preservative-treated wood and to maintain is water-repellent preservative (WRP), which is clear and retains the original color of the wood. If you want to change the color, the next easiest finish to use (although not as easy to apply) is a semitransparent oil-based stain. Waterborne semitransparent stains, which may be required where VOC (volatile organic compound) levels are highly regulated, are quite easy to apply but aren't as durable as the oil-based variety (although new, improved compounds are continually appearing on the market). If you want to paint the wood, choose a paint that's a high-performance architectural coating for the deck surface and the recommended primer for that paint. Apply a water-repellent sealer before painting the wood.

- ✓ **Water-repellent-treated wood.** A few wood-treating companies offer preservative-treated $^5/_4$x6-inch radius-edged decking that includes a guaranteed water-repellent surface. Although this wood is convenient to use and probably worth the cost, take precautions and apply WRP (water-repellent preservative) to the deck periodically. Make sure that you follow all the manufacturer's recommendations.

- ✓ **Cedar or redwood.** Do not assume that these woods are immune to moisture and sunlight degradation. They require finishes. Choose a sealer that offers UV (ultraviolet) inhibitors and includes a preservative if the lumber contains any sapwood. Semitransparent stains are equally effective and prevent weathering for an even longer time. If you paint either wood, use an oil-based stain-blocking primer to prevent the natural tannins in the wood from bleeding through the paint. Apply two topcoats of acrylic latex.

- ✓ **Tropical hardwoods.** A clear sealer or WRP is the best choice for a hardwood deck. You can also leave the wood alone to weather naturally to a soft grayish color and perhaps renew it periodically with a light sanding.

- ✓ **Wood alternatives.** Most plastic "wood" is designed to be left alone. Vinyl decking is colored all the way through the material and retains its original color indefinitely. Wood-polymer composites weather to a light gray color that's permanent, or you can apply stain or paint as you would with wood. Unlike wood, this material is not subject to shrinking and swelling, which cause finishes to deteriorate more quickly.

Do you speak finish?

As you read the labels and manufacturer's specifications for deck finishes, you may think that you're reading a foreign language or looking at a can of alphabet soup. The following list can help you decipher the abbreviations and compounds:

✔ *ACQ (ammoniacal copper quaternary ammonium)* is a waterborne preservative that's offered as a nontoxic alternative to other compounds used for preservative-treated lumber.

✔ *ACZA (ammoniacal copper zinc arsenate)* binder is a water-based preservative used in hard-to-penetrate woods.

✔ *Bis (tributyltin) oxide* is a slightly yellow antifouling paint.

✔ *CCA (chromated copper arsenate)* is the most common agent used in preservative-treated lumber and is usually green.

✔ *Copper-8-quinolinolate* is used to protect against mold, mildew, wood rot/decay fungi, and wood stain fungi.

✔ *Copper naphthanate* is a preservative that's available to consumers for site applications. Available in clear form.

✔ *Film-forming* is a type of finish that forms a hard surface film.

✔ *Latex stain* is a water-based penetrating stain.

✔ *Mildewcide* is a compound added to paints and stains to inhibit mildew.

✔ *Penetrating* refers to preservatives that work by soaking into the board instead of by forming a film.

✔ *Penta (pentachlorophenol)* is a crystalline compound used as a wood preservative, fungicide, and disinfectant.

✔ *Polyphase (3-Iodo-2-propynyl butyl carbamate)* is a mildewcide.

✔ *Preservative* is any agent that retards microorganisms and insects from damaging wood.

✔ *Sealer* is any agent that prevents moisture from penetrating the wood.

✔ *Semitransparent stain* is stain that colors the wood slightly and allows the wood grain to show through.

✔ *Solvent* is the agent in stains and paints that dissolves solids and improves flow until you apply the product.

✔ *TCMBT (2-Thiocyanomethylthio benzothiazole)* is a mildewcide.

✔ *UV*, or *Ultraviolet*, refers to ultraviolet radiation from the sun.

✔ *UV inhibitor* (also called *UV blocker*) is an agent added to certain stains and sealers to inhibit UV radiation from breaking down wood fibers.

✔ *VOC (volatile organic compound)* refers to ingredients in paints, stains, and sealers that *volatize*, or evaporate, easily and are a potential source of air pollution.

✔ *Waterborne* characterizes preservatives, sealers, and paints with water-soluble main ingredients rather than oil-based compounds.

✔ *Water-repellent* is the capability to prevent moisture from penetrating wood.

✔ *WRP (water-repellent preservative)* is a compound that combines the water-repellent qualities of a sealer with the microorganism- and insect-destroying qualities of a preservative.

✔ *Zinc naphthanate* is a mildewcide.

Preparing the Deck for Finishing

For most decking materials, apply the finish right away. If lumber is left unfinished for very long, the wood surface begins to weather enough to cause any finishes that form a film on the surface to adhere incorrectly.

 If you bought "green" deck lumber that was neither air-dried nor kiln-dried, let the deck dry out for two to four weeks before finishing it. If water beads on the surface of the boards and does not penetrate, the preservative treatment applied at the factory contained some water repellent or you applied some prior to installing the boards. In such a case, wait two to three months before applying the finish. You should leave no wood unfinished for longer than three months.

If preservative-treated boards have a filmy residue on them, remove that residue with soap and water that you apply with a stiff brush *before* you apply a finish. If pine or Douglas fir lumber has pitch on the surface (pitch bleed), the pitch prevents a finish from adhering correctly. Try to remove the pitch by using mineral spirits or turpentine. Otherwise, you must replace the board. (You can prevent this problem by using kiln-dried lumber, which is heated enough to "cook" the pitch into a solid form.)

Applying a Deck Finish

Before finishing the deck, apply the finish to a test patch or some scrap lumber from your deck-building project. Choose a day on which the air temperature is between 40 and 90 degrees F and try to avoid working in direct sunlight. Apply WRP and stains by using a brush or pad to increase penetration (see Figure 13-1). Beware of overapplying; more is not necessarily better, because an excess can lead to filming, which impedes the correct penetration of the product. Read the product label carefully and follow all directions.

In applying stain, coat the full length of each board. Otherwise, you risk lap marks wherever you apply fresh stain over stain that's drying. Apply only as much stain as the wood can absorb. Avoid puddles.

If you're not sure how a semitransparent stain is going to look, experiment with scrap lumber or a hidden part of the deck. To avoid any risk, apply a WRP first and live with the deck for a few months. You can always coat it with a semitransparent stain later.

Figure 13-1:
Apply sealer or stain by using a brush to ensure uniform penetration of the product into the wood.

If you are painting your deck, apply a WRP specified as having 1 percent or less of water repellent. Observe the recommended drying time on the label before covering the WRP with primer and paint. Except for redwood and western cedars (which require an oil-based, stain-blocking primer), use a latex primer. For the deck surface, apply a "high-performance architectural coating" or at least an oil-based or urethane-modified alkyd paint. For railings or the understructure, you can use ordinary exterior latex or acrylic-latex paint.

Maintaining Your Deck

All wood decks are vulnerable to water, sunlight, and abrasion and must be maintained. Otherwise, the wood weakens and cracks, accelerating the advance of mildew, mold, and other wood-destroying agents. Keep the following points in mind:

✔ If your deck has a water-repellent preservative or clear sealer, renew it every year. Semitransparent stains last two to three years before needing renewal. You can possibly apply WRP over a stained deck if the pigments haven't worn off. Paint requires constant upkeep. If moisture gets under the paint, it deteriorates very quickly. Always choose products formulated with a mildewcide.

✔ If the deck is weathered, you can renew it with a brightener specifically designed for decks. The brightener removes any stains, mildew, or algae that may have a foothold in the wood cells and brightens the weathered surface to make it look like new lumber. Never use chlorine bleach to brighten a deck. Bleach leaves a whitish residue and may impede the effectiveness of the deck finish. (It also damages plants.)

After treating the deck with a brightener (following the instructions on the label), brush the deck to remove loose debris. After observing the recommended drying time, apply a deck finish the same as you would for new wood.

In addition to renewing the deck finish, keep the deck clean. Sweep or hose off the deck weekly (at least the stairs and other high-traffic areas). Clean out leaves, dirt, and needles that get trapped between decking boards. Inspect the deck once or twice a year. Look for loose nails, screws, and bolts and reset or tighten them. Probe wood members by using a sharp nail or screwdriver to look for rot, especially under the deck in the ledger area and around beams. Remove dirt and plant growth that may have accumulated around the base of posts.

If you discover rotted boards, remove and replace them immediately by following these steps:

1. **For a decking board, remove the rot by cutting out a section that spans at least two joist bays, as shown in Figure 13-2a.**

   Center the cuts over joists and apply preservative to cut ends of boards.

2. **Nail the replacement boards into place, as shown in Figure 13-2b.**

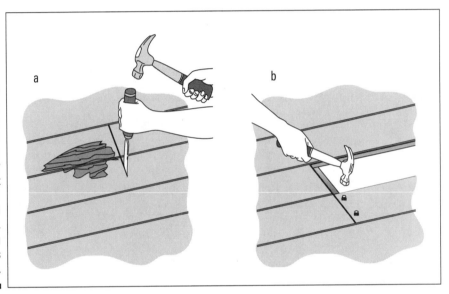

Figure 13-2:
Repair a rotted decking board by cutting out the affected section and replacing it, centering the joints over joists.

If a joist is rotted, provide temporary reinforcement by attaching a piece of preservative-treated wood to one side and then nailing the decking boards to the reinforcement. Remove any rotted wood from the original joist and apply preservative to the exposed areas first. Attach the reinforcing piece by using galvanized 10d common nails. Eventually, you should replace the entire joist by removing or cutting the nails or screws that hold the decking boards to it, sliding out the old joist, and inserting a new joist. By the time such a fix is necessary, however, you're likely to find that many other joists are rotted and you must remove all the decking to replace them.

Part III
Building a Patio

The 5th Wave — By Rich Tennant

"Come on, Jeanette, honey. Chew it up and spit it out. Daddy doesn't have all day."

In this part . . .

Although patios are as ancient as civilization itself, they are enjoying a surge of popularity as homeowners in all regions of the country rediscover the benefits of these simple, elegant, and enduring structures. New materials, such as concrete pavers, and improved construction techniques, such as compacted sand bases, make patios as appropriate for the frozen North as the arid Southwest. In these eight chapters you'll find an overview of patio materials, tips for planning your project, and step-by-step techniques for building a patio out of concrete, brick, stone, concrete pavers, or tile.

Chapter 14

Choosing Patio Materials

· ·

In This Chapter

▶ Surface impressions

▶ Concrete

▶ Brick

▶ Pavers

▶ Stone

▶ Unglazed tile

▶ Borders

· ·

The major planning decision for a patio is choosing what material to use for the surface. Whether concrete, stone, concrete pavers, brick, or tile, the paving material represents 70 percent to 90 percent of the patio budget and has the greatest effect on the overall patio design.

In making your choice, review the design principles presented in Part I, especially in Chapter 3. You must also consider the inherent properties of each material, such as color, texture, and shape. Some materials, such as concrete, for example, produce large, seamless expanses of paving. Others are modular, ranging in size from the relatively small forms of brick and tile to large adobe pavers or irregularly shaped flagstones.

Besides studying the information that I present in this chapter, you want to research your choices by visiting local masonry yards and building-materials suppliers. Ask to take home samples. Some yards have a free checkout system, similar to that of a library. Or you can buy a few pieces; they're sure to prove useful around the garden.

Surface Impressions

What is the best paving material for your patio? As you consider the various options presented in this chapter and from your own investigation, consider the following factors:

✔ **Color.** The single attribute that has the greatest visual effect is color. Most earth tones and neutrals, especially in variegated patterns, blend well with garden settings, but you should consider the subtleties of hue and shade. Terra cotta and brick colors complement greenery but have strong red or orange tones that seem artificial or overwhelming in some settings. Very light colors and sometimes dark colors call attention to the patio surface, which could be a distraction if the surrounding garden is more important. Mid-tones ensure that the patio surface plays a background, or supporting, role. Bold colors create interesting accents or contrast. Color also affects the capability of the patio to absorb or reflect sunlight, which could be a factor in exposed locations.

✔ **Texture.** Smooth surfaces tend to be monotonous and may become slippery, but you can relieve them by accenting borders. Excessively bumpy surfaces create the risk of tripping, may impede the movement of wheeled toys, and may make furniture wobbly.

✔ **Scale and proportion.** For small patios in confined spaces, choose brick, tile, or small stones. For expansive patios in wide-open spaces, choose flagstones, large pavers, or concrete divided into sections that you separate by borders of brick or stone.

✔ **Durability.** No patio is immune to cracking and settling, but control joints and steel reinforcement minimize the risk. Brick and stones that absorb moisture are vulnerable to frost damage and moss. Brick wears down from heavy foot traffic — although most residential patios don't generate such amounts. Materials that you can set on a sand base, not on rigid concrete, are more likely to endure unstable ground or areas with severe winters.

✔ **Drainage.** A patio constructed on a concrete slab sheds water, which may be a problem if you have few places for it to go or it covers vital tree roots. A patio that you construct out of pavers set in sand, on the other hand, doesn't shed water — a problem for a patio next to a leaky basement or crawlspace.

✔ **Regional or historical connection.** Many materials, such as brick or local stone, have a long tradition in some areas. Others evoke a particular country or design tradition that you may want to duplicate. In both cases, you don't need to mimic other patios, but you do want to avoid artificiality. Be aware of the overall context of your patio in respect to local traditions.

✔ **Availability.** Make sure that the material you select is available. Most stone and some brick is distributed within a small geographic region, although choices are abundant within most regions. Consider, too, ease of transportation and storage. All masonry materials are heavy, but some materials, such as pallets of flagstones, are difficult to handle because of their size and awkward shapes. Bricks, concrete pavers, and tile stack easily and are fairly easy to move because of their relatively small sizes. Concrete, which you can pump into place, is the easiest material to move.

✔ **Ease of installation.** Choose a material that you can install. The easiest installations are of brick or pavers on a sand base. Concrete is easy to place but requires skillful handling and finishing. Setting bricks in a mortar base and grouting the joints requires great patience, but the bricks themselves are easy to lift and handle. Stones of irregular thickness are difficult, but not impossible, to keep level. Some stone is very difficult to cut.

✔ **Borders.** You can overcome some of the limitations of certain materials by planning borders to create contrasting colors, textures, and lines. Concrete, for example, is less monotonous if you break it up into sections with dividers of a contrasting material. You may also use for a border materials that aren't appropriate for the dominant patio surface, such as wood. As you evaluate various materials, imagine them with or without a border to test their usability.

✔ **Cost.** In pricing materials, make sure that you verify the unit of measurement. Materials are priced by the square foot (tile), by cubic yard (concrete), by unit (brick), or by weight (stone). Generally, concrete is the least-expensive material. The most expensive is flagstone set in mortar on a concrete base. As you price various materials, factor in the delivery cost.

Concrete

No material offers more versatility than concrete. A reinforced concrete slab provides a durable base that you can cover with other paving materials or finish in a remarkable variety of textures and colors (see Figure 14-1). Concrete adapts easily to various patio shapes and site conditions and is relatively easy to transport and place (although finishing the surface requires considerable skill). It's an unforgiving material; you must place it quickly and finish it correctly or you're stuck with unsatisfactory results for a long time. Concrete's only limitations are a tendency for large slabs to expand and contract and an unavoidable propensity for cracking. You can minimize both problems by using *control joints* (grooves that you cut into the fresh concrete to contain cracking), *expansion buffers* (strips of compressible material that you place between large sections of patio or between the patio and the house foundation), *additives* in the concrete mix (to minimize damage from freezing/thawing cycles), and *surface textures* that disguise cracks (such as faux flagstone).

Figure 14-1:
Concrete is
often as
dazzling
and elegant
as it is
strong and
versatile.

Recently, a revolution occurred in concrete finishing. Until five or six years ago, most concrete patios were finished with a smooth surface or exposed aggregate (a pebbly surface). A few had embossed patterns resembling cobblestones or tile, and some had pigments of one color mixed into the concrete. Now, embossing techniques include large-format, free-form designs that resemble huge slabs of natural stone or realistic patterns of cut stone. These stamped finishes are even more dramatic because of staining techniques that color the concrete permanently in variegated streaks and mottled washes. If you associate concrete with drab slabs, you may be surprised by these breathtaking developments.

Besides these new embossed, or stamped, finishes, you have a choice of traditional finishes such as exposed aggregate, troweled finishes (slick, smooth surfaces that you create by working the concrete with a trowel), broomed finishes (striated surfaces that you create by dragging a broom across the fresh concrete), and a pitted surface (which you create with rock salt). For interesting effects, you can combine two or more finishes in one patio for contrasting textures and shapes.

For information about estimating and ordering concrete, see Chapters 6 and 9. As a rule, plan on one cubic yard of concrete for 80 square feet of patio that's 4 inches thick.

Brick

Brick is a long-standing favorite for patio paving, from ancient times to modern do-it-yourself installations. With thousands of colors, textures, and patterns from which to choose, you can use brick to blend in with almost any garden design. Although permanent installations require setting bricks in a mortar bed over a concrete slab, you can create a serviceable patio quickly and fairly cheaply by setting bricks in a sand bed (see Chapter 19).

Made from clay fired at extremely high temperatures, bricks have subtle variations in color and surface features that give installations a rich texture. The basic rectangular shape enables you to lay bricks in many different patterns, from basic grid designs to intricate woven, herringbone, and circular patterns. Although most bricks are the classic "brick-red" color, many lean toward orange and even yellow hues. Used bricks, which are expensive and difficult to find, have white blotches from old mortar that give them a unique charm.

Types of brick

Not all brick is suitable for patios, but certain variations of the most common type are. Referred to as *common, standard,* or *building* brick, it's the least-expensive brick and varies the most in color and shape, giving installations a rustic appearance suitable for patios. Not all common brick can withstand constant exposure to freezing and thawing cycles. Choose type SW (severe weathering) for areas with subzero temperatures, and SW or MW (moderate weathering) for areas where temperatures frequently dip below freezing but seldom below zero. Avoid type NW (nonweathering) for patios. These categories are also labeled as SX, MX, and NX. Be wary of used bricks for extreme weather conditions; old bricks absorb moisture too easily.

Common brick varies widely in appearance. Bricks manufactured by a sand-mold process have a somewhat tapered shape, rounded edges, and smooth texture. Wire-cut bricks have sharp edges and a rough texture. *Clinker brick* has a rough surface with smooth patches, called *flashes,* that's caused by overburning. Another type of brick, *face brick,* has a smooth, durable surface to resist weathering. It's intended for buildings and walls and is too slippery for patios. *Paving brick,* which is half the thickness of common brick, is stronger but more expensive. Designed for walks, patios, and other traffic areas, it has straight, even sides for mortarless installations.

Buying brick

Besides knowing something about the different types, colors, and textures of brick, you should also be aware how bricks are sized. They vary in size, but always have modular dimensions that enable them to fit into different patterns. The basic module is 4 x 8 x 2½ inches. Actual dimensions vary to take the mortar joints into account and because of discrepancies in manufacturing methods. Some bricks, for example, may be 3½ inches wide; others may be 3¾ inches. Paving brick is usually a full 4x8 inches wide to enable you to make mortarless installations. If you obtain bricks from different sources or are trying to match an existing installation, check the sizes first.

In estimating bricks, figure on five bricks per square foot of patio surface. Add about 5 percent to your total order for waste. A block of 500 bricks weighs about one ton, so if you transport them yourself, you may need to make several trips. If you buy small quantities over time, make sure that the lots don't vary in color or size.

Pavers

Modular concrete pavers have swept the patio scene as the ideal paving material for do-it-yourself installations. They're also widely used for public works projects, such as sidewalks, plazas, and park paths, because they're easy to maintain, remove, and replace. They're cheaper and more durable than brick but lack the rich variations of color and texture, although manufacturers are continually striving to create natural-looking tones with as much variation as mass production can manage. Choose pavers that have color embedded throughout; otherwise, color applied only to the surface wears off.

Shapes vary from mock bricks to hexagon and herringbone patterns. Most enable you to set up a mortarless, interlocking pattern. Some patterns — including the one shown in Figure 14-2 — require two different shapes of paver; most pavers are designed for a one-size-fits-all approach. Although pavers come as thick as 3⅛ inches, those between 1½ and 2½ inches are adequate for patios.

Pavers are intended for installation over a sand bed. Such installations are extremely stable if you provide solid borders, compact the sand, and compact the pavers after installing them. Many paver designs have rounded edges to prevent sharp transitions between pavers as they settle and move at different rates. The angled shape of most pavers requires you to cut pieces to fit along the straight edges of the patio, which you can do by renting a tile saw or buying a masonry cutoff blade for your power saw.

Figure 14-2:
You can install modern concrete pavers such as these over a bed of sand, just as you can traditional brick, making them an ideal do-it-yourself material.

Stone

Stone is as old as the hills and, like hills, can be rugged or smooth. Stone is suitable for a variety of patio styles. You can use it to evoke permanence, rustic informality, sophisticated elegance, or a strong regional flavor, depending on the type and cut of stone.

If you enjoy puzzles and have an artistic flair, you can't beat the ultimate jigsaw puzzle: installing a patio of irregular flagstones, such as those shown in Figure 14-3. The biggest challenge is keeping the surface level and smooth; unless stone is *gauged* (cut to uniform thickness), it can vary in thickness from half an inch to two inches. Unlike flagstones, stone that's cut into uniform sizes, such as slate, is no more difficult to install than brick or tile. Just the price tag may be hard to handle. You can buy it in completely uniform sizes or in modular sizes based on a four-inch grid that you can install in either random or regular patterns.

Basalt, bluestone, granite, limestone, sandstone, and slate are common types of stone for paving. In some areas, particularly the arid Southwest and Mediterranean climates, soft-pink shades of flagstone are prized because of the way they blend with the natural hues of the surrounding landscape. If you live in an area with cold winters, avoid sandstone and limestone. They absorb water, which freezes and causes the stone to crack and break up.

Some stones that don't absorb water, such as granite, become very slippery if wet. The best stone is rough enough for good traction but smooth enough for tables and chairs. Investigate which types of stone stain easily. You don't want to spend money on a new patio and have it look like a pizza joint. You should also consider the type of foundation that you plan to use — sand or concrete — because a sand bed requires thicker stones.

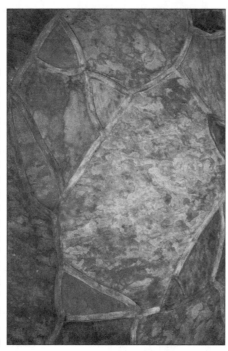

Figure 14-3:
Thanks to a concrete base and grouted joints, the flagstones that make up this patio can endure harsh weather and constant wear for years to come.

Flagstone is sold by weight and is usually packaged on pallets. Consult with your supplier about the amount needed to cover your patio. Typically, one ton covers 80 to 120 square feet, but coverage varies dramatically depending on the thickness of the stone. Plan to buy 5 to 10 percent extra if you're fitting irregular flagstones together. Cut stone is sold by weight or by the square foot.

Although you may have access to places where you can collect your own stone — open fields and streams (with permission) — such stone is seldom suitable for patios. Field stone and river rock lend themselves more to walls than paving.

Unglazed Tile

Unglazed tile, like brick, has a natural look and blends into many garden settings. Unlike brick, you can't arrange it in different patterns because its usually square shape is limited to a regular grid. As a result, the lines that the grout joints between the tiles create may have a stronger visual effect than the tiles themselves, which seem to recede into the background. To emphasize or minimize this effect, depending on your desired look, vary the color of the grout.

Four types of unglazed tile are intended for outdoor paving. (Never use glazed tile for a patio surface — it's too slippery.) One type, called *pavers,* comes in sections that are 12 inches square or larger and range from irregular rustic designs (the traditional Mexican paver) to smooth, uniform designs. Most pavers are earth-colored, ranging from yellow-orange to reddish-orange tones.

Patio tiles and quarry tiles are usually smaller than pavers. Patio tiles come in terra cotta and other natural colors and, because of variations in thickness, size, and shape, have a rustic look. Quarry tiles are more uniform in size and resemble cut quarry stone.

Recently, the field has seen an explosion of ceramic tile designs that resemble various types of stone. They vary in size from 4 to 12 inches square, including some rectangular shapes. They're less expensive and more uniform in size than cut stone is but convey the same warm, natural effect. They're especially effective in creating a Mediterranean look with Classical overtones.

Tile is sold by the square foot. All installations require a stable concrete slab for a base. Because most unglazed tile absorbs water, it may not be appropriate for areas with cold winters. If you live in such a climate, consult with a professional tile installer about your patio.

Borders

Patio materials that you install on a sand bed require a permanent edge to hold them in place. Even those that you install on a mortar bed or a concrete slab that requires only temporary forms may look better with some kind of border. As you investigate patio options, consider the type of border that would look best. Your options include bricks laid flat or on end, stones, a concrete curb, wood timbers (either laid horizontally or cut up into short vertical sections set into concrete), 2-by lumber set on edge, and concealed plastic edging held in place with spikes.

If your patio is formal and has a strong axis or symmetrical shape, a border (see Figure 14-4) of contrasting material can enhance the sense of order. If your patio has an informal design or is surrounded by plants, a visible border may interfere with the blending between patio and garden. In such a case, if you need an edging to contain the patio, use concealed plastic edging intended for that purpose or 2-by lumber set on edge. The natural color and texture of the wood blend into the garden.

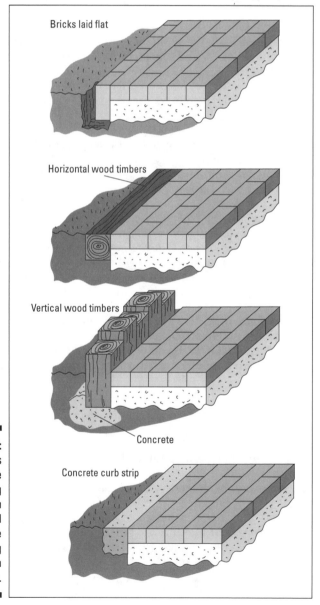

Figure 14-4: Borders hold loose paving materials in place and make interesting design accents.

Bricks laid flat

Horizontal wood timbers

Vertical wood timbers

Concrete

Concrete curb strip

Chapter 15

Before You Dig

In This Chapter

▶ Ordering materials

▶ Hauling in and hauling out

▶ Lining up tools

▶ Prepping yourself (getting yourself ready)

*B*efore you can go outside and play in the dirt, you need to do your homework. In the case of a patio, that means ordering materials, getting a permit (if required), planning how to transport and store materials, hiring help, and getting tools.

Most of this preparation is similar to that for building a deck (see Chapter 8), but a few twists are unique to patio building. For one thing, you probably don't need a set of detailed working drawings. Although building a patio is more challenging than building a deck if you've never worked with concrete or masonry, the actual structure is simple and doesn't pose any risk of collapse. Unless it involves retaining walls, footings for a shade structure, or an extensive drainage system, a patio is nothing more than a few layers of some heavy materials. Specifications needn't be more than a dimensioned plan view and a cross-sectional view to show the base. Patio materials are also easier to store than deck lumber is, and construction disrupts the house even less. For these reasons, the paperwork and logistics for building a patio are simpler than they are for a deck.

Ordering Materials

To estimate the quantity of materials you need, start with the overall dimensions of your patio and compute the total area. If the patio is a simple geometric shape, such as a rectangle, or you can divide it into such shapes, you can calculate the area by multiplying the length times width of each section and adding them together. If the patio is free-form, with irregular shapes, draw it to scale on graph paper and count the squares that it covers. (Make sure that you convert the total number of squares into square feet if each square represents less than one square foot.)

If, for example, an L-shaped patio has one leg measuring 15 by 25 feet and a smaller leg measuring 8 by 8 feet, the total area is 439 feet (15 x 25 = 375 and 8 x 8 = 64). If you shape a free-form patio like a kidney, with the longest dimension 28 feet and the width at the midpoint 12 feet, you can't apply the formula for rectangles (length x width) to this patio to find the area; the curves prevent the patio from filling out to the corners of a full rectangle. The easiest way to figure the area of this type of patio, therefore, is by drawing it to scale on graph paper and counting the squares it covers.

Next, convert the surface area to the volume of each material that you need, starting with the paving. If it's concrete, multiply the surface area by the thickness of the slab, which is usually four to six inches (use fractions of a foot). Then convert the answer to cubic yards. (See Chapter 6 for more information on estimating concrete amounts.) If the paving is brick, figure five bricks per square foot. If it's tile or dimensioned stone, simply use the square footage. If the paving is flagstone, consult with the supplier about how many tons you need.

Other materials to order include sand and gravel for a base (see Chapter 16); reinforcing steel for concrete (see Chapter 17); drain pipe and fittings (see Chapter 16); mortar and grout for setting brick, stone, or tile (see Chapters 18, 19, and 20); and edging, or border, materials (see Chapter 14). You must also anticipate any underground utility lines that you plan to run under the patio, such as wires for outdoor lighting or pipes for water, and have the materials on hand. If you're pouring a concrete slab, don't forget lumber for form boards. Finally, order any specialty or finishing materials you need, such as concrete stain, stones for seeded aggregate, expansion joint material, and plastic sheeting to cover a concrete slab while it cures.

Hauling In and Hauling Out

As with decks (see Chapter 8), decide where and how you're going to transport materials after they're delivered (or you pick them up). Following are a few other things to keep in mind:

> ✔ Try to plan the job so that you need to move materials only once. Most you can store out in the weather, except bags of cement or concrete mix. If you have sand delivered, cover it with a tarp to keep cats out of it.

✔ Investigate renting a portable conveyor system to move large quantities of sand and gravel from the driveway to a backyard job site. Otherwise, recruit as many able-bodied helpers and borrow as many wheelbarrows as you can.

✔ Do as much as possible to facilitate easy access; heavy wheelbarrows invite scraped knuckles and twisted backs. Build sturdy ramps and bypasses for stairs and other obstacles. Remove gates or fence sections that constrict passage.

✔ If you plan a flagstone patio, clear a large area next to the job site to sort out and lay out stones.

✔ As for debris such as excavated soil, rocks, unused masonry materials, and broken or cut stone, most are "clean" materials that you can work into the garden or find other uses for around the house. If not, offer it to neighbors or friends.

Lining Up Tools

A patio involves fewer tools than decks and other carpentry projects, but many are specialized one-use tools that you can buy or rent. (See the relevant chapters, 16 through 21, for more information.) You probably need to rent at least one large piece of equipment or hire a service for it. Such equipment includes the following items:

✔ A miniature tractor with a scoop loader and possibly a backhoe to excavate and transport bulk materials

✔ A portable conveyor to transport bulk materials

✔ A plate compactor or vibrator to compact base materials or mortarless paving

✔ A concrete pumping service to transport concrete from a ready-mix delivery truck to your job site

✔ A concrete vibrator to consolidate fresh concrete

✔ A tile saw for cutting brick, tile, or stone; a concrete-cutting saw if you're altering an existing patio

✔ And (gasp) a jack hammer to "erase" mistakes

Investigate rental prices, delivery costs, and operating techniques for such equipment and plan your job carefully to minimize downtime for these machines. As Figure 15-1 suggests, renting such equipment can make the work much easier.

Figure 15-1:
Renting a
tile saw
such as this
one makes
the tedious
parts of
patio-
building
much
easier,
especially if
you don't
have
helpers.

Prepping Yourself

Concrete and masonry work present interesting paradoxes. Sometimes you're handling tons of material; other times, you're on your hands and knees performing fastidious, intricate tasks. Sometimes you're rushing to beat the setup time of concrete or mortar; other times, you're inching along at a leisurely pace, fitting and fussing with stones or bricks. For the most part, you have a wide margin of error because you're building a free-standing structure that may not even require precise edges and borders. On the other hand, shoddy work becomes a permanent landmark in your landscape.

If you're comfortable with such contradictions, you're ready to patio. If not, get inspired by seeking out some patio projects that you can watch to gain confidence. Don't underestimate the physical demands of building a patio; make sure that you're in shape to dig, haul, lift, and kneel . . . a lot. If this patio is your first masonry project, you may want to do the excavating yourself and hire a professional to install the patio base and paving materials.

Chapter 16

Preparing the Base

· ·

In This Chapter

▶ Site prep

▶ Layout

▶ Excavation

▶ Subsurface drainage

▶ Underground utility lines

▶ Gravel base

▶ Edging

▶ Sand setting bed

· ·

*P*atio construction is simple: Dig a hole and fill it with a patio. This image emphasizes the fact that a patio involves a lot more than the surface. The most important component of a patio is what you don't see — the base. Whether poured concrete or compacted sand, a stable base provides a firm bed for the paving materials and protects the patio from buckling, settling, and flooding. You must install even a poured concrete base over a bed of sand or gravel, or it sustains cracking and settling problems.

The process of building a base is similar for any type of patio, whether the surface is concrete, stone, brick, pavers, or tile. Building a base starts with preparing the site and assessing slope and drainage conditions and includes laying out the patio perimeter, excavating a hole to the correct depth, installing drainage lines where necessary, running underground utility lines, installing edging materials, and laying down a bed of gravel. You may need to vary this order of tasks, depending on site conditions and the type of edging and paving materials that you use.

Site Prep

If your patio site is level and clear to begin with, you don't need to do much before layout, but if your patio site has uneven ground, trees, an old patio, or similar obstacles, remove them before starting your layout. Rough-grade ground that varies more than a few inches in height by removing the high spots. Remove trees and plants from the patio site and dig out all stumps or roots to at least 12 inches below the ground; otherwise, they may cause the ground to collapse under the patio as they rot away. Don't fill holes with loose dirt. Leave them open until after you excavate for the patio base and then fill them with compacted base material. Break up and remove old paving by using a sledgehammer or a rented 60-pound electric jack hammer.

While demolishing old paving, wear eye protection and heavy clothing. Paving is very resistant to downward pressure but yields readily to uplifting pressure, so use sledgehammer blows only to crack the paving and a heavy pry bar or pick to get under it and break it up.

If you aren't absolutely certain that gas, phone, electrical, or plumbing lines don't lurk in the ground where you're digging, call your local utility companies to come out and verify.

Can I use my old patio for a base?

If you want to use an existing concrete patio as a base for new paving materials, make sure that it slopes away from the house at least 1/8 inch per foot, has no cracks or settlement problems, and has a surface that mortar can adhere to. The biggest problem with most older patios is that they list toward the house, trapping water against the house foundation. Such a condition only gets worse and you should not reuse the patio. Most patios, after a few years, also develop cracks. If the patio has strong reinforcing steel (which most don't), the cracks should stabilize and may not "telegraph" through to the paving material if you cover them with a reinforcing membrane embedded in the setting mortar. Otherwise, cracks in a poorly reinforced patio get worse over time and cause the paving to crack and settle. If the existing patio is sound and the only problem is a painted or very smooth surface, you can *scarify,* or roughen, the surface to ensure adhesion of the setting mortar for new paving materials. You can rent a scarifying machine for this purpose.

Layout

The procedure for laying out a patio is similar to that for a deck (see Chapter 9) in that you place *batterboards* (stakes with a crosspiece) at the corners and string lines between them to delineate the perimeter of the structure. Layout for a patio is somewhat different from that of decks, however, because you may have more curves or free-form shapes to deal with, you must adjust the string lines to account for a sloping patio surface to ensure adequate drainage, and you need a grid of secondary string lines to guide excavation.

For curved edges, lay a garden hose directly on the ground, sprinkle flour or chalk along the hose, and remove it (see Figure 16-1). For precise curves, follow these steps:

1. **Drive a stake into the ground where the center of the circle or arc is located.**

2. **Using the stake as the pivot point, tie one end of a rope to it, measure along the rope the length of the radius, tie a stick to the rope at that point, and swing the stick along the ground like a compass.**

Mark the curve with flour or chalk.

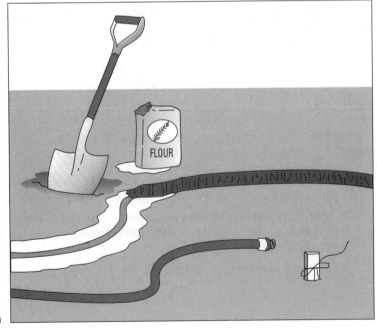

Figure 16-1: One way to lay out a free-form patio is to use a garden hose and flour.

After you outline the patio, set string lines up around the perimeter. For correct drainage, the string lines on each side of the patio must slope away from the house at a rate of $1/8$ inch per foot. To achieve this slope, follow these steps:

1. **Set the crosspieces of the two batterboards along the outer edge of the patio at a lower height than the crosspieces against the house; lower them one inch for every eight feet of patio.**

2. **Set the crosspieces for the string line that runs parallel with the house and defines the patio's outer edge at a height that matches the sloping string lines where they intersect.**

   The string line for the outer patio edge should be level.

After laying out the string lines or curved chalk lines for the perimeter of the patio, you need to finish the grid. To do so, follow these steps:

1. **Drive 2x4 stakes around the outside edge of the perimeter layout every four or five feet so that they're aligned in pairs across the patio from each other.**

2. **String lines between the pairs of stakes, tying them at a height that causes them to barely touch the perimeter string lines.**

3. **After stringing these lines, make any necessary adjustments and mark each stake where you tied the string to it.**

   After you finish, you have a sloped grid that mirrors the plane of your future patio. Use the grid to guide excavation for the base and installation of the edging and bedding materials, as shown in Figure 16-2.

Excavation

After the string lines are in place, excavate for the patio by following these steps:

1. **Mark an outline of the patio on the ground in flour, chalk, or spray paint, using the layout lines as a guide (see Chapter 9).**

2. **Remove any sod or old lawn by slicing it into strips with a square-edged shovel and then forcing the shovel under the strips and lifting them off the ground.**

   Reuse the sod elsewhere or haul it away.

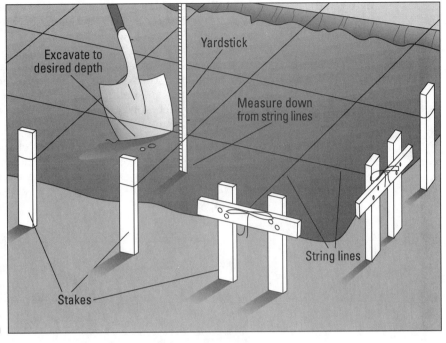

Figure 16-2:
A grid of string lines enables you to excavate to a uniform depth and avoid overdigging.

Labels in figure: Excavate to desired depth · Yardstick · Measure down from string lines · String lines · Stakes

3. **Excavate the soil within the patio area to the desired depth, measuring down from the string lines a uniform distance to keep the bottom of the excavation flat and correctly sloped.**

   For a small patio, you can do the digging yourself or with a few helpers and wheelbarrows. For a large patio, rent a small tractor with a front loader. Make sure that you can get it into your backyard. Keep the edges of the excavation as straight as possible, unless the soil is too loose to hold its shape.

4. **After digging out the soil, moisten the bottom of the excavation and compact it with a rented power compactor to consolidate any loose soil and minimize future settlement.**

Subsurface Drainage

For most yards, you don't have severe drainage problems to solve; water that runs off the patio flows away from it into the rest of the yard. In some cases, however, it doesn't, such as in a situation where the patio is located between the house and a hill sloping down to it. In such a case, you must install a drainage system to divert water away from the patio and house. You can accomplish this task in either of the following two ways (see Figure 16-3):

- Use surface gutters to intercept water coming down the hill and a subsurface drain line uphill from the patio site. The subsurface line should run parallel to the house at a depth slightly below the patio base and carry water to an outlet at least 10 feet beyond the side of the house or to a storm sewer system.

- Install a catch basin within the patio itself or a concrete channel around the edge of the patio. Both devices are covered by a grate and are connected to four-inch diameter drain pipes that carry the water away. You can buy prefabricated catch basins and drain channels at building supply outlets or masonry yards.

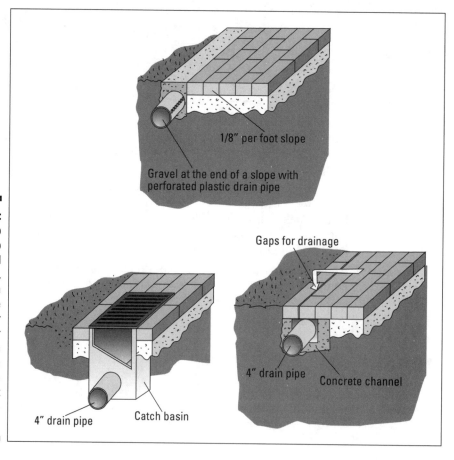

1/8" per foot slope

Gravel at the end of a slope with perforated plastic drain pipe

Gaps for drainage

4" drain pipe
Concrete channel

4" drain pipe
Catch basin

Figure 16-3:
If your patio has no natural drainage, install a subsurface interceptor drain or catch basins in the patio that connect to drain lines.

If you install either type of drainage system, excavate the pipe trenches at the same time as you excavate for the patio. Slope the trenches toward the termination point at a rate of $1/8$ inch per foot. Place two inches of drain rock below perforated drain pipes and another eight inches above it, with a layer of filter fabric between the rock and soil backfill. For solid drain pipes that merely carry water to another point, cover the pipe with four inches of sand to protect it from any sharp rocks in the backfill. See Chapter 9 for more information on dealing with water.

Underground Utility Lines

If you're running water lines, drain lines, or wiring under your patio, excavate trenches at the same time that you excavate for the patio. For water lines, use flexible copper tubing, available in half- or three-quarter-inch diameters, to avoid needing to solder elbows or other fittings. Bury the tubing in sand to protect it from puncturing. Make sure that drain pipes slope at least $1/4$ inch per foot for plumbing drains and $1/8$ inch per foot for drainage lines.

If you're running electrical wiring for standard house voltage (120 volts for lighting or outlets; 240 volts for such things as swimming pool equipment), excavate trenches at least 6 inches deep for metal conduit, 18 inches deep for plastic conduit, and 12 inches deep for Type UF (direct-burial) cable. (These depths are for standard 20-amp circuits.) After installing the wiring, backfill the trench with sand. Where the wiring emerges from the ground, you must protect it by surrounding it in rigid metal conduit with liquid-tight fittings.

If you're pouring a concrete slab and pipes or conduit must emerge through it, wrap them in insulation or similar material to cushion them from the abrasion that expansion and contraction of the concrete causes.

If you know that you're going to run wiring or plumbing under the patio someday but aren't sure exactly how much or what size, bury under the patio two- or three-inch-diameter plastic piping that you can access at both ends. Then, in the future, you can run pipes or wiring through it without disturbing the patio. Cap the ends to prevent critters from nesting in it.

Gravel Base

For the gravel base, use crushed rock, sometimes referred to as *road base,* or pea gravel designated as *class-five gravel.* Both types of rock have rugged edges that lock the gravel together into a solid mass after you compact it, providing a firm base for other materials and minimizing future settlement.

To estimate how many cubic yards of gravel you need, calculate the area of the patio surface and multiply it by the depth of gravel (four to eight inches). Make sure that you convert the depth into fractions of a foot (four inches equals .33 foot; six inches equals .5 foot; eight inches = .67 foot). Convert the total cubic feet into yards by dividing by 27. Add 5 to 10 percent for compaction and waste.

If you can have gravel delivered directly to the patio site, have the truck dump it in several small piles within the excavation to make spreading it easier. If the gravel is delivered to your driveway or the street, plan on hauling it to the backyard in wheelbarrows, a rented conveyor, or a rented tractor with a dump loader. Most construction wheelbarrows hold four cubic feet of material, but two cubic feet of gravel is a very heavy load, which means 14 trips per yard. Round up plenty of help or rent a conveyor or a tractor with a dump loader.

How deep should I dig?

Assuming that the surface of your patio is at ground level, dig deep enough for the thickness of paving material, plus a 2-inch sand bed or 4-inch concrete slab, plus 4 to 8 inches of compacted gravel base, as shown. If, for example, your patio is 2-inch-thick concrete pavers set on a sand bed and you live in an area with mild winters, excavate 7 to 8 inches below ground level, or *grade* (2 inches of pavers plus 1 to 2 inches of compacted sand plus 4 inches of compacted gravel).

If you live in an area with extremely cold winters, plan on at least 8 inches of compacted gravel. (Consult with local experts.) Excavation

depths of 18 inches or more aren't unusual. If you're pouring a concrete slab, plan on 4 inches of concrete plus 4 to 8 inches of compacted gravel (also shown), depending on winter conditions. In some regions where winters are severe, concrete patios must have an 8- to 12-inch-wide footing around the perimeter, deep enough to extend below the frost line, which requires a trench deeper than the rest of the excavation.

Conversely, if you live in an area without freeze-thaw cycles and your patio site is on undisturbed "virgin" soil that drains well, you may get by with only a 2-inch thick sand bed and no gravel base. Check with your local building department. In no case should you excavate next to your house deeper than the foundation without consulting with a qualified professional.

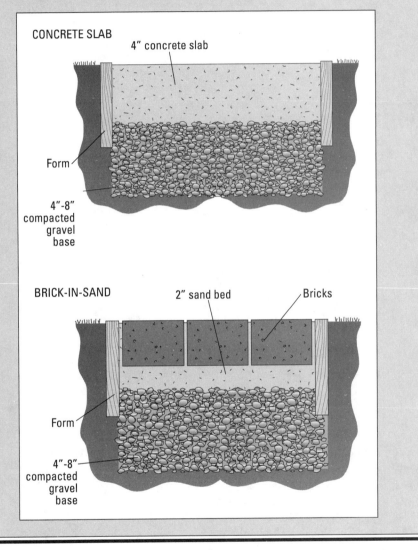

CONCRETE SLAB

4" concrete slab

Form

4"-8" compacted gravel base

BRICK-IN-SAND

2" sand bed

Bricks

Form

4"-8" compacted gravel base

Spread the gravel to a uniform depth throughout the patio area, using the string lines as a guide. Build up the gravel half to three-quarters of an inch above the finished level to allow for compaction. Using a rented power compactor — the type with a vibrating plate, as heavy duty as you can manage — compact the gravel to a solid, uniform mass (see Figure 16-4). If the base is deeper than four inches, spread out the gravel and compact it in layers, or *lifts*, no more than four inches deep. Add gravel to low spots as necessary.

Edging

Install edging materials on the edge of the compacted gravel. Re-establish the perimeter layout lines and, using a plumb bob, align the edging with these lines. Measure down from the string lines to the top of the edging every few feet to keep the top of the edging at the correct height.

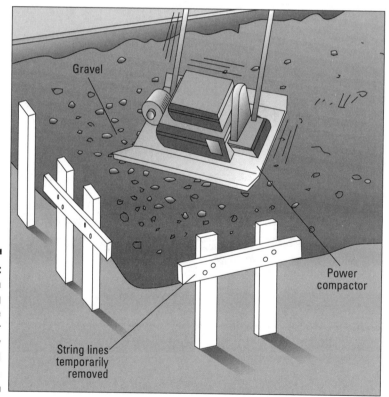

Gravel

Power compactor

String lines temporarily removed

Figure 16-4:
Rent a vibrating plate compactor to solidify the gravel base.

Among the easiest edgings to install are pressure-treated timbers, sometimes called *landscape timbers,* and pressure-treated 4x4s. Follow these steps:

1. **Before installing the timbers or 4x4s, drill ⁵/₈-inch diameter holes through them, from top to bottom, 12 inches from each end and approximately every 3 feet.**

2. **Set each timber in place on the gravel base, aligning it with the string lines and making adjustments to the base as necessary.**

3. **After the timber is in position, drive two-foot lengths of half-inch rebar (reinforcing steel) through the holes into the ground until the tops are just below the top of the timber.**

   For soft soil, drill three-quarter-inch holes through the wood and use longer lengths of half-inch galvanized pipe. Look for a plumber or builder who's discarding such pipe.

Another edging material that's easy to install is 2-by boards set on edge, which you can secure to 1x2 stakes that you drive along the outside edges of the boards. Nail the stakes to the boards by using 8d galvanized box nails.

As you drive nails through stakes into boards, hold a sledgehammer against the opposite side of the board to keep it from kicking away from the stake.

To make an edging out of bricks set in an upright position (called *soldiers*), place a straight board along the outside of the perimeter line and set the bricks in place, on end, against the board. Backfill the space along the outside of the bricks, tamping the soil gently to keep from disturbing the bricks. You may need to set a straightedge against the inside faces of the bricks as a temporary stop until you install the paving.

To build a concrete border strip, follow these steps:

1. **Install a double row of 2x6s for forms, four to eight inches apart, with the tops at the finished level of the paving (unless you plan to cover the concrete with a contrasting paving material).**

   Secure the boards to steel or wooden stakes with 8d duplex nails. Make sure that the sides are plumb.

2. **Suspend lengths of half-inch rebar between the forms 1¹/₂ inches below the top and, for deep footings, 3 inches from the ground.**

   Where rebar is spliced together end-to-end, lap the ends 20 inches and tie them together with tie wire.

3. **Fill the forms with concrete, screed (or level) off the top with a wooden float, and, after the concrete stiffens, finish the top by using a steel trowel and then round over the outside edge by running an edging tool between the concrete and outside form board.**

Sand Setting Bed

Certain paving materials, such as brick or concrete pavers, can be installed directly on a half- to two-inch-thick bed of sand without the need for a concrete slab (see Chapters 18, 19, and 20). One of the keys to a successful patio installation by using this technique is a firmly compacted sand bed. Make sure that you install the bed with the same slope as you need for the finished patio. In most installations, you pack the paving material so firmly together that the paving sheds rainwater as if the surface were a solid membrane.

All sand is not the same. For a sand bed, choose a washed, well-graded angular type of sand with a maximum particle size of $3/16$ inch, the type used for concrete aggregate. Do not use "masonry sand" for a bed thicker than half an inch.

If your gravel base is loose material that doesn't compact firmly, install a layer of *geotextile fabric* between the gravel and sand bed. This clothlike material, also referred to as *filter fabric,* is available from masonry suppliers and prevents the sand from "draining" down into the gravel.

Installing the sand bed is similar to installing a gravel base, except that you need to screed the sand to create a uniformly smooth bed. Follow these steps:

1. **Set long 2x4s in place three feet apart as temporary screed guides.**

   Rather than setting a screed guide in place every three feet, you can use just two, leap-frogging them as you go. They should be the same width as the patio. Keep the tops flush with the top of the edging material by driving an 8d nail into the top of the board near each end and bending the nails over so that they hook over the edging. Secure the board with additional nails or temporary stakes.

2. **Construct a screed.**

   Cut a 2x4 approximately four inches longer than the distance between the screed guides and a scrap of plywood four inches wide and five inches shorter than the 2x4. Center the plywood on the 2x4 and adjust it so that one edge extends below the 2x4 exactly the same distance as the thickness of the paving material less $3/8$ inch (for sand compaction). Screw or nail the plywood to the 2x4. The screed resembles a paddle with a long 2x4 handle across the top.

3. **After spreading out the sand, set the screed on the guides and drag it across the sand by using a back-and-forth sawing motion, as shown in Figure 16-5.**

   The screed should level the sand so that, after you compact the sand and set the paving on top, the surface of the paving is flush with the top of the edging.

4. **Fill in low spots with extra sand.**

5. **Repeat this process until the sand bed for the entire patio is screeded.**

6. **Remove the temporary screed guides and fill in the voids with sand; then wet the sand and compact it by using a power compactor.**

Figure 16-5:
Use a screed and guides to level a sand bed for setting paving directly on it.

Chapter 17

Installing a Concrete Patio

. . . .

In This Chapter

▶ Preparing the forms and steel
▶ Preparing for the pour
▶ Placing the concrete
▶ Smoothing the concrete
▶ Finishing the concrete
▶ Curing

. . . .

*A*concrete slab is a relatively easy and inexpensive patio to install — and even easier to construct if it's a foundation for other paving materials, such as flagstone or brick. The actual placing of the concrete — technically, it's *placed,* not poured, although using the word *pour* is customary — is not as important an event, in spite of the high drama, as what happens before and after the pour. If you focus on preparing the base, building the forms, setting the reinforcing steel, estimating the volume of concrete that you need, getting enough help, getting the necessary tools available for finishing the surface, and giving the concrete sufficient time to cure correctly, you should find that handling tons of wet concrete is no more stressful than playing in the mud.

If, however, you find that you like reading about some special concrete application in this chapter but have no desire to try it, consider hiring some help. Many specialty contractors can help you with things like special colored and textured finishes.

Concrete, the wonder material

That concrete structures are so strong and durable is truly a wonder. By itself, concrete is quite brittle and breaks more easily than does most stone. It also responds to temperature changes by expanding and contracting readily. Concrete is vulnerable to damage from freezing weather and buckling or settling ground.

All these weaknesses, however, you can overcome. Reinforcing steel gives concrete incredible strength. Installing concrete slabs over a resilient base of sand or gravel absorbs ground movement and prevents water from accumulating under the slab and freezing. Adding to the concrete mix *air entrainment*,

which is an ingredient that causes the concrete to trap millions of microscopic bubbles within itself, prevents it from absorbing water that could freeze and pop off sections of concrete from the surface. (In areas where freezing is common during winters, order concrete with at least 6 percent air entrainment to make the concrete resistant to damage from frost and de-icers.)

Of course, the concrete mix itself must have the correct proportions of cement, sand, gravel, and water, and you must also place it correctly to ensure a compact mass. See Chapters 6, 9, and 14 for more information.

Preparing the Forms and Steel

Review the techniques in Chapter 16 for excavating and installing a gravel base. Follow these steps:

1. **Build temporary forms for the concrete by setting 2x4s on edge around the patio perimeter and holding them in place with steel or wooden stakes.**

2. **Place the stakes along the outside edge of the boards every three to four feet and at joints between boards, driving them just below the top edge of the forms.**

3. **Adjust the boards so that the tops are at the finished height of the slab and then secure the stakes to the form boards with 8d duplex nails (see Figure 17-1).**

   Because most concrete patios are 4 inches thick and 2x4s are $3^1/2$ inches wide, a half-inch gap lies between the gravel base and the form boards; you need to backfill this gap with soil before you place the concrete.

If the patio is on sloping ground and must rise several inches above grade on the downhill side, build the forms out of 2-by lumber wide enough to accommodate the height of the slab. Drive 2x4 stakes two to three feet apart and brace the tops with additional stakes driven diagonally into the ground. Nail the stakes together at the tops by using 8d or 16d duplex nails. If the edge is higher than 18 inches, consult with a professional builder about constructing a retaining wall first, compacting backfill behind it, and installing the patio slab over it.

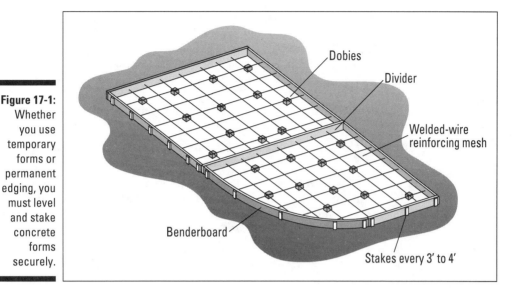

Figure 17-1:
Whether you use temporary forms or permanent edging, you must level and stake concrete forms securely.

Dobies

Divider

Welded-wire reinforcing mesh

Benderboard

Stakes every 3' to 4'

If the patio abuts the house foundation, install a strip of expansion joint material, available at concrete and masonry suppliers, against the foundation to absorb pressure from the concrete patio as it expands during hot weather.

If you plan to build steps to the house or into the garden, you may build the forms at this time or, to simplify the process, wait until you finish the patio slab — but before you install paving over it. (See Chapter 21 for information about building concrete and masonry stairs.)

Curved forms

If the patio has curved sides, build curved forms out of *benderboard* (thin boards intended for landscaping use and available from building supply outlets) or use quarter-inch plywood ripped into four-inch-wide strips. Double up the boards, bend them to the desired shape, and stake them in place. Make sure that the inside edges of the forms are flush where curved sections join straight 2x4s.

Permanent forms

If the forms are a permanent border, use heart redwood, cedar, cypress, or preservative-treated lumber specified for ground contact. Follow these steps:

1. **Treat the wood, especially cut ends, with water-repellent preservative before installing it.**

2. **Drive stakes one inch below the tops of the boards and trim the stake tops at a 45-degree angle to shed moisture.**

3. **Drive a galvanized 16d nail into the inside face of the forms every 16 inches just enough to hold the nails in place without penetrating the boards so that the nails become embedded in the concrete and bond the concrete and boards tightly together.**

4. **Before placing the concrete, cover the tops of the boards with strips of masking tape to prevent spilled concrete from staining the wood.**

Dividers

If you're dividing the patio into sections for a decorative effect or to make the task of pouring the concrete in stages easier, follow these steps:

1. **Set 2x4 divider boards on edge to create sections no larger than 10 feet wide.**

2. **Use the same lumber that you would for permanent edging (see the preceding section).**

3. **Space 16d galvanized nails along both sides of each board every 16 inches to lock them into the concrete.**

4. **Cover the tops with masking tape to protect them from stains.**

Reinforcing steel

The easiest type of reinforcing steel to install is *welded-wire reinforcing mesh*. This mesh comes in five- and seven-foot-wide rolls and is often referred to as *6-6-10-10 mesh* because it consists of 6x6-inch squares formed by 10-gauge wire running in both directions. In estimating the amount to buy, figure on overlapping sections at least six inches.

To install the mesh, follow these steps:

1. **Dampen the gravel base to further compact it.**

2. **Roll out the mesh.**

Straighten the mesh as much as possible to prevent it from coiling back into a roll. Wear gloves.

3. **Cut the mesh by using a hacksaw, bolt cutters, or a circular power saw with a metal cutoff blade.**

   Overlap sections at least six inches. Leave an inch and a half to two inches of clearance between the mesh and perimeter forms. This distance is called *concrete cover* and is the amount of concrete that you need to protect the steel from exposure to moisture-laden air. For the same reason, and to ensure maximum reinforcing strength, the steel must clear the bottom of the concrete by two inches (three inches if the concrete is placed directly on the ground).

4. **To ensure that you get the mesh embedded in the center of the slab, set two-inch *dobies* under the mesh every two to three feet.**

   These small concrete blocks, available at building materials suppliers, have wires embedded in them that you can twist around the reinforcing mesh.

An alternative to using wire mesh is to fabricate a grid of $^3/_8$- or half-inch-diameter rebar, which comes in 20-foot lengths. Cut the rebar by using a rented rebar cutter or a circular power saw with a metal cutoff blade. Space the bars 12 inches apart, wire them together at each intersection with tie wire, and set the grid on two-inch dobies.

If you're building a patio in an area with cold winters, it must have a footing around the perimeter of the slab that extends below the frost line. For steel reinforcement, lay two half-inch horizontal rebars along the bottom of the footing trench, held off the ground with three-inch dobies. Tuck the wire reinforcing mesh down into the trench and secure it to the outer rebar with tie wire. All steel should clear the sides of the trench by at least three inches. For trenches two feet or deeper, suspend additional pairs of horizontal rebar every 12 inches, holding them in place with tie wire tacked to the forms.

Preparing for the Pour

For information about estimating and ordering concrete, see Chapters 6, 9, and 14. If the concrete truck can't get close enough to your patio site to reach most of it with its chute (about 16 feet long), order a pump truck along with the ready-mix delivery.

To get ready for the pour, assemble tools for handling and finishing the concrete. Depending on what method you use to finish the concrete (see the section "Finishing the Concrete," later in this chapter), you need some or all of the following tools and equipment to pour your concrete:

- Gloves
- Rubber boots
- Knee pads (for trowel finishing)
- Skin cream (for after the pour)
- Hose
- Buckets (two or three for cleanup, carrying concrete, and so on)
- Wheelbarrow (for extra concrete)
- Square shovels
- Heavy hammer or maul (for tapping forms)
- Pole or rod (for jabbing concrete to consolidate it)
- 2x4s (straight pieces in assorted lengths, for screeds)
- Wood or magnesium float (for rough finishing)
- Darby (a large float, for rough finishing larger areas)
- Bull float (a float with a very long handle, for rough finishing very large areas)
- Edger (for rounding perimeter edges)
- Brick trowel (for smoothing concrete along forms)
- Jointer (for cutting control joints, or grooves)
- Push broom (for exposed aggregate finish)
- Hose with nozzle (for exposed aggregate finish)
- Steel trowel (for very smooth finish)
- Stamping pads (for stamped finish)
- Plywood squares (for kneeling on)
- Plastic sheeting (for covering concrete to cure it)

Besides assembling tools and equipment, line up two to four helpers, depending on the size of the patio. If you intend to have the concrete pumped, make sure that the driver knows beforehand how many feet of hose are necessary and clear the shortest path to lay the hose. Designate an area for cleaning up equipment and slopping excess concrete; don't use the street or gutter.

If you anticipate a very hot day, suspend a large tarp overhead, if possible, to shade the patio site. If you're working in autumn and the site has trees, rig screening to prevent leaves from falling onto the wet concrete; a few leaves can mar a fresh patio surface.

If the patio is wider than 18 feet (20 if you can find a long enough screed board; see the section "Smoothing the Concrete" later in this chapter) and has no divider boards, install temporary screed guides between the perimeter forms to create sections no wider than 18 feet. Use straight 2x4s for the guides, cutting them to length to fit between the perimeter forms and placing the guides so that their tops are flush with the tops of the forms. Secure each end by driving two 16d duplex nails through the perimeter form into the end of the guide.

Placing the Concrete

While waiting for the concrete truck to arrive, spray the forms and gravel base with water to keep them from drying out and absorbing water out of the concrete mix. Once the truck arrives, things happen quickly (see Figure 17-2).

To place concrete in the forms, start in one corner and move the truck chute or pumper hose around to distribute the concrete evenly. As it falls into place, jab the fresh concrete up and down with a rod or shovel to consolidate it so that it fills up all voids and settles evenly. Don't overwork the concrete, or the solids sink and water accumulates on the surface too soon. Using a heavy hammer, tap the outsides of the forms and divider boards to release air bubbles trapped against the forms. Place just enough concrete to pile it slightly higher than the tops of the forms.

Figure 17-2: A concrete pour is a beehive of activity. The supplier plans for about five minutes per yard of concrete to unload the truck.

Smoothing the Concrete

After filling the first section of patio forms with concrete, have one crew continue placing concrete in adjacent sections and another *strike off*, or *screed*, and then float the concrete in the first section (see Figure 17-3). To do so, follow these steps:

1. **Lay a long, straight 2x4 or 2x6 (called a *screed*), on edge, across the concrete so that both ends rest on form boards.**

2. **Drag the 2x4 along the length of the section to make the concrete surface flat and even with the tops of the form boards, moving the screed in a side-to-side sawing motion as you proceed.**

   Do about three feet of screeding at a time, going back over the same segment before proceeding to the next.

3. **Shovel away the excess concrete as it builds up in front of the screed and fill in low spots as you move across the slab.**

4. **Repeat this process for each section.**

5. **After placing and screeding all the concrete, and before water collects on the surface, smooth the concrete further by using a wood or magnesium float, which resembles a trowel.**

   This process forces the heavier aggregate slightly below the surface so that the lighter particles and paste float on top of it, producing a smoother texture. It also levels high and low spots. It does not produce a fine, smooth finish (this requires troweling the surface with a steel trowel after the concrete begins to set), but it prepares the surface for any decorative finishes or the installation of paving materials.

   To float small areas that you can reach easily, use a darby, working it back and forth in a sawing motion. For large areas, use a bull float, which has a long handle. Keep the leading edge up slightly as you glide it back and forth over the concrete, using a steady motion.

6. **After floating the slab, smooth the concealed edges of the concrete and free them from the form boards.**

   Simply slip the blade of a brick trowel or mason's trowel down between the forms and the edge of the concrete, approximately one to two inches, and run it around the perimeter of the slab with a slicing motion.

7. **Have some lunch and wait for the concrete to begin setting up before doing the final finish.**

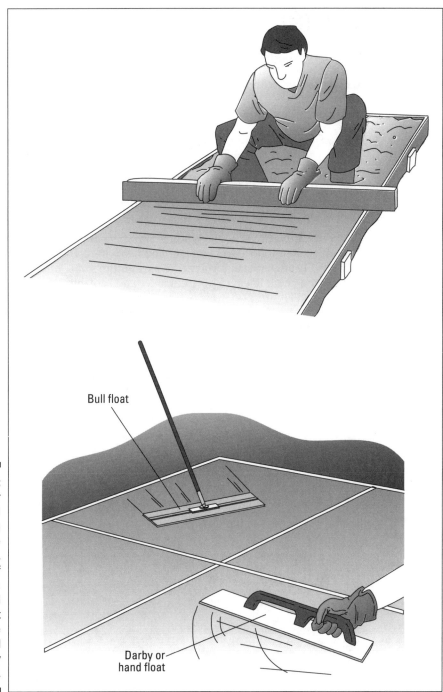

Figure 17-3:
After placing and consolidating the concrete, level it off by using a screed and then float the surface with a bull or darby float.

Bull float

Darby or hand float

Finishing the Concrete

After the water evaporates from the surface of the floated concrete and your foot sinks no more than a quarter inch if you place pressure on the surface, you can proceed with the finishing steps as follows:

1. **Edge the concrete.**

   Use a small hand tool with a curved lip along one edge. Slide this tool along the edges of the concrete, holding it against the form boards to guide it. Keep the leading edge slightly raised and apply steady, even pressure on the tool as you glide it back and forth.

2. **Cut control joints across the slab, unless the slab has permanent dividers.**

   Control joints are straight grooves running across the concrete, no more than 10 feet apart. First, snap chalklines where you want to cut the joints. Then, using a straight 1x6 as a guide, run a *jointer,* or *groover,* over the chalk lines. (This item is a hand tool similar to an edger, as shown in Figure 17-4.) Use one that makes grooves one inch deep. As you work your way toward the center of the slab, set squares of plywood on the concrete to kneel on — one for your knees and one for your feet. Make two passes with the jointing tool.

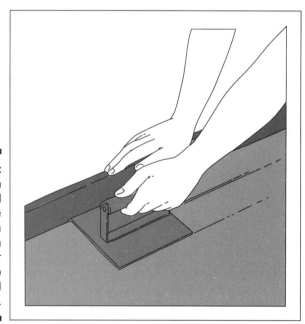

Figure 17-4: Use an edging tool to round the edges of a slab and a jointer, or groover, to cut control joints.

3. **Finally, float the surface again, this time using a hand float.**

This process leaves an even, slightly rough finish that's suitable for a rustic patio surface. To achieve a smooth surface, which is desirable for patios only if you follow with a rock salt or travertine finish (see the sections on those types of finishes, later in this chapter), go over the slab with a steel trowel. The concrete must have no surface water and must be stiff enough to support your kneeling on small plywood squares. If the consistency is just right, the trowel "sings" with a distinct sound and glides over the concrete without any drag, leaving the surface smooth and glossy.

For large slabs, professionals use a power finisher called a *whirlibird* (because its rotating trowels resemble helicopter blades).

Exposed aggregate finish

To create an *exposed aggregate (pebbly) finish,* follow these steps:

1. **Float the slab lightly to keep from pushing the larger stones too deep into the concrete.**

2. **After floating, wait for the watery sheen to evaporate from the surface of the slab.**

3. **After the concrete can support your weight on knee boards, brush away the top layer of hardened paste by using a stiff nylon push broom, brushing just enough to expose the aggregate.**

4. **Using a pump sprayer, coat the surface of the concrete with a curing agent and cover it with plastic sheeting.**

5. **After 24 hours, sweep the concrete again, this time spraying at the same time with a fine mist of water.**

Expose only the top half of the stones.

6. **Cover the slab again with plastic sheeting for final curing.**

If you want to liven up the dull, gray color of the aggregate you can "seed" the concrete with decorative stones, such as black river pebbles, white pebbles, or a multicolored mix (see Figure 17-5). Do so right after floating by spreading the stones over the wet concrete with a shovel or by hand. Then embed them into the concrete with the bottom of the shovel, a board, or a wood float until they sink just below the surface. Wait for the surface water to evaporate and proceed with exposing the aggregate.

Wood float

Multicolored pebbles

Figure 17-5:
By seeding the concrete surface with decorative stones, such as black or white river pebbles, you can create a distinctive exposed-aggregate finish. You expose the aggregate with the help of a push broom.

Broomed finish

You can create a very simple decorative finish with a nonskid texture by dragging a dampened broom over the concrete just after floating it. Use a push broom with nylon bristles specifically designed for concrete finishing. Pull the broom gently in straight, curving, or wavy strokes and repeat the same pattern across the slab.

Rock-salt finish

A rock-salt finish has a smooth, flat surface punctuated by small pits, or *indentations,* that give it an interesting, nonslip texture. This type of finish, however, is not a good one for areas with freezing weather. You can apply this finish to concrete that you've floated or broomed or, if you want a smooth surface, finished with a steel trowel. Follow these steps:

1. **While the concrete is still workable, scatter rock salt over the patio and press it into the surface with a hand float.**

   Leave a bit of each salt particle exposed.

2. **Cure the slab by covering it with plastic sheeting (see the section "Curing the Concrete," later in this chapter); do not use water.**

3. **After five days, remove the sheeting and spray the concrete with water to dissolve the salt.**

   Use a brush to help clean the slab.

When dissolving the salt, avoid contaminating adjacent flower beds with the salty water by either flushing it profusely or diverting the runoff to a safe location.

Travertine finish

Traditional *travertine* is a manufactured, stonelike material consisting of aggregate immersed in a cementitious matrix that hardens around the stones and is then sliced and polished. A travertine concrete finish mimics the actual material. This type of finish, which is quite easy to do, combines the concrete with a material that has a different texture and color: *mortar.* The result is hundreds of flat "islands" of mortar in a "sea" of concrete. The surface is heavily textured and is not advised for areas with freezing weather. Follow these steps:

1. **Prepare the "sea" by edging and floating the slab and adding a broomed finish for better adhesion.**

2. **Mix white portland cement with sand, water, and a color pigment of your choice.**

3. **Dip a dash brush (available at concrete or masonry suppliers) into the mortar and throw globs of the mortar onto the concrete by snapping the brush.**

4. **After the slab is firm enough to support your weight on knee boards, go over the surface with a steel trowel, flattening and spreading the mortar globs.**

Stamped-pattern finish

You can buy or rent stamping pads to produce a wide variety of finishes, from regular tile forms to random flagstone patterns. Such finishes are most effective if the concrete is colored (see the following section). Some stamping pads resemble cookie cutters and merely cut grooves into the concrete to resemble grout lines. Others are fully shaped and give the "cells" several different surface textures or shapes. Most are fairly small, enabling you to create a repetitive pattern by leapfrogging two identical stamp templates across the slab. To do so, wait for the floated concrete surface to stiffen slightly. Then place both pads on the concrete, carefully aligning them. Step onto one pad to press it into the concrete. Then, as you step over to the second pad, lift the first one up and place it on the other side of the pad on which you're standing. Repeat this process until you complete the entire patio. Use a bricklayer's jointing tool to clean up the grooves.

A few stamping pads are very large, made out of a rubberized material that you can quarter-turn for each "embossing" to create a stonelike surface over the entire slab that doesn't repeat itself (see Figure 17-6). For this type of surface, hire an experienced concrete finisher who has such pads and is experienced in using them.

Coloring concrete

The easiest way to color concrete, although expensive, is to blend pigment into the concrete mix. Mineral oxide or synthetic iron-oxide pigments are available from concrete suppliers in colors such as brown, white, green, pink, and cream. For soft tones, use one and a half pounds of pigment for every sack of cement (nine pounds per yard of concrete). For deep tones, use seven pounds per sack (42 pounds per yard). The concrete is colored throughout, with no variation.

Figure 17-6:
Stamping
pads enable
you to
create a
concrete
finish that
resembles
paved
surfaces or
textured
stone.

For *variegated color,* you have two options. One is the dry-shake method, which involves sprinkling powdered pigment over the surface of the slab before floating it and then blending the pigment into the concrete as you float the slab. Make sure that you follow the directions on the label. By varying the amount of pigment and even using alternate colors, you can create streaks and blotches of color. You don't get much chance to practice, however, and the results are permanent. And the color is only skin deep and so can wear off.

A more permanent way to apply color to the surface is by using concrete stain, which you apply after the concrete cures for at least three months. Following are the steps involved in this process:

1. **First, wash the slab with a solution of water and trisodium phosphate (TSP) or phosphate-free heavy-duty cleaner.**

   Follow the manufacturer's instructions, rinse thoroughly, and avoid contaminating nearby plants.

2. **Etch the surface of the concrete with acid, as recommended by the stain instructions.**

   Use either muriatic acid or phosphoric acid, as specified, and follow all safety precautions. This nasty stuff is very caustic and requires you to wear rubber gloves, full goggles, and old clothes. In mixing acid with water, always add the acid to the water (and *not* the other way around).

3. **Using a hose with a strong spray, rinse away the acid thoroughly (protecting plants from exposure).**

4. **After the concrete dries thoroughly, apply the stain according to the manufacturer's instructions.**

   Vary the concentration of stain to achieve subtle color changes and experiment by adding streaks and washes of a second color.

Curing the Concrete

Concrete hardens by a chemical process called *hydration,* which takes several days to complete (28 days for full hardening, but only 5 days to achieve a strength adequate for residential projects). This chemical reaction requires water. If water evaporates from the concrete too quickly, hydration ceases and the concrete fails to attain maximum hardness. Because a concrete patio has a large surface area, evaporation can occur easily and quickly. You have several ways to keep the concrete from drying out. One is to keep a constant spray of water from a sprinkler or soaker hoses on the concrete. Another is to cover the patio with old carpets, straw, or burlap and keep it moist. The key to both techniques is to keep the concrete constantly wet; cycles of wet and dry cause severe cracking.

The third and easiest way to cure concrete is to cover the patio with plastic sheeting. Anchor the edges with stones or sand and tape joints where they overlap. Leave the plastic on for five days (seven days in cool weather below 70 degrees F). You want to make sure that the temperature isn't going to dip below 50 degrees F while the concrete is curing. If it does, insulate the top of the plastic with fiberglass insulation batts or old carpets and blankets.

Chapter 18

Installing a Flagstone Patio

* *

In This Chapter

▶ Choosing a foundation

▶ Tooling up

▶ Piecing the puzzle together

▶ Filling the sandbox

▶ Building for forever

▶ Stones gathering moss

* *

F lagstone is one of the most beautiful patio surfaces. The natural stone combines wonderfully with plants and evokes a unique warmth, style, and texture. It's also one of the most expensive patio surfaces. Depending on where you live, a flagstone patio can cost you more than 5 to 10 times as much as a simple concrete patio. (That's because different types of flagstone are quarried in different parts of the world, so transportation figures heavily into the cost.) Flagstone also takes a certain amount of creativity to lay down attractively, and because of the wide seams and natural unevenness of the stone, flagstone can be tough on patio furniture or wheeled kids' toys. Some types of flagstone also stain easily. But if you have the bucks and you're committed to an extraordinary patio, you can't go wrong with flagstone.

Choosing a Foundation

You can lay flagstone and dimensioned stone on a bed of compacted sand or, for a more stable patio, on a mortar bed spread over a poured concrete slab. A sand bed requires permanent edging to keep the sand from shifting and doesn't work as well for irregular flagstones as for dimensioned stone, brick, and pavers, all of which you can butt together into a tight formation.

If you use flagstones, however, you can fill in the joints with soil and then plant ground-hugging plants therein for a very soft-textured, natural-looking patio. Plants or no plants, the flagstones in this type of patio are eventually going to shift and settle because the sand can shift by oozing up between the stones. The stones are less likely to shift if they're large and thick.

You can also stabilize the patio even more by filling the cracks with dry mortar mix and then wetting the whole thing. After the mortar sets, it expands slightly and locks the stones in place and, more importantly, seals the compacted sand. Although not much stronger than Humpty Dumpty's shell, this method may give you a serviceable patio for several years if the base is solid and the ground stable.

The most durable flagstone patio is set over a concrete slab — either a new slab (see Chapter 17) or an existing patio in sound condition (see Chapter 16). If you construct a new slab, you don't need to finish the surface beyond the first floating, which leaves the surface rough enough for mortar to adhere to.

Tooling Up

Before building a flagstone patio, you must prepare the site (see Chapter 16), order materials, and round up some tools. Besides the stones, you need enough sand for a two-inch-thick bed or enough mortar for a three-quarter-inch-thick bed and grout between the joints. If you install a sand bed, you should also buy enough weed-control fabric to cover the bed (unless you plant groundcover between the joints).

If you use mortar to install the stones, figure on one cubic yard of mortar for every 300 square feet of patio. Use Type M mortar, which is designed for exterior paving and consists, by volume, of one part portland cement, one-quarter part hydrated lime, and two and three-quarters parts masonry sand. (The "parts" add up to an aggregate that has slightly less volume than their sum because of blending of the larger and smaller particles.) Have the masonry supplier calculate the materials based on these proportions or ask for a recommendation for your area. You can always add colored pigment to the grout to make the joints blend with or contrast with the stones.

You should also buy muriatic acid to clean stains off the stones from any mortar that spills. If the concrete slab has a smooth surface, you should buy *latex bonding agent* (a gluelike substance) to spread over the concrete to ensure a tight bond between the concrete and mortar.

In addition to the supplies, you need some or all of the following tools to install a flagstone patio, depending on the type of foundation you have:

✔ Gloves

✔ Goggles or safety glasses

✔ Knee pads

✔ Knee boards (for laying stones in mortar)

✔ Tape measure

✔ Hose

✔ Buckets

✔ Wheelbarrow

✔ Square shovels

✔ Screed (for leveling sand or mortar; see Chapter 17)

✔ Power compactor (for installations on sand bed)

✔ Straightedge (2x4)

✔ Mason's level (four-foot; resistant to drop damage)

✔ Cold chisel (stonemason's, for scoring stone to cut)

✔ Brick set (for cutting stone)

✔ Club hammer ($2^1/_2$ to 3 pounds, for chisel)

✔ Mason's hammer (for chipping edges)

✔ Rubber hammer (for seating stones)

✔ Pipe (two-foot piece of galvanized pipe, for cuts)

✔ Mortar hoe (for mixing mortar)

✔ Pointed trowel (for placing mortar, grout)

✔ Jointing tool (for smoothing grout joints)

✔ Damp rags (for wiping off excess mortar)

✔ Plastic sheeting (for curing grout between stones)

Unlike with a concrete pour, you can install flagstone without many helpers. You should have at least one helper, however, to assist with large stones and to speed up the work.

Piecing the Puzzle Together

Flagstone comes in all shapes and sizes, so the first step in installing a flagstone patio is to lay out the pieces in an attractive way. You just want to make sure that all the small or large pieces aren't bunched up in one area. Strive for an even distribution of sizes and shapes while minimizing the amount of cutting you need to do. You also want to keep the joint size as consistent as possible — about three-quarters to one and a half inches apart for flagstones set on sand and about two to three inches apart for mortar installations, depending on the size of stones.

Do a dry layout in a clear, open area close to the patio site. If you don't have space in which to lay out the entire patio, at least sort the stones into groups of small, medium, and large sizes.

To cut flagstone, follow these steps, as shown in Figure 18-1:

1. **Set the stones in place, tucking the piece you intend to cut under the adjacent stone.**

2. **Using a pencil or sharp object, scribe the outline of the top stone onto the lower stone, taking into account the thickness of the joint.**

3. **Using a cold chisel, a pitching chisel (used in stonemasonry), or a brickset, score the cutting line by tapping on the chisel with a club hammer or maul as you move the chisel along the stone.**

   Wear gloves to protect your hands from hammer blows and sharp edges.

4. **After scoring the stone, place a short length of pipe under it, centering the pipe below the scored line.**

5. **Center the brickset on the line and strike the brickset with a sharp blow of the hammer.**

   The stone should break along the line.

6. **Complete the break and clean up the rough edges with a mason's hammer or mallet and chisel.**

If you're installing dimensioned stone with straight edges, you can make straight, smooth cuts by using a power saw with a masonry cutoff blade. Use an electric circular saw or a gasoline-powered masonry-cutting saw. Set the blade depth to score a line an eighth to a quarter of an inch deep. Then tap the stone to break it along that line (as described in Step 5 of the preceding list).

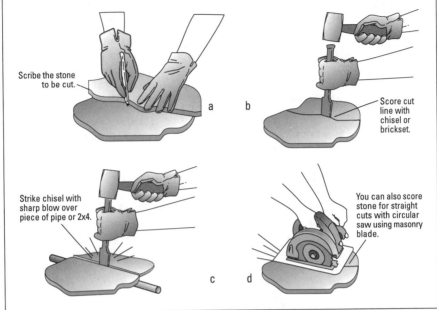

Figure 18-1:
To cut flagstone, score a cutting line and, using a hammer and brickset or wide pitching chisel, strike a brisk blow on the line.

Scribe the stone to be cut.

Score cut line with chisel or brickset.

Strike chisel with sharp blow over piece of pipe or 2x4.

You can also score stone for straight cuts with circular saw using masonry blade.

a b c d

Filling the Sandbox

For instructions about preparing a sand bed for patio paving, see Chapter 16. After installing the gravel base, edging, and sand bed, lay weed-control fabric over the sand if you're not filling the cracks between stones with mortar or planting soil. Also dampen the sand to settle it. Then follow these steps:

1. **Start laying stones in one corner, maintaining even joints.**

2. **Tap each stone with a rubber mallet to set it snugly into the sand.**

3. **After you have several stones in place, lay a mason's level across the tops to check for level and evenness.**

Where necessary, add or remove sand under stones or reset them. As you lay stones farther from the patio edge, set plywood knee boards on the stones to distribute your weight. Use a longer straightedge with the level on top of it to check evenness.

4. **After setting all the stones, a job that may take several days, fill in the cracks with sand, soil, or dry mortar.**

   If you use sand, choose a sharp-edged type, such as *fines* from crushed stone, that locks into place. Spray the joints with water as you sweep the sand into place to facilitate compaction. If you fill the cracks with soil, pack it firmly to stabilize the stones. (See the section "Stones Gathering Moss," later in this chapter, for suggested plants to use.)

   For mortar joints, shovel dry mortar mix into the cracks, sweeping it and tamping it into place. Wet the surface with a fine spray of water. Don't apply too much too fast. Spray for about 10 minutes, take a break, and then do it again. Repeat this process until the mortar is thoroughly wet. Then go back and fill in any voids with dry mortar and moisten it as needed. Wipe away excess mortar with damp rags. After the patio sets for 24 hours, clean off mortar stains with a solution of one part muriatic acid added to ten parts water (following the safety precautions on the label). Then keep the surface lightly moist or cover it with plastic sheeting for five days to cure the mortar.

Building for Forever

If you construct a new concrete slab as a base for your flagstone patio, finish it only to the point of screeding and floating (see Chapter 17). Let it cure for at least 24 hours before installing paving over it. For existing patios or new slabs with a smooth surface, roughen the surface and apply a latex-modified bonding agent over the patio before spreading mortar onto it.

If all the stones are of uniform thickness (not likely with flagstone but possible with dimensioned stone), set up screed guides around the edge of the patio, staking them in place so that the tops are exactly one inch above the surface of the slab. Using the guides to screed the mortar makes keeping the mortar and stones level an easy task.

Mix enough mortar to cover about 10 square feet at a time. You may need to play around with the consistency, adding more or less water or concrete to get the mix to a point where it's just firm enough to support the stones but oozy enough for the stones to make full contact with the mortar.

After your mortar is ready for you to lay down the stones, follow these steps:

1. **Lay down enough mortar — about an inch thick — to set the first two or three stones, screeding it if the stones are of uniform thickness (see Figure 18-2).**

   If the stones are not of uniform thickness, use a pointed trowel to shape the mortar into furrowed ridges so that it "grips" the stone as you set the latter into place.

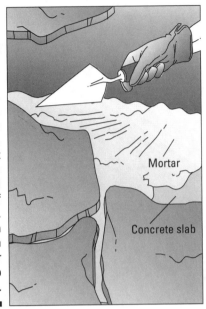
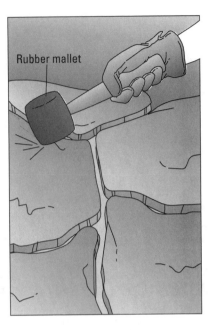

Figure 18-2:
Lay down only enough mortar for a few stones at a time, furrowing it to ensure full adhesion of the stones. Tap each stone with a rubber mallet to seal it.

Mortar

Concrete slab

Rubber mallet

2. **Tap each stone a few times with a rubber mallet to seat it.**

   Check every three or four stones with a level or straightedge to see whether they're even across the top. Make adjustments by adding or removing mortar or resetting the stone. Use knee boards and clean the stones with a wet rag as you go.

3. **After setting all the stones, cover the patio with plastic sheeting for 24 hours and then grout the joints with mortar, adding pigment to color the mortar if you want.**

   Use a pointed trowel or a *grout bag* (a canvas bag that tapers to a pointed opening) to guide mortar into the cracks without spilling it onto the stones, as shown in Figure 18-3. After the mortar stiffens, smooth the joints by using a brick mason's jointing tool or a small trowel. Clean excess mortar off the stones with a wet rag.

4. **After you finish setting the stones, cover the patio with plastic sheeting or keep it moist for at least three days.**

   Clean up any mortar stains with a mixture of one part muriatic acid to ten parts water (see the preceding section).

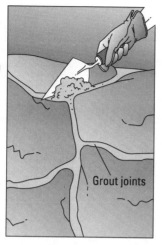

Figure 18-3:
Use a
pointed
trowel or a
grout bag
to guide
mortar into
the cracks
between
stones.

Grout joints

Stones Gathering Moss

Unlike rolling stones, a flagstone patio begs you to tarry and let the moss grow under your feet. Planting ground-hugging plants between flagstones is a wonderful way to give your patio a rustic, country-garden look. But not just any plants work, and even those that do require special care.

The best plants for this purpose can take some foot traffic, can withstand the intense heat that builds up on a sunny patio, and can reseed themselves each year. The list that follows includes several such plants; experiment with them to see which ones work best for your patio. Start out by trying a few plants in areas with the least amount of activity. Not many plants can withstand heavy foot traffic. Water the plants regularly; they dry out much more quickly than they would if they were planted under normal conditions.

The following plants grow in full or partial sun and make suitable ground-covers for planting between flagstones:

- Blue Star Creeper, *Laurentia fluviatilis*. Compact, with blue flowers.
- Chamomile, *Chamaemelum nobile*. Aromatic herb with daisylike flowers.
- Common aubrieta, *Aubrietia deltoidea*. Gray perennial foliage and colorful flowers.
- Cranesbill, *Erodium reichardii*. Dark green leaves and cute flowers.
- Creeping thyme, *Thymus praecox articus*. Fragrant herb.
- Dichondra, *Dicondramicrantha*. Tender plant with deep green, round leaves.

✔ Irish or Scotch moss, *Sagina subulata.* Wonderfully textured foliage plants.

✔ Lippia, *Phyla nodiflora.* Tight plant, but flowers attract bees.

✔ Sweet alyssum, *Lobulariamaritima.* Colorful annual, easy to start from seed.

You can also use many lawn grasses between flagstones, but you must mow them regularly. Korean grass, *Zoysia tenuifolia,* however, is one grass that stays dwarf and doesn't need much mowing.

To plant between stones, either scatter seed and see what comes up or dig out small holes in the joints and plant from six-packs. Make sure that you water often.

Chapter 19

Installing a Brick Patio

● ●

In This Chapter

▶ Choosing a foundation

▶ Rounding up tools and materials

▶ Choosing a pattern

▶ Laying bricks in sand

▶ Laying bricks in mortar

● ●

*A*mong patio materials, brick offers the widest variety of styles and levels of complexity. Perhaps the easiest patio to build is a brick-in-sand patio. It's like playing with blocks; you simply set bricks next to each other on the sand in whatever pattern you choose. Even some mortar installations quickly become routine as you repeat the same operation over and over again, although many patterns are very complex and require great skill.

The main advantages of brick, from the point of view of installing the material, are wide availability, the relatively light weight of each brick, and the modular dimensions that make various interlocking patterns possible. The main disadvantage is that the small size of units makes keeping the patio surface absolutely flat a difficult task, which isn't necessarily a bad thing — some variation in height adds to the texture of the overall installation (but can be maddening if your patio furniture keeps teetering).

Choosing a Foundation

As with flagstone, you can install bricks in a bed of compacted sand or on a mortar bed over a concrete slab (see Chapter 18). A sand bed, of course, is the easier installation and, if built correctly, makes an excellent patio base. It also enables water to flow back into the ground if the bricks have spaces between them, which is important if you build your patio over tree roots. As with most building techniques, however, you face a tradeoff: If you leave space between the bricks so that water can seep through, you weaken the cohesive strength of the paving.

A good compromise is to space the bricks only a quarter inch apart and pack the spaces firmly with sand. Narrower spaces impede water seepage. Larger spaces cause the sand to shift and the bricks to sink; the sand also washes out easily.

Another factor to consider with sand beds is weeds. Weed-control fabric, which was developed for landscaping use, is the best solution to this problem. Install it between the sand and bricks. It blocks weeds from reaching daylight but lets water soak through the fabric.

If you build your patio over a sand bed, figure on spending some time each year maintaining it. The crisp edges of bricks create tripping hazards as they settle and shift, so you need to constantly bring them back into alignment. Simply pry out individual bricks and remove or add sand to level them. You may also need to replace bricks, so buy extras when you build the patio.

Setting bricks in mortar on a concrete base offers the chance for more intricate patterns and, of course, creates a more solid and durable patio. The mortared joints add variations in texture, color, and pattern. The bricks are also less likely to absorb moisture and attract moss. After you build the patio — assuming that the concrete slab is sound — you're done with it. The only thing left to do is rearrange furniture or plants from time to time and enjoy patio life.

Rounding Up Tools and Materials

Besides bricks, you need to order sand or mortar and round up some tools. For information about a sand bed, see Chapter 16. If you buy mortar, choose Type M for exterior applications (see Chapter 18). The amount you need depends on the size of bricks and the joint width. Typically, for bricks that measure $3^5/_8$ x $7^5/_8$ inches and are set with $^3/_8$-inch joints, 100 square feet of patio requires approximately 7.5 cubic feet of mortar. This includes a half-inch mortar bed under the bricks. See Chapter 14 for information about choosing and ordering bricks.

Use the following list of tools and equipment for your project, depending on whether you install the bricks in sand or mortar:

- ✔ Gloves
- ✔ Goggles or safety glasses
- ✔ Knee pads
- ✔ Tape measure

- Hose
- Wheelbarrow
- Square shovels
- Screed (for leveling sand; see Chapter 16)
- Power compactor (for installations on sand bed)
- Straightedge (2x4)
- Mason's level (four feet; resistant to drop damage)
- Mason's twine
- Brick tongs (for carrying bricks)
- Brick set (for cutting bricks)
- Mason's hammer (for chipping edges)
- Wet saw (for precise cutting) or . . .
- Power saw with masonry cutoff blade
- Rubber mallet and scrap of 2x6 (for seating bricks)
- Framing square (for checking alignment)
- Mortar hoe (for mixing mortar)
- Brick trowel (for placing mortar, cleaning bricks)
- Jointing tool (for smoothing mortar joints)
- Damp rags (for wiping off excess mortar)
- Plastic sheeting (for curing mortar between bricks)

As for needing helpers, a brick patio is one of the few types that you can truly do solo, if necessary, although having help is always nice, if for nothing else than the company. A brick-in-sand patio is particularly suitable for "little helpers" — a can't-miss family project that everyone can enjoy.

Choosing a Pattern

Centuries of bricklaying have produced several time-honored patterns that lend themselves well to a modern patio (see Figure 19-1). The easiest pattern to lay is bricks lined up next to each other in even rows. This pattern, called *jack-on-jack,* creates a predictable grid of joint lines. Staggering each row so that the joints fall at the midpoint of bricks in the adjacent rows creates a pattern called *running bond.* Other patterns, such as *basketweaves* and *herringbones,* involve placing bricks at angles to each other.

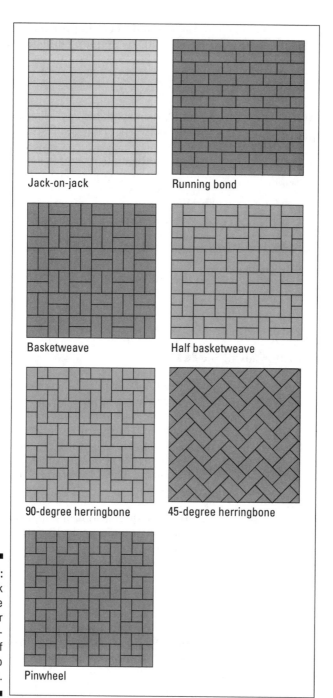

Jack-on-jack

Running bond

Basketweave

Half basketweave

90-degree herringbone

45-degree herringbone

Pinwheel

Figure 19-1:
These brick
patterns are
suitable for
do-it-
yourself
patio
installations.

In choosing a pattern, consider the amount of cutting you must do. Jack-on-jack, runningbond, and basketweave patterns require cutting only a few bricks, if any. Herringbone and pinwheel patterns require cutting many bricks in half, and 45-degree herringbone patterns involve numerous angled cuts.

The most difficult patterns to install are curved designs. The rows change in length as the arcs of a curve expand outward, making adjustments to the alignment and brick spacing for each row necessary. As you get closer to the center of a circle or curve, you must cut bricks to a tapered shape so that they fit, changing the angle of the taper for each row. Such patterns are possible but require a great deal of patience.

After you decide on a pattern, measure the size of the module that you intend to repeat and calculate whether it fits evenly into the width and length of your patio. If possible, adjust the spacing between bricks so the bricks fit evenly and don't require trimming along one side. If you must trim bricks, adjust the layout so that the cut bricks are at least half a brick wide (or long).

Laying Bricks in Sand

If the gravel base is not a material that compacts solidly, such as class-five gravel (which compacts better than other grades, such as pea gravel) or road base (a mixture of sand, gravel, and rock with angular, not smooth, edges), install a layer of geotextile fabric. This fabric is designed to cover drainrock in subsurface drainage systems between the base and the sand bed. Spread, screed, and compact one half to two inches of sand over the gravel base or filter fabric, as shown in Figure 19-2 (see also Chapter 16). Install the edging as described in Chapter 16.

Check a few bricks to make sure that the dimensions are uniform. If so, pack them together tightly as you lay them. If not, lay bricks loosely. After you set bricks on the sand bed, they should lie just slightly higher than the edging to give them room to settle after you compact them later.

When you're ready to lay the bricks, follow these steps:

1. **Dampen the sand bed.**

2. **Tie a length of mason's twine to two loose bricks and, using them for anchors, stretch the line parallel with (and one brick's width away from) the starting edge.**

   Use this line, rather than the edging, to align the row of bricks. Move the line over and use it as a guide for each row of bricks.

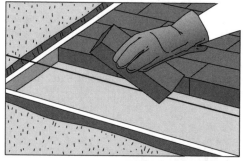

Figure 19-2:
Laying
bricks in
sand
involves
screeding
and
compacting
the base,
using twine
guides,
setting and
leveling,
and
compacting.

3. **Set each brick in place without sliding it.**

   Tap the brick lightly with a rubber mallet to snug it into the sand —
   avoid displacing any sand.

   As you work your way across the patio, use knee boards to distribute
   your weight. They should be larger than the knee boards you use for
   concrete finishing or mortar installations; use half sheets of plywood if
   possible.

4. **After laying several bricks, lay a straightedge or mason's level across
   your work.**

   From time to time, use a long straightedge to check how even the brick
   surface lies over a large area. Reset bricks as necessary to align them.

   As you come to edges of the patio where you must cut bricks to fit,
   either cut as you go or leave voids and cut all the partial bricks to fit at
   the same time by renting a masonry saw for an hour or two. (See the
   nearby sidebar, "Cutting bricks.")

5. **After all the bricks are in place, compact the patio.**

   To do so, spread a layer of fine sand over the patio and then sweep it
   back and forth so that it falls into the brick joints. With the excess sand
   still on the surface, go over the patio with a vibrating plate compactor,
   which you can rent. Sweep again, as necessary, to force sand into the
   joints, and compact the bricks again. Thorough compaction is essential
   for locking all the bricks into a tight unit. The result is a firm patio
   surface that should last for many years.

Laying Bricks in Mortar

A reinforced concrete slab, either new or existing, makes an excellent base
for installing bricks in mortar. (For instructions on building a slab, see
Chapter 17.) The slab should have a rough surface for the mortar to adhere
to. If not, rough up the concrete by using a *scarifier,* a machine that you can
rent, which is something like a rototiller for concrete. Then apply a latex-
modified bonding agent over the patio surface.

After the surface is ready, follow these steps:

1. **Set up screed guides around the slab to ensure that the finished brick
   surface is even.**

   Stake 2-by boards so that the tops extend above the slab a distance
   equal to half an inch of mortar plus the thickness of one brick. Make a
   screed board that spans the patio as well. The screed should have ears,
   or extensions, that straddle the guides, enabling the rest of the screed
   to extend below the tops of the guides exactly the thickness of one brick.

Cutting bricks

Always wear safety glasses or goggles while cutting bricks. The easiest way to cut a brick is by using a brickset and hammer. Score the brick on all four sides by tapping it with the brickset and hammer. Then, laying the brick on a firm surface, place the brickset on the scored line, with the beveled edge facing the "bad" side of the cut, and whack! Strike the brickset sharply with the hammer. Clean up the rough face of the cut with the chipping end of a mason's hammer, a brickset, or a brick trowel.

For perfectly smooth cuts, use a circular power saw with a masonry cutoff blade (as shown in the accompanying figure) or rent a wet saw, normally used for tile and stonecutting. If you use a circular saw, clamp the brick in a vice or a portable workbench that has an adjustable clamping surface. Start with shallow cuts and increase the blade depth for successive cuts. To cut with a wet saw, set the brick on the movable table and slowly feed it into the spinning blade. If the saw has a stationary platform and a movable blade, lower the blade slowly onto the brick and move it back and forth as you slice through the brick.

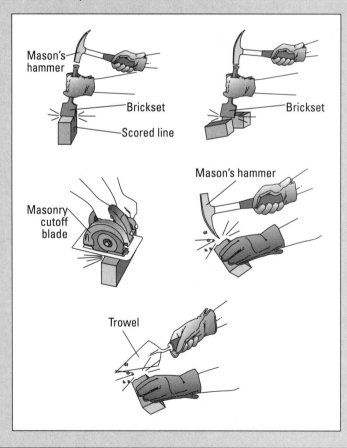

Mason's hammer
Brickset
Scored line
Brickset
Masonry cutoff blade
Mason's hammer
Trowel

2. Before laying the bricks, check to see whether you need to wet them.

Some bricks are "dry" and absorb water from the mortar, inhibiting a strong bond. To test, choose a few bricks randomly and scratch a circle on each one about the size of a quarter. Place half a teaspoon of water in each circle and time how long the brick takes to absorb it. If the time is less than 90 seconds, wet the bricks before laying them. Either soak them in a tub of water or lay them out and spray water on all six sides. Give the surfaces time to dry before laying them, or the mortar doesn't bond.

3. Mix your mortar.

Follow the instructions on the mortar mix bag. Mix enough mortar to cover about 10 square feet at a time.

To test the mortar for the correct consistency, spread some out and trowel it into a series of small ridges. If they crumble, add water. If they dissolve or slump, add dry ingredients. If they hold their shape and the trowel slides easily across the mortar, the consistency is just right.

4. Start laying your bricks, as shown in Figure 19-3.

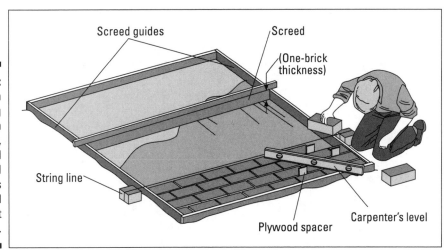

Figure 19-3:
When setting bricks in mortar, spread mortar and lay bricks over a small area at a time.

Screed guides

Screed

(One-brick thickness)

String line

Plywood spacer

Carpenter's level

Starting at one corner, spread some mortar over the concrete and screed it level. Lay bricks in the mortar according to the pattern you chose, aligning them with a string line, framing square, or straightedge (see the earlier section, "Laying Bricks in Sand"). Tap each brick in place with a rubber mallet or lay a board over several bricks and tap it with a mason's hammer. Place spacers between the bricks to maintain uniform joint size — scraps of $3/8$- or $1/2$-inch plywood work well. You must work quickly; the mortar becomes unworkable after an hour or so, depending on the weather. If necessary, mix several batches of mortar.

As in laying bricks in sand (see the preceding section), move string lines along as you work your way across the patio. Make cuts and fit bricks into place as you go rather than wait. (See the sidebar "Cutting bricks," earlier in this chapter, for cutting techniques.) Scrape excess mortar off of bricks immediately, using a damp rag to wipe off stains.

5. **After you finish laying all the bricks, cover the patio with plastic sheeting and wait at least 24 hours to grout the joints.**

Buttering bricks

If you've laid brick before (or feel confident that you can pick up the craft quickly), you can avoid the two-step process of laying bricks one day and grouting the joints the next day by "buttering" two sides of each brick before you set it in place. This process eliminates the grouting step but slows down the laying step and, if you aren't sure-handed, plops mortar everywhere but where you want it. But if you have the knack, these are the motions:

1. **Holding the brick in one hand and a brick trowel in the other, scoop some mortar onto the trowel and scrape it onto one edge of the brick in one motion.**

2. **Scoop more mortar onto the end of the brick.**

3. **Knock off excess mortar along the edges of the brick, beveling both globs of mortar as you do so.**

4. **Slam the brick into place, aiming the mortar globs against the two bricks already in position while at the same time packing it down on the mortar bed firmly.**

5. **If necessary, tap the side of the brick with the trowel handle to seat it.**

   The mortar between joints should compress firmly, without leaving any voids, and should maintain the desired joint width of $3/8$-to $1/2$-inch.

6. **Scrape excess mortar from bricks immediately and wipe away stains with a damp rag.**

6. Grout the joints.

Mix mortar and carefully place it between the bricks by using a brick trowel or a *grout bag* (a canvas bag that tapers to a pointed opening, which you fill with mortar and squeeze to force mortar out of the opening). If you use a trowel, sling the mortar down into the joints with a sawing motion. Wipe off excess mortar.

7. After the mortar stiffens, smooth the joints by using a brick mason's jointing tool.

You can also use a short length of half-inch diameter copper tubing bent into a slight curve. Clean excess mortar off the bricks by using a damp rag.

8. After the mortar sets, go over the joints with a stiff brush to knock off excess mortar.

Sweep the excess away and cover the patio with plastic sheeting or keep it moist for at least three days. Clean up any mortar stains by using a mixture of one part muriatic acid to ten parts water (see Chapter 18).

Chapter 20

Installing Concrete Pavers and Tile

● ●

In This Chapter

▶ Paver foundation

▶ Paver tools and materials

▶ Paver techniques

▶ Setting tile

▶ Grouting tile

● ●

*I*nstalling concrete pavers is similar to installing bricks on a sand base. The material lends itself well to do-it-yourself installations because the pavers are relatively inexpensive (especially compared to brick or stone) and have two design features that overcome the limitations of sand-bed installations: interlocking shapes that stabilize the paving and beveled edges that smooth out slight differences in height between pavers. These features, combined with the inherent strength of the concrete, make pavers almost foolproof.

Tile is a different story. It's the most brittle of materials. Most tile requires a concrete foundation and precision placement to ensure straight grout lines. Setting and grouting are time-consuming, and you must seal some tile for moisture protection. Nevertheless, tile is a beautiful paving material that dresses up a patio as nothing else can. You can also use it as an accent material for borders and *feature strips* (trade lingo in the tile biz) to contrast with large expanses of concrete.

Paver Foundation

Install pavers over the same type of sand bed that you'd use for flagstones or brick (see Chapters 18 and 19). For complete instructions on how to prepare the base and sand bed, see Chapter 16. Check the manufacturer's recommended depth for the sand base. (Some specify a maximum of one inch.) That you compact the sand bed fully by using a vibrating plate compactor, which you can rent, and that the patio has permanent edging are important considerations in laying a foundation.

Plastic edgings that were developed specifically for concrete pavers are available, as the following list describes:

- ✔ One type consists of long, flexible strips of vinyl that resemble an inverted T as you install them. The continuous vertical fin is stable enough to hold the pavers in place but thin enough to conceal with turf grass, bedding soil, or other landscaping materials placed against the patio. Simply set the edging in place around the perimeter of the bed and drive plastic spikes, available with the edging, into holes along its base to secure it.

- ✔ A second type of edging holds in place pavers that extend above the surrounding ground. It has a wide, beveled flange along its outside edge to provide a gradual, trip-free transition between the ground and raised patio paving. Because this type of edging is rigid, you must saw *kerfs,* or slots, into it to bend it around curves.

You can also use more conventional edgings, such as timbers, brick "soldiers," or a concrete curb. Whichever type of edging you choose, use it to contain the sand as well as the pavers.

Another consideration for the foundation is weed control. The most effective barrier is weed-control fabric, which you can buy where landscaping materials are sold. Simply roll it out over the sand bed before you install the pavers. It blocks weeds and allows rainwater to soak into the ground.

Paver Tools and Materials

Besides pavers, you need edging materials, sand for the bed, and weed-control fabric. Figure on two inches of compacted sand. For information about ordering pavers, see Chapter 14. The following list includes tools you need to prepare the foundation and install pavers on a sand bed:

- ✔ Gloves
- ✔ Goggles or safety glasses
- ✔ Knee pads
- ✔ Tape measure
- ✔ Hose
- ✔ Wheelbarrow
- ✔ Square shovels
- ✔ Screed (for leveling sand; see Chapter 16)

A new life for old concrete

An alternative patio paving material is chunks of broken concrete — primitive pavers — that you can install over a sand bed. If you're demolishing an old patio or walk, save the larger pieces that have a smooth surface. Keep intact pieces as large as possible. Set them in a sand bed as you would flagstones, leaving two- to three-inch-wide joints. Unlike with flagstone, you probably don't have many pieces to choose from, so maintaining a uniform joint size is usually hard. This irregularity, however, adds to the rustic appeal of this type of paving. It also creates voids that you can use as pockets in which to plant groundcover. After you finish the layout, fill the joints with gravel, sand, or soil for plants (see the following figure).

- ✔ Power compactor (vibrating-plate type)
- ✔ Straightedge (2x4)
- ✔ Mason's level (four-foot; resistant to drop damage)
- ✔ Mason's twine
- ✔ Brickset (for cutting pavers)
- ✔ Mason's hammer (for chipping edges)
- ✔ Wet saw (for precise cutting) or . . .

> ✔ Power saw with masonry cutoff blade
>
> ✔ Rubber mallet and scrap of 2x6 (for seating pavers)
>
> ✔ Framing square (for checking alignment)
>
> ✔ Brick trowel (for scooping sand, digging pavers)

As with laying bricks in sand, you can install a paver patio by yourself or with helpers, especially youngsters. Get the whole family involved.

Paver Techniques

After compacting the sand bed, dampen it and lay weed-control fabric over the top. (The fabric should sink into the sand somewhat as you install the pavers.) Make sure that you familiarize yourself with the layout pattern of the pavers; some have intricate shapes that nest together in a certain way. Select several pavers randomly from the lot to look for color variations. Most lots have a set proportion of color variants; they may be randomly mixed together or stacked in a particular order. Strive for an installation that has random variations.

Following are some tips on installing pavers:

> ✔ Install pavers starting in one corner. The pavers should protrude above the edging slightly, to leave room for compaction. Set each one into place so that it fits snugly against the others, hand tight, as shown in Figure 20-1.
>
> ✔ Place a board over several pavers and tap on it to level them. (Complete this operation later by using a power compactor.)
>
> ✔ Use knee boards to support your weight as you work your way across the patio.
>
> ✔ Use mason's twine stretched across the patio as a guide for aligning pavers that have a strong grid pattern (see Chapter 19).
>
> ✔ Cut pavers to fit odd shapes by using a power saw with a masonry cutoff blade, as described for bricks in Chapter 19, or a paving stone cutter, which you can rent.
>
> ✔ Fit cut pieces into place as you work your way across the patio to ensure a tight fit of all pavers.

After you complete the installation, spread a quarter inch of fine sand over the patio. Then go over the patio with a vibrating plate compactor, vibrating high spots until they settle into place. Sweep away the excess sand and hose off the patio for a final cleanup.

Figure 20-1:
Fit pavers snugly against each other. When all the pavers are in place, spread sand over the patio and go over it with a vibrating compactor.

Setting Tile

Although you can conceivably lay some tiles in sand by using the same techniques as for flagstones (see Chapter 18), most installations require a sound concrete slab at least four inches thick. Prepare it the same as you would for laying flagstones or brick (see Chapter 18). Set up screed guides around the slab to level the mortar to a one-inch-thick bed. Use the following tools for setting and grouting tile:

- ✔ Mortar hoe and mixing container
- ✔ Square shovel
- ✔ Notched trowel (for spreading tile mortar)
- ✔ Mason's twine
- ✔ Half-inch plywood spacers
- ✔ Rubber mallet
- ✔ Tile cutter or power saw with masonry blade
- ✔ Tile nippers (for trimming tile edges)
- ✔ Jointing tool (for finishing tile joints)

Mix the setting mortar a bit stiffer than you would for bricks, using one part cement and four parts sand. Spread it by using a notched trowel recommended by the tile supplier. Spread enough mortar for about 10 square feet of tile and screed it to a uniform thickness of 1 inch. To align the first row of tiles, string mason's twine across the patio, anchoring it with stones or bricks.

As you set each tile, lower it into the mortar with a slight twisting motion to make full contact with the mortar. Tap the tile with a rubber mallet. Use half-inch strips of plywood as spacers between tiles to maintain a uniform joint size (see Figure 20-2). After setting four or five tiles, check them with a level or straightedge to make sure that the surface is flat. Use knee boards as you work your way across the patio. Clean spilled mortar from the tile surface immediately.

Figure 20-2: Set tiles in a mortar bed half an inch to one inch thick, using spacers between the tiles to keep joint sizes even.

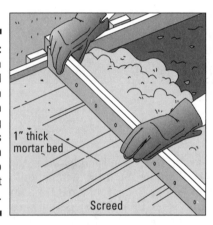

1" thick mortar bed

Screed

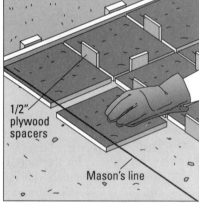

1/2" plywood spacers

Mason's line

Figure 20-3: After filling the joints with grout, use a joint tool to pack the grout.

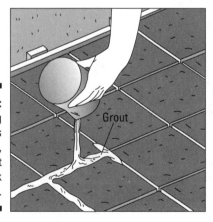

Grout

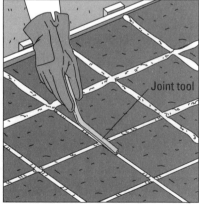

Joint tool

Cutting Tile

Make cuts by using a circular saw with a masonry blade, a rented wet saw, or a snap cutter that you can rent or buy.

To use a snap cutter, follow these steps:

1. **Set the tile in place so that your cutting mark aligns over the center of the cutter.**

2. **Holding the cutter handle in the raised position, quickly slide it across the tile with enough downward pressure for the cutting wheel to score a line.**

3. **Quickly bring the handle back to the center of the tile and lower the handle slowly and firmly to snap the tile in half.**

After you set all the tiles, cover the patio with plastic sheeting for at least 24 hours.

Grouting Tile

Remove the plywood spacers and dampen the joints. The mortar for grouting should be thinner and richer than setting mortar. Mix one part cement with three parts sand and enough water to create a slippery consistency that stays firm but that you can pour out of a container. A can with a bent opening for a spout makes an excellent grout spreader. You can add colored pigment to this grout or buy premixed "sanded" grout of the desired color.

Whenever you're ready, grout the tile by following these steps:

1. **Using a container with a spout or a grout bag to control the flow of grout, fill the joints carefully with the grout (see Figure 20-3).**

2. **Wipe away spills immediately with a damp tile sponge.**

3. **As the grout begins to stiffen, smooth the joints by using a joint tool, packing the grout into the joints and leaving a slick sheen on the surface.**

   The grout should be slightly concave and even with the edges of the tiles.

4. **After the grout sets, wipe excess grout away from the joints with a tile sponge, rinsing it frequently in clean water.**

5. **Cover the patio with plastic sheeting for at least three days to enable the grout to cure.**

6. **Clean off any grout stains with a solution of one part muriatic acid added to ten parts water, following the safety precautions listed on the label.**

Sealing tile

Some types of unglazed ceramic tile, like the Spanish pavers pictured, are very porous. Although the unglazed surface improves traction for greater safety, especially if the tiles are wet, water can seep into the tiles and, if it freezes, crack and break them. Unglazed tile also encourages the growth of moss and algae, which make the patio slippery.

You should apply a sealer to such tile. Check with the supplier where you buy the tile for a recommendation. Apply the sealer before grouting the tiles so that the grout doesn't leave stains. You can apply most sealers by using a paint roller or pump sprayer, according to instructions on the label. Many sealers are quite caustic and may damage plants if the spray wanders over to them, so cover nearby plants with plastic sheeting. Avoid contaminating the ground by applying the sealer carefully under ideal weather conditions and, if necessary, covering the ground around the perimeter of the patio with plastic sheeting.

Chapter 21

Building Patio Steps and Benches

- -

In This Chapter

▶ Laying out stairs

▶ Building forms for stairs (concrete base)

▶ Paving stairs (brick, flagstone)

▶ Building a patio bench (brick, block, stone)

- -

*I*f the floor of your house is more than eight inches above the patio surface or you have a change in levels between the patio and garden, you must build steps. Sometimes the appropriate measure is to build a wooden platform and steps for access from the house, much like a small deck (see Chapter 12). For most patios, however, you should use masonry materials that blend with the patio.

For the safest and most durable installation, build a base of reinforced concrete and finish the surface with a decorative treatment to match the patio or cover it with bricks, flagstones, or other paving. For garden steps, which can be more rustic, you can set stones, bricks, or pavers on a bed of gravel or sand, holding the gravel in place with landscape timbers or lengths of railroad tie spiked to the ground. As with any stairs, design the steps for safety, keeping risers and treads within consistent, allowable dimensions.

Laying Out Stairs

For overall stair requirements, refer to Chapter 5 for information on stair dimensions. Try to use a riser height and tread height — such as 6-inch risers and 15-inch treads — that's more restful than standard dimensions for indoor stairs. Of course, you must adjust these dimensions to fit the steps evenly between fixed levels, such as the patio surface and floor level of the house.

To find the precise distance between two levels, set the end of a long straightedge on the upper level and hold it out over the lower platform. Hold the straightedge level and measure from the bottom of it to the surface of the lower platform at the approximate location where you think stairs are to terminate. This distance is the total rise of the stairs, a figure that you must use for calculating individual riser heights (see Chapter 5). For steps that begin at the patio and lead into the garden, where you can grade the garden path to any level, plan whatever riser and tread dimensions seem ideal (or to match other steps around the patio). Start the layout at the patio and then grade the garden path to line up with the last step, wherever it comes out.

If you pave the steps with bricks or other dimensioned materials, try to adjust the riser height and tread depth to accommodate the modular dimensions. A flat brick stacked on top of a brick laid on edge, for example, yields a total height of $6^3/8$ to 7 inches, depending on the size of the bricks and thickness of the mortar. By factoring these dimensions with the height of the total rise, you may arrive at a riser height that enables you to use full bricks stacked in a particular way without needing to cut any.

A classic brick pattern for steps is to make the treads out of two rows of bricks laid on edge with the bricks aligned front to back and with the front edge resting on a row of bricks laid flat. The flat bricks, in turn, rest on the tread below, aligned along the back edge. This arrangement has an approximate riser height of $6^1/2$ inches and a tread depth of approximately $13^1/2$ inches.

If you build more than one set of stairs around the patio, try to use the same riser-to-tread ratio throughout all the stairs. Make each set of stairs at least 36 inches wide.

Building Forms for Stairs

If you intend to pave the steps, make sure that you know the thickness of the finish material before you build forms for the concrete base. This dimension may affect the riser height of the bottom step, depending on whether you finish the lower landing (or patio) or leave it as a concrete base that you cover with the same paving as the steps. If you intend to finish it, you should *reduce* the riser height for the bottom riser by the thickness of the paving material. If the risers are $6^1/2$ inches and the paving material is 2 inches thick, for example, the bottom riser for the concrete forms needs to be $4^1/2$ inches high; all other risers are $6^1/2$ inches. (Notice that the top tread of the concrete steps seems low, but after you cover it with the paving material, the paving should be flush with the top landing.)

Steps to the house

Use the following technique to build forms for two or three concrete steps (see Figure 21-1). For higher steps, consult with a professional builder.

1. **Rip the necessary boards.**

   First, rip several 2x8 boards to a width exactly equal to the riser height. (Remember that 2x8s are $7^1/4$ inches wide, so you may need to use 2x10s if the riser height is more than $7^1/4$ inches.) Rip boards for the bottom step to a narrower dimension, if necessary (see the preceding section).

2. **Assemble the forms for the bottom step.**

   You build a three-sided form to create a rectangular shape — the house's foundation serves as the fourth side. The boards for the two sides should extend all the way to the foundation. Set the forms on the patio surface and square them up by measuring the diagonals to make sure that they're equal. The form should be level across the front and slope away from the house at the same angle as the patio surface.

   Secure the form to the patio surface by placing 2x4 cleats around the outside of the form boards and attaching them to the patio with expansion bolts.

3. **Next, build another three-sided box for the second step and set it on the first form.**

   Cut the side pieces shorter than the bottom form by a distance equal to the tread depth (13 to 15 inches, for most stairs). If, for example, your bottom form sides are 48 inches long and you want a tread depth of 15 inches, you want side pieces for the second step that are 33 inches long.

   Before nailing the front board between the second step side pieces, set the saw blade of your circular saw to 30 degrees and bevel one edge of the board. Nail this board between the two side boards, flush with the ends, so that the bevel is on the bottom and facing out. (The inside face of the board should be the full riser dimension.) This bevel enables you to slide the finishing trowel under the form board as you pour and finish the concrete.

4. **Repeat this procedure for the next step.**

5. **Join the forms together.**

   Tie the boards on the sides of the form together by nailing 2x4 cleats to them every 12 to 16 inches. Brace the sides to the ground with diagonal bracing to keep them from bowing outward as you fill them with wet concrete. Stabilize the riser boards with two horizontal 2x4s, called *walers,* across the front of each board. Secure the ends of the walers to 2x2 cleats attached to the side forms with screws. Reinforce all the joints with straps, cleats, braces, extra nails, and screws.

6. **Make sure that you secure the forms to the patio; otherwise, they "float" and concrete pours out the bottom.**

   One technique is to place weights, such as bricks or stones, on the forms. Another is to nail the forms to cleats secured to the patio with expansion bolts.

7. **Cut and fit a sheet of expansion material — which you can buy at home centers or concrete supply outlets — against the house foundation.**

8. **Prepare the inside of the form structure cavity.**

   Then place large stones or chunks of concrete in the center of the cavity to reduce the amount of concrete you need. Leave enough clearance around the rubble for at least six inches of fresh concrete. Then place welded-wire reinforcing mesh inside the forms so that the wire clears the sides and top of the steps by two inches (see Chapter 18). Finally, cut a length of #3 (^{3}/$_8$-inch) rebar for the nosing (front edge) of each step — three inches shorter than the riser form — to place in the fresh concrete approximately one inch from the edge.

9. **Pour the concrete.**

   Pour concrete in the bottom step first. Wait 15 or 20 minutes for it to set and then fill the second step and then the third. Consolidate the layers of concrete by jabbing a rod up and down in the concrete, but don't overwork the mix. Place the length of rebar in the nosing of each step, embedding it an inch or so. Then screed each step to level the concrete across the top and remove excess concrete, float it by smoothing it with a wood or magnesium float, and wait for the bleed water to evaporate. Then either cover the steps with plastic sheeting for curing if you intend to pave them later or hand-float them to a moderately smooth texture for safe traction.

10. **Leave the concrete to cure for at least five days before you strip away the forms.**

Adding design flair

If you build a low set of steps from the house to the patio (with less than four risers so that no handrail is required), plan a platform outside the door and wrap steps completely around the platform so that they fan out from the door in all directions. Consider a circular design or build 45-degree angles where the steps change direction. Another way to make steps more attractive is to integrate planters or benches into the design, which you can do quite easily by using the riser height as a module for planning the bench or planter height. Three riser heights, for example, makes a convenient height for a bench if the risers are six inches or less in height. Two risers of 7^1/$_2$ inches would also work.

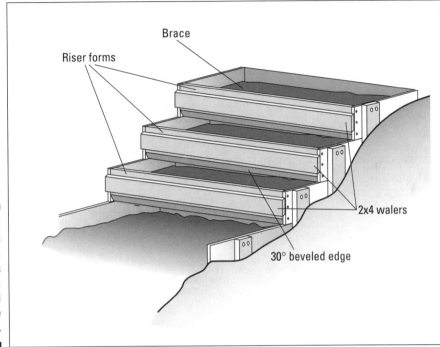

Brace

Riser forms

2x4 walers

30° beveled edge

Figure 21-1:
Use 2x8
lumber to
build forms
for a
landing and
two or three
steps.

Garden steps

Garden steps, which you build on the soil, are much easier to form than porch steps because you can secure the forms by driving stakes directly into the ground and you don't need to extend the side forms of the lower steps as far. You do, however, need to excavate soil from inside the forms to create a flat, level base. The bottom of the excavation should be a series of stepped terraces that mirror the steps themselves and not a sloping ramp. Excavate deep enough so that the concrete at all points is at least six inches thick (see Figure 21-2). Plan for a two-inch layer of gravel, which doesn't conform to the same profile as the excavation but should stay on the level platforms. You may find that building the forms first, before excavating, is easier — that way, you have guides to gauge the depth of digging.

Build the forms as a series of three-sided boxes stacked on top of each other, essentially the same way as you would porch steps. Cut the side boards, however, so that they're just long enough to extend no more than three or four inches beyond the riser of the next step up (in other words, three to four inches longer than the tread depth). Hold the forms in position with stakes. Bevel the bottoms of the riser forms (see the preceding section).

Figure 21-2: In excavating for garden steps, dig out a series of level-bottomed terraces, deep enough for at least six inches of concrete.

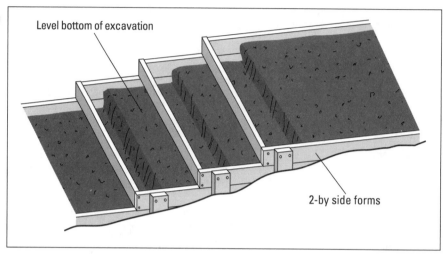

Level bottom of excavation

2-by side forms

After building the forms and excavating the soil, place two inches of gravel on the level soil. Cut and place reinforcing mesh and cut rebar for the step nosings (see the preceding section). Before pouring the concrete, dampen the soil and gravel so that it doesn't absorb water from the concrete mix. Then pour, finish, and cure the concrete, as I describe in the preceding section.

Paving the Stairs

After building a concrete base for the steps, cover it with bricks, stones, or other paving materials by following these steps:

1. **Mix mortar according to the directions given for flagstone in Chapter 18 or for brick in Chapter 19.**

2. **Wet the bricks, if necessary.**

   Some bricks are "dry" and absorb water from the mortar, inhibiting a strong bond. To test, choose a few bricks randomly and scratch a circle on each one about the size of a quarter. Place half a teaspoon of water in each circle and time how long the brick takes to absorb it. If it takes less than 90 seconds, wet the bricks before laying them. Either soak them in a tub of water or lay them out and spray water on all six sides. Give the surfaces time to dry before laying them, or the mortar doesn't bond.

3. **Start laying the paving.**

   Start on the bottom riser. Spread a half-inch-thick layer of mortar and set stone into it, using spacers to keep joints even, or lay bricks against it. After completing the riser, spread mortar above it on the tread. Place the paving along the front of the tread so that it overhangs the riser by about one inch. Cover the entire tread. If you need to cut bricks or dimensioned stone, place the cut pieces at the back of the tread. The paving should slope toward the tread nosing at a rate of an eighth to a quarter inch per foot to prevent water from puddling.

After completing the first riser and tread, proceed with the others the same way, working your way up the steps. Place spacers between paving units to keep joints even. After completing the stairs, pack the joints with mortar and smooth the mortar by using a jointing tool. Wipe off excess mortar immediately by using a damp rag.

4. **Cover the stairs with plastic sheeting and leave the mortar to cure for at least three days.**

   If any mortar stains remain on the paving units, wash them off by using a solution of one part muriatic acid in ten parts water, following safety precautions on the label.

Building a Patio Bench

A masonry bench, although somewhat uncomfortable, blends beautifully with a patio and the garden around it, beckoning you to stay a while. Plan it as the focal point of the patio design or integrate it into a low wall or steps.

The dimensions for a bench are 15 to 18 inches high, at least 15 inches deep, and as wide as you desire. Although a relatively small structure, a bench is a substantial pile of masonry and requires lots of expensive material if it's solid brick or stone.

A more economical approach — and easier to build — is to construct a core of concrete blocks and cover them with a veneer of flagstone, brick, or tile. Concrete blocks are typically $7^5/8$ inches high and $7^5/8$ inches deep, so stacking them two high and two deep creates the desired height and depth dimensions for a bench.

Building the core

To build with block, follow these steps:

1. **Spread one inch of mortar on the patio or a concrete base for about three blocks.**

2. **Set the first block onto the mortar and press it down until the mortar is only $^3/8$ inch thick.**

   Make sure that the block is not upside down; the flanges on the top side are wider than the bottom.

3. **Pick up some mortar on a trowel and** *butter,* **or spread, it onto one end of another block. Set that block against the first one, pressing it into place.**

4. **Continue laying blocks until you complete the first row.**

5. **Using a level, check to see whether the blocks are level and plumb.**

   Check by using a straightedge to see whether they're also aligned in a straight line.

6. **Build the second row behind the first, using the same technique.**

   To lay the second course (or vertical layer), spread mortar on the first row of blocks and set the second row of blocks on it. Turn the first block sideways so that it straddles both rows of the first course. (Blocks are $15^5/_8$ inches long, exactly the width of two $7^5/_8$-inch blocks with $^3/_8$ inch of mortar between them.) This overlapping joint staggers the layout of blocks so that vertical joints don't align over each other, which would result in a weak arrangement.

   As you lay blocks in the second course, embed wall ties, which are strips of corrugated galvanized metal, into the mortar before setting blocks on it. Place a tie every 12 to 16 inches, embedding about half of it in the mortar and leaving 2 to 3 inches protruding. As you cover the finished block core with paving, you can strengthen the bond between the bench's core and veneer by embedding the exposed portion of the wall ties in the mortar between paving units.

Applying the veneer

After completing the core of concrete blocks, leave the mortar to cure for at least seven days, keeping it moist. Then apply the stone or brick veneer.

For bricks, follow these steps:

1. **Apply mortar to the concrete blocks and along the patio or slab where the first row of bricks goes down.**

2. **Lay the first course of bricks.**

   Start by setting the corner brick in place. For successive bricks, butter one end with mortar and push it in place against the previously laid brick.

3. **After completing the first course, spread mortar over the top and lay the second course of bricks.**

   As you reach the wall ties, bend them, if necessary, to embed them in the mortar before you lay the next course of bricks.

4. **After you complete the sides, cover the top of the entire structure with bricks, the same as you would a patio.**

5. **Pack the joints with mortar, smooth the mortar by using a jointing tool, and cover the bench with plastic sheeting or keep the mortar damp for at least five days.**

For a flagstone veneer, as shown in Figure 21-3, follow these steps:

1. **Lay out a dry run of stones on the patio, using the same dimensions as the sides of the concrete block core.**

2. **Place the largest stones along the bottom, for the first course; then spread mortar onto the concrete blocks and set the bottom course of stones in place.**

   Put spacers between the stones to keep them from slumping together.

3. **Lay the other courses in order.**

   As you lay the next courses, cut stones as necessary to fit (see Chapter 18).

4. **After completing the sides, cover the top with mortar and set the stones.**

5. **After all the stones are in place, fill the joints with mortar.**

   Leave the spacers in place but protruding far enough that you can take them out later. Tool the joints and clean excess mortar off of the stones by using a damp rag.

6. **After the mortar sets, remove the spacers and fill the holes with mortar.**

7. **Cover the bench with plastic sheeting and leave the mortar to cure for at least five days.**

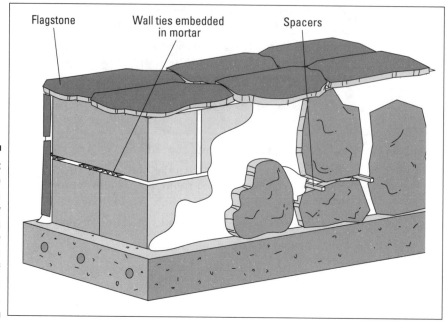

Flagstone

Wall ties embedded
in mortar

Spacers

Figure 21-3:
One way to
build a
masonry
bench is
to apply
flagstone to
a core of
concrete
blocks.

Part IV
Deck & Patio Amenities

The 5th Wave   By Rich Tennant

"Some guy comes around here about three years ago selling in-deck catapults. Since then, summers have been real uneasy around here."

In this part . . .

Today's decks and patios are more than outdoor platforms. They are exciting living spaces with trellises, screens, planters, storage bins, barbecues, fireplaces, lighting systems, and plants providing the extra ambiance. These four chapters present design and construction techniques for building these amenities. Even if you already have a patio or deck, you can adapt any of these add-ons to enhance it and create a personal backyard retreat.

Chapter 22

Building an Overhead

A patio or deck roof enhances outdoor living in many ways, from providing shade to delighting the eye. If you want an overhead structure, first ask yourself why. Is it for shade? Decoration? Relief from the wide-open sky? Rain protection? Design balance? By clearly answering this question, you have a head start in planning the location, size, shape, dimensions, overall appearance, orientation, and details of your roof.

If shade is your goal, for example, you must take into consideration the position of the sun relative to the living area of your patio or deck at different times of the day and year. You may find that the area directly under the overhead isn't shaded at all during hot summer afternoons or that a slatted canopy blocks sunlight only if you orient the slats in a particular direction. If decoration is your goal, the shape, proportions, and finish details of the roof assume primary importance. For rain protection, you can design a standard roof structure with conventional sheathing and shingles, or you can integrate panels of tempered glass, acrylic, or polycarbonate plastic into a more traditional patio roof design.

You may discover that you're not really sure why you want an overhead. If so, consider less-complicated alternatives, such as a few market umbrellas or an awning, to give you more flexibility for experimenting than a permanent structure does.

Designing an Overhead

For general planning suggestions, see Chapter 3. In addition, consider the following design issues as you plan your overhead:

- **Free-standing or attached to the house.** For an attached structure, such as the overhead in Figure 22-1, the height of the house's roof overhang determines some of your design options. If the overhang is at least nine feet above the patio or deck surface, you can probably tuck the patio roof under the eave if the patio roof is level. Otherwise, plan to attach the overhead to the house roof itself or build a free-standing structure that clears the roof eave.

- **Made in the shade.** For minimum shade, where overheating isn't a problem, plan a structure without any canopy above the rafters or a canopy consisting of very few slats. For more shade, space slats no farther apart than their depth. If the slats are 2x4s, for example, space them 3¹/₂ to 4 inches apart. If you orient the slats east to west, they provide shade except during early morning and late afternoon hours. If you orient them north to south, they admit the sun at noon but provide shade in the late afternoon. For maximum shade, of course, build a solid roof. To avoid heat buildup, plan the roof with a vented ridge or similar openings. A good compromise between an open structure and a solid roof is to plant vines, such as grapes, clematis, or wisteria, that fill out the canopy during the summer and drop their leaves in the fall.

- **Scale and proportion.** Plan the overhead large enough for comfortable seating under it (at least 10 feet square) and high enough to leave approximately 8 feet of clearance. (The clearance below supporting beams may be less — a minimum of 7 feet is typical for most codes.) For overall dimensions, see the pertinent sections of Chapter 3. Balance the overhead with other vertical elements in the landscape, such as trees or the house itself, to keep it from overwhelming the patio or deck. As you plan individual components, such as posts and beams, consider the overall scale. A 4x8 beam, for example, may be strong enough to span between posts, but a 6x12 beam may be a more appropriate size visually.

- **Views.** An overhead structure affects views. It blocks certain views, especially of the sky, but it can also frame views of the horizon for a pleasing effect. Use stepladders, poles, and other devices to mock up the location of your overhead to make sure that it doesn't obstruct desirable views.

- **Overall look.** By varying the size of structural members and the finished details, you can make an overhead structure appear light and airy or massive and dominant, refined and elegant or rustic and comfortable. Fix in your mind which of these attributes blend best with your patio or deck and plan the structure's color, size, details, and

Figure 22-1:
An overhead structure provides an inviting place to relax or entertain on your deck or patio.

shape to correspond. If your home and landscape have a formal style, align the overhead with a clear axis, keep the design symmetrical, and choose elegant details. If your home has traditional architecture, plan an overhead with a Victorian or other well-defined motif by adding a gingerbread of intricate scrollwork or lattice and finishing it with white or richly colored paint. If your home and landscape are rustic, plan posts of natural timbers and a canopy of peeled poles and branches, reminiscent of a Southwestern ramada. For other effects, use Classical columns or massive stucco-covered pillars instead of posts or a canopy of brightly colored fabric instead of wooden slats. Each element of the overhead contributes to the overall look.

✔ **Structural rigidity.** Although a patio roof seems like a much simpler structure than other roof systems, it must be designed to withstand the same loads and stresses. First, the footings must be adequate to support the weight of the entire structure plus any snow loads. Secondly, the structure must attach securely to the footings. Third, the individual beams, rafters, and lattice members must be large enough and strong enough for the spans (see Tables 22-1 and 22-2). Finally, the structure must be rigid enough to withstand lateral forces; this requires strong connections between all members and, if necessary, knee braces or similar diagonal bracing.

✔ **Durability.** As does any outdoor structure, an overhead must resist deterioration that constant exposure to sun, rain, snow, and other elements causes. All connections must be corrosion-resistant. Wood members must be at least eight inches above the ground unless they're treated with a preservative specified for ground contact. Wood members must also be well-secured to resist warping and cracking and should be treated with a preservative and sealer (see Chapter 13).

Figure 22-2 illustrates the basic components of most overhead designs. The following two tables recommend the minimum sizes for beams and rafters, based on the distance they must span and the space between members.

These tables are valid only for a simple, flat roof structure with a canopy of lattice or other lightweight material. They help you design an overhead using average lumber typically available for garden construction. If you wish to build something with longer spans, with a solid roof, or for areas with high wind or snow load factors, refer to the code requirements of your local building department or consult with a professional designer. For more information about using span tables, see Chapter 5.

Table 22-1	Maximum Beam Spans between Posts			
Beam Size*	Beam Spacing (Joist Span)			
	8'	10'	12'	16'
2x8	9'6''	8'6''	8'0''	7'6''
2x10	12'0''	11'3''	10'6''	9'6''
2x12	14'6''	13'6''	12'9''	11'6''
4x6	9'6''	8'9''	8'3''	7'6''
4x8	12'6''	11'6''	11'0''	10'0''
4x10	16'0''	14'6''	14'0''	12'6''
4x12	19'6''	18'3''	17'0''	15'6''

*Table assumes construction grade or #2 grade or better for species group A or B. Assume longer spans for structural grades of Douglas fir and Southern pine. Beams are on edge. Spans are measured center-to-center. Check local codes. (See Chapters 5 and 6.)

Table 22-2	Maximum Rafter Spans or Beam Spacing			
Rafter size*	**Rafter Spacing**			
	12''	**16''**	**24''**	**32''**
2x6	14'6''	13'0''	10'6''	6'8''
2x8	19'0''	17'0''	13'10''	9'3''
2x10	20'0''	20'0''	17'0''	11'3''
2x12	20'0''	20'0''	20'0''	12'6''

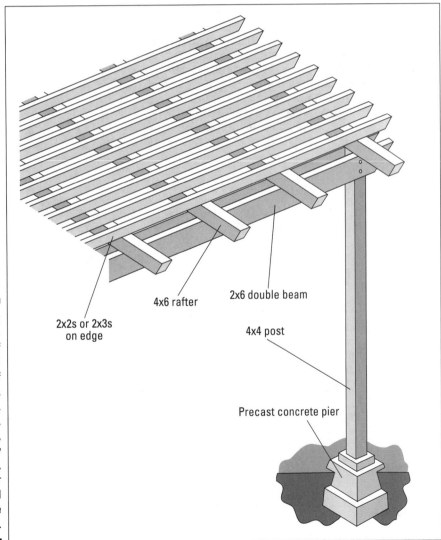

Figure 22-2: The structure of an overhead consists of footings, posts, beams, rafters, canopy material, and a ledger if attached to the house.

2x2s or 2x3s on edge

4x6 rafter

2x6 double beam

4x4 post

Precast concrete pier

Building Footings

Footings must support the weight of the structure and anchor the posts against lateral sway. Two systems are possible, as shown in Figure 22-3. One is concrete footings, which support wooden posts or masonry pillars. Excavate, form, and pour this type of footing the same way as you would for a deck post (see Chapter 9). If you incorporate the footings into a concrete patio, make the tops of the footings level with the patio surface and embed the type of post anchor or column support that holds the bottom of the wooden post approximately one inch above the concrete surface. Make sure that the brackets for anchoring the posts to the footing are the correct dimension for the posts and that you orient them all in the same direction (brackets facing the same way).

The other footing system is to set posts or poles directly in the ground, burying them far enough to reach below the frost line. Bury the posts deep enough so that $1/3$ of the total post length is below the ground. This technique stabilizes the posts against lateral sway but requires longer (more expensive) posts and subjects them to possible decay. Use 8x8 posts or eight-inch diameter poles treated with preservative that's rated for ground contact (.40 pcf — which is .40 pounds of preservative per cubic foot of wood). Dig holes for the posts below the frost line and place six to eight

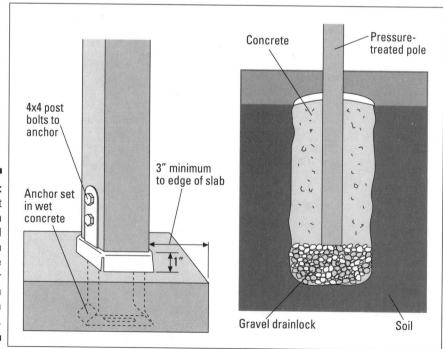

Figure 22-3: Support posts for an overhead with concrete footings or bury them directly in the ground.

4x4 post bolts to anchor

Anchor set in wet concrete

3" minimum to edge of slab

1"

Concrete

Pressure-treated pole

Gravel drainlock

Soil

inches of drainrock in the bottom of each hole. Set the posts in place and brace them. Backfill the holes with concrete or alternating layers of gravel and soil, compacting each layer to a depth of approximately six inches. Slope the concrete or top layer of soil away from the post.

Installing Posts

The simplest posts to install are single timbers, such as 4x6s or 8x8s. Simply rough-cut them to length, set them into the footing brackets, brace them, and secure them with bolts. Then trim the tops to the required height before you install the beams.

Decorative options

You have several ways to decorate plain posts. One is to run a router along all four edges of each post, using a round-over bit for a curved edge, a straight bit for a chamfered edge (a 45-degree bevel), or a more ornate bit for a fancier profile. You can also dress up the base of each post by attaching 1-by lumber around the bottom to create a simple box. For more detail, trim the tops of the 1-by boards at a 45-degree angle, miter the corners by cutting the ends of each board on a 45-degree bevel, and add strips of molding around the box. Another decorative technique is to ring the post near the top with one or two grooves by using a router with a V-shaped or U-shaped bit.

A more elaborate type of post is a built-up post. By sandwiching three or more pieces of lumber together, you can create a post with an interesting profile. Sandwiching a 4x8 between two 2x6s, for example, creates a post that's $7^1/_4$ inches wide in one dimension and $7^1/_2$ inches in the other, with elegant stepped edges that produce pleasing shadowlines. This technique enables you to conceal the post anchor and other connecting hardware by covering them with the outer layers of the "sandwich." To do so, you need to remove some of the wood from the back side of the outer boards to make space for the protruding post anchor and any bolts or nuts.

Because this type of assembly has joints that can trap moisture, use preservative-treated lumber and coat every piece with sealer before assembling them.

You can attach beams to built-up posts in two ways. One way is to trim the outer boards shorter than the core and attach a pair of 2-by beams to the sides of the core, resting them on the outer boards. The second is to cut the core piece shorter than the outer boards and nest a 4-by beam between the two longer pieces so that it rests on the core. Either way, you can connect the beam to the post with half-inch machine bolts.

Another variation on the basic wooden post is to build a plywood box around it and cover the box with shingles, stucco, or other siding material. The sides can be straight, tapered, or stepped. Use preservative-treated plywood and provide screened holes for ventilation. Fabricate a sheet-metal cap to fit over the top of the box to keep rain out.

Nonwood posts

A nonwood option for a post is to build a pillar of concrete blocks, fill it with reinforcing bars and concrete, and cover the outside with stucco. Embed a post anchor in the concrete at the top of the post to hold the beam.

You can also buy prefabricated columns for posts, complete with *plinth blocks* (fancy tops and bottoms). Most are hollow; are made out of wood, fiberglass, or plastic; and fit around a steel post that does all the heavy lifting. Have a welder fabricate the steel post with a square plate at the bottom for bolting to the footing and a saddle, or U-shaped bracket, at the top for the beam. Embed anchor bolts, also called *J-bolts,* in the footing concrete to align with the four holes in the bottom plate. Set the steel pole over the bolts, attach the nuts, and slide the column down over the pole or cut it in half and fit it around the pole.

Attaching Beams

The techniques for installing beams for an overhead are similar to those that you use for a deck (see Chapter 10). Follow these steps:

1. **Trim the posts to the same level and install a post cap or other post-to-beam connector at the top of each beam.**

2. **Trim the beams to length.**

3. **If you want to cut decorative shapes into the ends of beams, do so before lifting them into place.**

   To outline an S shape or other design for cutting, make a template out of plywood by cutting out the shape with a jig saw. Then trace the outline onto the end of the beam and cut it with a reciprocating saw or, for 2-by lumber, a jig saw with a long blade.

4. Lift the beams into place.

Set a sturdy stepladder next to each post and, from the ground, lift the end of each beam onto the stepladder. Then, using a second stepladder at one end, lift the end of the beam into the bracket on top of the post. Do the same at the other end. Measure the distance between posts at the base and, if necessary, make adjustments to the beam at the tops of the posts to duplicate the same dimension. To do so, tap the posts — not the beam — with a sledgehammer until the beam is aligned. If the span is too long for one beam, splice two beams end-to-end; make sure that the joint is over a post.

5. Secure the beams to the post brackets with bolts.

6. Install knee braces at the outside corner posts.

You may not need the braces if the posts are buried directly in the ground without footings. Cut 3-foot braces out of 2x6s, with a 45-degree angle at each end. Bolt them to the post and beam by using two half-inch-diameter machine bolts with malleable washers at each connection. To camouflage the braces, add decorative trim or cut a graceful curve into the braces before installing them, which makes them appear less obtrusive.

Connecting an Overhead to the House

To connect an overhead to the wall of a house (see Figure 22-4), attach a ledger the same way as you would for a deck (see Chapter 10). Unlike with a deck ledger, however, you don't have a floor joist inside the wall to bolt into; you must align the bolts for the overhead ledger with the studs inside the wall. You also don't need to install sheet-metal flashing behind the ledger if it's under the roof overhang where rain can't reach it. However, use caution when attaching a ledger to the house wall so that you don't damage any plumbing, wiring, or mechanical ducting. After installing the ledger, lay out and attach joist hangers the same way as for a deck ledger.

If the roof overhang is too low to place the overhead below it, attach the overhead to the roof itself. This practice is advised only if the overhead is an open, lightweight structure, such as an arbor or lattice-type shade structure. A solid roof presents drainage and leakage problems. To attach the frame of an open, lightweight overhead to the roof, lay a 2x6 across the roof where the overhead rafters are to attach. Then place short 2x6 blocks under the long 2x6 at each roof rafter location. These blocks raise the 2x6 and create gaps under it so that rainwater and melted snow aren't dammed.

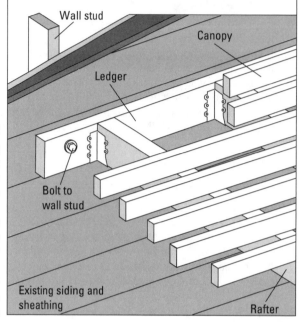

Figure 22-4: Connect an overhead to the house by bolting a ledger to the wall (as shown) or installing a 2x6 cleat to the roof.

Labels in figure: Wall stud · Canopy · Ledger · Bolt to wall stud · Existing siding and sheathing · Rafter

Installing Rafters

For techniques for laying out the rafter spacing on the beams and ledger (or roof cleat), see Chapter 10. If you want to cut a decorative design into the ends of the rafters, do so before installing them (see the section "Attaching Beams," earlier in this chapter). Then install them, attaching one end to the ledger by placing it in a joist hanger and resting the other end on a beam. Secure the rafter to the joist hanger with 16d galvanized or stainless-steel joist-hanger nails. To attach the rafter to a beam, toenail it (that is, drive nails into it at an angle) by using three 8d galvanized common nails. Reinforce the joint with a hurricane tie (a bracket for attaching rafters to beams or wall plates) or a rafter tie or by installing blocking between the rafters (see Chapter 10).

Completing the Canopy

The canopy, or screening, that goes on top of the rafters may be lattice, lath, 2x3s or 2x4s set on edge, fabric, shade cloth, woven reeds, clear plastic, or similar material. If the rafters provide sufficient shade or mass or the overhead is only a decorative structure with no practical function, you don't need to apply any screening.

If you install lattice panels, use a spray gun to apply stain, paint, or clear sealer before installing the panels. Plan the layout so that you stagger end joints and center all seams between panels over framing members. To cut panels, use a chalk box to snap a chalkline on the panels and then cut along the line by using a circular power saw. Attach the panels by using 6d galvanized box nails. Cover the outside edges of the panels with 1x3 or similar trim and nail a 2x6 around the perimeter of the structure, covering the edges of the panels and the 1x3 trim piece.

To install 2x3s or 2x4s, space them about the same distance apart as their depth ($2^1/_2$ to 3 inches for 2x3s; $3^1/_2$ to 4 inches for 2x4s). Because the ends of the 2-bys are free and prone to warping, install blocks of the same material along each rafter between the members. Drill two pilot holes in each block and nail the block to the rafter by using 8d galvanized box nails.

To install a conventional roof, cover the rafters with plywood or other structural panels, leaving $1/_8$-inch gaps between panels. Slope the rafters at a rate of 3 inches of vertical rise for every 12 inches of horizontal run. For a more attractive appearance from below, use 2x6 or 2x8 tongue-in-groove pine decking instead of panels or use plywood siding with the good side facing down. After installing the sheathing, cover it with 15-pound felt roofing underlayment and install composition shingles over it, following the instructions on the package.

To install clear plastic panels, such as acrylic or polycarbonate, drill holes through the panels along the edges that align over framing members. Space the holes every 6 to 12 inches, and drill them a quarter inch larger than the screw size. Place a rubber washer or similar gasket over each hole and a stainless steel fender washer (a washer with a small hole) on top of it, and drive a $1^1/_2$-inch stainless-steel screw down through the washer, gasket, and hole. Tighten the screw enough to hold the panel in place but not too snugly. This arrangement enables the panel to expand and contract without cracking at the screw locations.

Apply stain, sealer, or other finish to the structure as soon as you complete the canopy (see Chapter 13).

Chapter 23

Screens, Dividers, Planters, and Storage

Screens, planters, and storage compartments benefit a deck or patio in many ways, from defining spaces to controlling clutter. These basic amenities are quite easy to design and build. Most screens and planters are variations on a few basic components, and storage options run the gamut from recycling an old mailbox to constructing an elaborate shed that rivals any home. This chapter presents ideas and building techniques for several simple structures. As you plan your own projects, review the design principles in Part I, especially in Chapter 3, for more information about add-ons, options, and features.

Building Screens and Dividers

Screens and dividers, such as the ones shown in Figure 23-1, are really fences. Most are free-standing and supported by posts that are separate from the deck posts. The most important structural component is the posts. After you erect them (or if you're using the same posts that support the deck), you can fill in the spaces between them with any material you want, from elegant arrangements of lattice to solid barriers of vertical fencing, horizontal siding, or decorative panels. You can also build dividers out of masonry materials, such as brick, stone, or concrete block, to blend with patio pavings.

Figure 23-1:
Built-in screens and planters, as shown here, help make a deck or patio feel more like home.

Installing posts

To keep the posts in a straight row, stretch a string line about six inches above the ground, where the inside or outside edges of the posts align. At four- to six-foot intervals — depending on the strength and dimensions of your screening material — mark hole locations for the posts along the string line. Excavate 14-inch-diameter holes at least 24 inches deep, keeping the sides of the holes straight. Place four to six inches of one-inch drainrock in the bottom of each hole. Then follow these steps:

1. **Soak the bottom of each post in preservative (see Chapter 10).**

2. **Set the two end posts in the holes first.**

   Align each post with the string line and, using a level to bring it to a plumb (vertical) position, brace it in both directions with steel stakes or sharpened 2x4s driven diagonally into the ground and nailed to the sides of the post.

   To prevent the bottom of each post from kicking out of alignment, tap a 16d nail into the bottom before placing the post in the hole. The protruding nail locks into the rocks.

3. **After placing and bracing the two end posts, string a line between them near the top.**

4. **Place the other posts in their holes.**

   Align each post with both string lines, use a level to keep it plumb in the other direction, and brace it.

5. **After all the posts are in place, mix sacks of premixed concrete in a wheelbarrow and fill the holes.**

   Tamp the concrete with a stick to consolidate it and smooth the top by using a trowel, mounding the concrete around the post just above the ground.

Posts for deck screens

Screens on decks may be free-standing (with separate posts; see the preceding section) or built into the structural system of the deck. If you support the screen with the same posts that support the deck, extend the posts above the deck surface five to eight feet, depending how tall the screen must be. For decks more than three feet high, use 4x6s or 6x6s for the posts, to resist wind loads against the screen.

If you erect posts for a free-standing screen next to the deck, align the screen posts with the outside edge of the deck and bolt them to the deck's outside joist or header. The deck stabilizes the tall screen, and the screen posts add to the stability of the deck. For screens that are low or have an open design that lets the wind flow through, you may attach the posts to the side of the deck as you would railing posts. (See Chapter 12 for more information on installing railing posts.)

Attaching lattice panels

One of the easiest screening materials to install is prefabricated lattice panels, which measure four by eight feet. You can buy panels with frames attached, which are handy if you use full panels and none need to be cut. Simply set them between the posts and drive galvanized deck screws through the panel frames into the posts, or into stringers and cleats installed just for that reason (see Figure 23-2).

If you provide your own frame, one method is to install 2x4 rails between the posts to create a box frame and then cut pairs of 1x1 nailing strips to fit around the inside of the box. Attach the first strip of each pair to the insides of the box members, set the lattice panel in place against these strips, and lock it in place with the rest of the strips. You don't even need to nail the panel itself to anything; the nailing strips hold it in place.

Another method for installing panels is to cut grooves into the posts and 2x4 rails by using a router, eliminating the need for nailing strips. You can also buy posts and 2x4s with grooves already cut into them for this purpose. After installing the posts, install the bottom rail with the groove facing up. Slide the lattice panel into place between the posts until it rests in the groove of the bottom rail. After installing all the panels, install the top rail across the tops of the posts and lattice panels with its groove facing down.

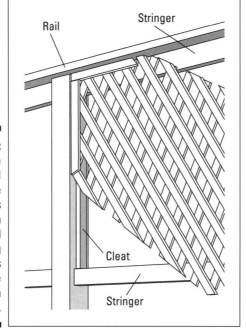

Figure 23-2: Cut lattice to size and install the panels between posts and rails, using trim pieces to hold the panels in place.

Creating slatted screens

If lattice panels are too predictable, you can customize your own screen by arranging 1x1s, 1x2s, 1x4s, 2x2s, and similar small-dimensioned lumber into a trellislike pattern. Vary the spacing between members — for example, place three vertical 1x1s close together, widen the next gap, place the next three 1x1s close together, and so on. Arrange horizontal and vertical members much as you'd weave various sizes of yarn into a fabric.

After you decide on a pattern, lay it out and assemble it in panels that fit between the posts. Secure all connections by using a 2d or 3d galvanized box nail to minimize warping and twisting. Install the panels between posts, using galvanized deck screws.

Building solid screens

For more privacy, build a "fort screen" by filling in the space between the posts with boards, panels, or siding materials. Vertical boards and solid panels require horizontal rails to support them. Follow these steps:

1. **To install the bottom rails, measure the distance between posts and cut 2x4s to fit.**

   Take all measurements at the same level, which you can mark on each post by using a hydrolevel or a series of readings with a long carpenter's level. After cutting each 2x4, set it between the posts, aligning it with the level marks on the posts so that it's "on edge" (the narrow edges are on the top and bottom) rather than flat (the narrow edges are on the sides), because 2x4s sag if they span more than three feet when laid flat.

2. **Drill a pair of pilot holes at an angle through the post and into the 2x4s at each end and then drive 16d galvanized twist nails through the holes into the 2x4s.**

   Note that this technique is the reverse of toenailing the rails into the posts, which tends to split the rails.

3. **To install the top rail, trim the tops of the posts level, lay a long 2x4 over them (cutting it to length so that both ends align over posts), and nail it to the posts by using 16d galvanized twist nails.**

   Drill pilot holes for the nails at the ends of the 2x4. For a long screen, butt two or more long 2x4s together.

4. **To provide a nailing surface for the fence boards, attach 1x2 cleats to the bottom of the top rail, between the posts, so that the inside edge of the cleat aligns with the inside edge of the bottom rail below it.**

5. **After installing top and bottom rails, attach vertical siding boards to them.**

   Hold each board against the bottom rail and snug it up against the top rail. Secure the boards by using three 8d galvanized box nails or galvanized deck screws at the top and bottom.

Decorative options

Whether your screen is open latticework or a solid fence, you can dress it up to add some style to your yard. Buy *finials* (decorative balls) and attach them to the tops of the posts. If the screen is made of lattice panels, embellish the frame around them by installing curved trim at the corners or cutting pieces of 1x6 into a curved shape and attaching the pieces at the tops and bottoms of the panels.

Extend the posts 12 to 18 inches above the top of the screen and attach a narrow arbor to them. To do so, attach short crosspieces of 2x4 or 2x6 to the tops of the posts. Attach two long 2x4s across them, on edge, running parallel with the screen. Then top the long 2x4s with short 2x2s, spaced four to eight inches apart. For added flair, cut the ends of each piece into a decorative shape, such as an S-curve or a simple 45-degree angle, before installing it.

An option for dressing up a solid screen is to use the solid fencing material for the first 5 feet and then top it with a 16- to 24-inch-tall lattice screen. The variation in materials reduces the wall-like feeling of a fence, and you can soften it even more by trailing vines through the lattice.

Building Wooden Planters

Although attractive planters made out of wood, fiberglass, acrylics, ceramics, metal, and other materials are readily available at garden centers and other outlets, building wooden planters of your own has some advantages: You can design planters to match the dimensions and details of your deck; you can build larger planters than are available for sale; and you can incorporate the planters into the deck structure itself as built-ins.

Keep in mind that large planters are heavy. A planter two feet high, two feet wide, and six feet long holds almost a ton of moist soil — too heavy for a deck without reinforcement (see Chapter 5). If possible, place such planters within openings in the deck and support them on a concrete or gravel bed on the ground. Another option for large planters is to build a wooden enclosure with a shallow shelf and place container plants on the shelf, leaving most of the wooden planter empty.

Building the box

Wooden planters are variations on a box with four sides and a bottom (see Figure 23-3). Construct planters out of redwood, cedar, or preservative-treated wood (including plywood) and use corrosion-resistant screws or bolts. Because a box full of moist soil exerts considerable pressure against the sides, reinforce the corners by bolting the side boards to vertical 4x4s that you place inside the corners (by lapping the alternating boards at each corner, log-cabin fashion). Or you can attach a band of 2x4s or other trim boards around the top of the box and bolt them together at the corners. Don't forget drainage holes in the bottom; cover them with screening to prevent soil loss.

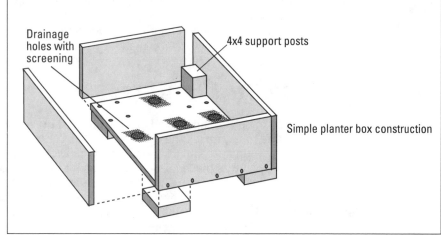

Drainage holes with screening

4x4 support posts

Simple planter box construction

Figure 23-3: A wooden planter is a variation on a simple box.

Decorating the box

The beauty of a planter is in the details (and, of course, the plants). Start with a frame around the top of the planter by using 2x6s or 2x8s laid flat and mitered at the corners. To give them adequate support, attach a band of 2x4s around the outer edge of the box, flush with the top, and set the frame on them. Overlap the inside edges of the box by half an inch or so and attach the frame to the box by driving screws up into it, at an angle, from inside the box.

To embellish the box further, attach 1x2s or other small-dimensioned strips to the sides in a pattern that blends with your deck. These strips can be vertical pickets, spaced approximately one inch apart, that reflect the railing design; simple Xs to create a crisscross design; or horizontal 2x2s around the top and bottom to emphasize serene, horizontal lines. Many details are possible, including finials at the corners and ceramic medallions placed in the sides.

Preserving the box

To increase the longevity of wooden planters, treat all lumber with a water-repellent preservative. In addition, drill $5/8$-inch-diameter holes in the bottom of the planter for drainage and fabricate a liner out of heavy plastic, roofing felt, or sheet metal. Or obtain prefabricated liners and adapt the planter dimensions to them.

To keep deck boards from rotting, move portable planters to different parts of the deck periodically or build the planters into the deck so that the drain holes drain directly to the ground and not onto decking boards.

Building Masonry Planters

Many patios are built on sloping ground and require a short retaining wall along the uphill side to hold back the hill. Such walls offer marvelous opportunities for planting perennials and annuals to cascade down over the wall. Free-standing planters placed around the edge of the patio or within the patio to act as dividers are equally impressive additions to your patio. Brick, stone, and concrete blocks covered with a veneer are all attractive materials for these planters. You can incorporate them into benches or low walls for even greater effect (see Chapter 21).

To build a masonry planter, use the same techniques that I describe for building benches in Chapter 21. Planters should have concrete bases with openings in the center for drainage directly into the soil. An easy way to provide such drainage is to set short lengths of plastic pipe, such as two-inch-diameter PVC (plastic) pipe, vertically within the planter area before pouring concrete for the footing. Simply insert them into the gravel base and then trim the tops flush with the finished concrete surface. You can also build a box form the same size as the interior dimensions of the planter and pour concrete around it — something like a donut with a hole in the middle — and then lay the brick, stone, or concrete blocks on the reinforced concrete ring (see Figure 23-4).

After you finish setting the stones, bricks, or blocks and the mortar cures, *parge,* or coat, the inside of the planter with a cementlike coating that you would normally use for sealing basements, which you can obtain from a masonry supplier or home center. If you don't apply this waterproofing membrane, moisture from the soil oozes through the masonry walls and promotes grunge. You don't want that to happen.

Providing Storage

Outdoor storage is a fascinating challenge. Not only must stuff stay hidden and orderly, but the storage compartments must also resist rain, insects, and sunlight. Solutions range from pegs on a wall to custom-built sheds and cabinets. But before you take out your tools, investigate some ready-made storage options.

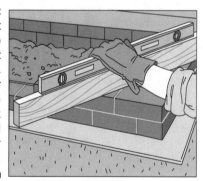

Figure 23-4:
Construct patio planters out of brick, stones, or concrete block covered with similar materials.

First, consider garden products intended for storing hoses, rakes, shovels, and other equipment, such as attractive containers for storing coiled hoses and free-standing racks. For concealed storage, consider weatherproof storage boxes and containers. Some are made for backyard use, but don't overlook truck boxes, rooftop carriers, RV stowaways, and containers for camping gear. Manufacturers are constantly improving the design and utility of these products, many of which are available only through mail-order catalogs. Begin your search at the library, browsing through specialty magazines.

Also look at novel uses for containers that aren't intended for outdoor storage. Wine and whiskey barrels, cut in half, are convenient for holding coiled hoses. Rural mailboxes are perfect for keeping trowels, pruning shears, and similar small items. With some imagination and fresh paint, you can convert many such objects into attractive storage containers.

Prefab sheds and outdoor cabinets offer another choice. Plans for a complete shed are beyond the scope of this book, but most homeowners are capable of assembling a prefabricated kit or even devising their own basic design. Just make sure that you weatherproof the structure with paint, roofing materials, and a raised floor. A lean-to tucked under the roof eave of the house is a fairly simple structure to build. Use the patio surface for the floor or pour a small concrete slab. Then attach framing to the side of the house and cover it with exterior-grade plywood. You can build a sloped roof and cover it with shingles or extend the walls up to a low-hanging roof eave. Install screened vents at the top and bottom of the shed to prevent mildew. Attach hinged doors, paint the exterior, install some simple shelves — the shed's ready for storage.

Go hog wild

Storage containers needn't be strictly utilitarian — faceless boxes that command attention but fail to delight. Give them some pizzazz. Elegance and whimsy come into play in this area. Much as you can with birdhouses, you can decorate the outside of a plain cabinet with painted stars, moons, flowers, animals, flowerpots, fake windows, or other inventions. You can also create an entire structure to resemble a specific building, from a backwoods outhouse to the Taj Mahal. If your yard is formal and elegant, buy a Classical column, cut it in half lengthwise, and mount the halves on either side of a shed door. Add some molded trim pieces, such as corbels, pediments, and pilasters (fancy stuff, readily available in plastic copies of Classical architectural forms from home centers). All these embellishments start with a basic box that you can construct from inexpensive waferboard or other construction panels.

Stowing below deck

The area beneath a deck offers lots of storage options (see Figure 23-5). Here are just a couple of ideas:

✔ To utilize the area below a deck for storing such items as firewood, pipes, lumber, bricks, roof gutters, a boat, and other bulky items, pour a concrete slab or lay pressure-treated 4x4s across concrete blocks to elevate these items above the ground.

✔ To protect objects from moisture (decks not being waterproof, after all), suspend corrugated roofing panels or similar lightweight membranes from the deck joists or make storage tubes out of large-diameter PVC pipes (4- to 12-inch), which are available from irrigation-supply outlets. Glue a cap onto one end of each pipe, stack the tubes under the deck, slide materials into them, and slip caps on the open ends for watertight removable covers. (Drill a small hole in the cap to release air pressure.)

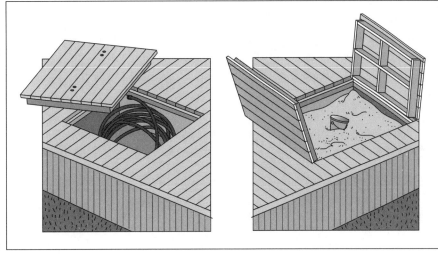

Figure 23-5:
The area under a deck offers useful storage space, as long as you provide protection from the elements.

Chapter 24

Building Barbecues and Fireplaces

For most people, outdoor living means outdoor cooking. Preparing food over an open flame appeals to ancient instincts and the latest grilling craze alike. Fire also warms you on chilly nights, extending the time that you can enjoy your deck or patio. You have several options for taming flames: Set up a cooking center around a portable gas grill, construct a permanent barbecue, build a fire pit, or build a traditional fireplace for outdoor use. You can go "whole hog" with each option, but even the most elaborate fantasies begin with the basics that I present in this chapter. For overall planning of a grill, barbecue, or fire pit, review Chapter 3's information on add-ons and cooking.

Always locate a grill or fire pit downwind from your house, your neighbor's house, and the place where cooks are most likely to stand. Above all else, make sure that you consult with your building department about requirements for a permanent barbecue, fire pit, or fireplace.

Enclosing a Portable Gas Grill

You can leave the gas grill on its stand and simply surround it with an enclosure or remove the grill from the stand and build it into a permanent base. Follow all manufacturer's instructions, including required clearances from combustible materials.

For patios, build an enclosure or base out of brick, stone, or four-inch-wide concrete blocks faced with tile, stucco, or stone. (For masonry techniques, see Chapters 21 and 23.) Build walls 32 to 34 inches high and create an alcove to tuck the grill into. Top the rest of the unit with a countertop made of poured concrete, natural stone, or $1^1/_4$-inch-thick pressure-treated plywood covered with tile backer board and tile.

Such a cooking center is too massive for decks, so think light. For a light-weight, noncombustible base, make a frame out of steel studs used for commercial construction. Follow these steps:

1. **Cut the studs by using tin snips or aviation shears and connect them by using sheet metal screws.**

2. **Sheathe (or sheet) the frame with tile backer board and cover it with tile, stucco, or faux stone.**

3. **Fabricate a countertop (with a cutout opening for the grill) by installing tile backer board and covering it with tile or dimensioned stone.**

   Use thinset adhesive for adhering the tile or stone. Avoid laminate countertops and wood undersurfaces, which deteriorate from exposure to the weather.

4. **After grouting the joints, apply a tile sealer, following instructions on the label.**

To complete the cooking center, you can adapt kitchen cabinets for outdoor use. Avoid cabinets constructed out of particleboard, which absorbs moisture easily, or those covered with laminates. Old plywood cabinets, especially with painted finishes, work well. Repaint all surfaces, inside and out. First, wash them with *trisodium phosphate* (TSP) or a similar cleaning product. Then roughen the surfaces by using sandpaper, vacuum the surfaces, and wipe them with a tack cloth to remove all dust. Prime the cabinets with a white-pigmented shellac. After the shellac dries, use a sprayer or foam roller to apply a finish coat of high-quality, oil-based exterior enamel. After the enamel dries, sand the cabinets lightly and remove dust with a tack cloth. Then apply a second coat of enamel.

Building a Brick Barbecue

The key components of a brick barbecue (shown in Figure 24-1) are not bricks, but rather the grill (for cooking), the grate (for the fire), and the ashtray or shelf (for catching ashes). The brickwork merely supports these working parts and provides an enclosure for the fire. The size and shape of the brick box, therefore, aren't critical, except that they must accommodate the dimensions of the metal grill and grate and support the grill at a convenient height for cooking. The grill and grate (and ashtray, if the brickwork isn't high enough for an ash shelf) are available at home centers, hardware stores, or masonry specialty suppliers. You can also buy a winch mechanism for raising and lowering the grill to control the heat. As for the optimum height for cooking, 30 to 34 inches works for most people. Place the grate four to six inches below the grill, and place the ashtray or shelf approximately four inches below that.

Build the barbecue on a concrete slab or reinforced patio surface. You don't need to use firebricks; Type SW or SX are adequate. (See Chapter 19 for information on brick types.) Follow these steps:

1. **First, lay out a "dry run" of the first course of bricks.**

   Arrange the bricks in a U shape into which the grill fits. Leave a ³/₈-inch gap between adjacent bricks for the mortar joints. Arrange bricks so that the sides and back are two, three, or more bricks wide, depending on how thick you want the walls and whether you want the barbecue to be symmetrical. (You may want one side of the grill wide enough to serve as a countertop or shelf.)

   After arranging the bricks, trace the outline onto the concrete base and make a sketch of your brick pattern. Then, before removing the bricks, fill in the center cavity of the U shape to make sure that the bricks fit for the base. The base may be only one course if you install a raised ashtray or seven courses high if the bricks themselves serve as an ash shelf.

   After dry-fitting the bricks, remove them. Now you're ready to lay the first course.

2. **Throw down a one-inch-thick layer of mortar for two bricks at the first corner and squish the corner brick into place.**

3. **Do the same thing at the second corner.**

4. **Stretch a string line between the two bricks, along the outer edge of the base, by tying each end to a brick and setting those bricks on the corner bricks.**

5. **Complete the first row of bricks, aligning the outside edges along the string line.**

   See Chapter 19 for bricklaying techniques.

6. **Finish the base, one brick at a time, by completing three of the sides and filling in the area between them.**

7. **Lay the second course of bricks over the first, setting the bricks on a one-inch thick mortar bed and staggering joints by turning the corner bricks 90 degrees (so that the bricks overlap at the corners).**

   Before you set the bricks into the mortar, embed ties (either corrugated wall ties or wire Z-ties) into the mortar to lock the two outer rows of bricks together.

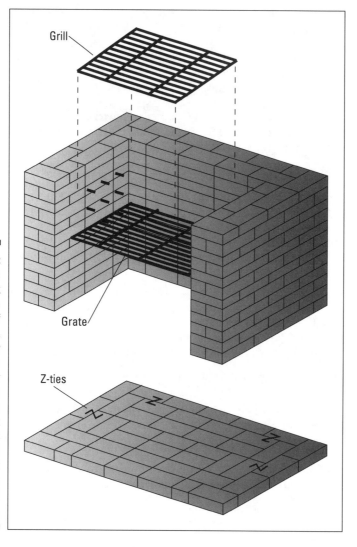

Figure 24-1:
The basic brick barbecue consists of a base, which may be high enough for an ash shelf, and a firebox enclosed by U-shaped walls that support a grill and grate.

8. **Lay the third course, using the same pattern as the first course. Continue building up the courses, alternating the brick patterns and embedding ties between every other course.**

   Guide your work by using string lines stretched between corners and a level laid over the bricks and held against the sides.

9. **After completing the seventh course, which is the level of the ash shelf, proceed with the U-shaped configuration.**

   If you've been using this shape since the second course, embed six metal pins in the mortar bed for the eighth course — three on each side of the firebox — to support the ashtray.

10. **As you build courses for the U-shaped firebox, embed pins in the mortar bed of the 10th and the 13th courses to support the grate and grill.**

    Use 7-inch lengths of $^3/_8$-inch rebar for the pins, spacing 3 on each side of the firebox. The pins should protrude three inches into the firebox opening. (You can also add the pins later by drilling into the brick with a masonry bit and setting the pins in expansive cement.)

11. **After you finish the brickwork, smooth the joints with a jointing tool.**

12. **After the mortar sets, clean off the surfaces by using a stiff brush, moisten the brickwork, and cover the barbecue with a plastic tent (plastic sheeting held away from the bricks by sticks) for five days so that the mortar can cure.**

Building a Fire Pit

Where allowed, a fire pit adds primitive ambiance to a patio. In its simplest form, a fire pit is a hole in the patio, lined by sand and surrounded by noncombustible materials for at least 20 feet. (Check local requirements.)

One refinement of this design is to place the pit inside a ring that's large enough to provide safe seating around the edge. (Make the seating ring a minimum of 12 feet in diameter, with the fire pit in the center.) Another refinement is to surround the fire itself with a low wall of masonry or stone, 8 to 12 inches high. This circular wall contains the fire and enables you to place a grill over it. It also keeps the fire pit tidy. A variation on this wall is a steel ring, or cylinder, which you can have made at a metal fabricating shop. Have it made from $^1/_8$-inch thick steel, 12 inches wide and rolled into a loop. You also need eight metal stakes to drive into the ground around it to hold it in place. You can then backfill the space around the ring with compacted gravel and continue the patio surface up to the edge or step the patio surface down to the lower edge of the ring for a seating pit.

Because of the clearance requirements for fire pits, they usually occupy the center area of the patio and become prominent focal points (see Figure 24-2). When not in use, they can be messy and unattractive. They work best, therefore, in rustic or very casual settings. A better alternative for stylish settings is a fireplace tucked into a corner of the patio.

Figure 24-2:
The simplicity of a fire pit makes it appealing in large patios with wide-open spaces.

Fireplace Basics

Fireplaces contain flames and direct the radiant heat more efficiently than an open fire does. They may also be located along the edge of a patio, thus saving space.

Unless you're experienced in masonry construction, however, or have training in designing a fireplace, you should not try to build one on your own. Codes governing fireplaces are very strict, and you must calculate fireplace dimensions carefully to ensure correct burning. Furthermore, chimneys must be high enough to create sufficient draft, which for most fireplaces is 10 to 12 feet, making them prohibitively tall near property lines — unless you make certain modifications.

If you want a fireplace, consider having a local craftsman build a brick, stone, or stucco-covered unit that blends into your patio design. Because the fireplace has a chimney, you can place the fireplace under a canopy or roof overhang, where the heat and ambiance create a cozy retreat even on drizzly nights.

Chapter 25

Providing Lighting and Irrigation

. . . .

In This Chapter

▶ Figuring out a lighting scheme

▶ Installing low-voltage lighting

▶ Extending your house wiring

▶ Irrigating deck and patio plants

. . . .

*T*wo indispensable improvements for any deck or patio are lights for the nights and showers for the flowers. Don't overlook these essential amenities or try to get by with a minimal treatment. Both improvements add style and convenience to outdoor living with far greater effect than their modest costs may suggest. Starter kits and modular components make both amenities excellent do-it-yourself projects.

Let There Be Light

If you think that lighting your deck or patio means putting up a few flood-lights, you're in the dark about outdoor design. Today's decks and patios bring high fashion into their lighting schemes (see Figure 25-1). Thanks to affordable, low-voltage outdoor lighting, this trend doesn't mean high expense, but it does mean sensible, strategic use of many different light fixtures — most of them simple in design — rather than one or two glaring floodlights.

Use the following guidelines to help you plan your lighting:

✔ **Light your yard, not the neighborhood.** Avoid lights that shine onto your neighbors' property. In fact, try to place all lights so that nobody can see the light bulb — only the results. You can't enjoy even the most exquisite patio or deck with a light glaring into your eyes.

✔ **Light up your lifestyle.** Identify your lighting needs. Some lighting is for traffic and movement; some is for activities, such as cooking or eating; some is to create moods, or ambiance; and some is for decoration.

Figure 25-1:
These clamshell lights not only add light, they add style.

✔ **Hide ugly fixtures.** Many outdoor lighting fixtures are works of art and should be on display, but you don't need to rely completely on these money-eaters. Use lots of plain, ordinary fixtures; just hide them.

✔ **Step into the light.** Light all stairs and traffic paths. To light stairs, set a fixture close enough to illuminate all the steps or install an in-wall fixture into the riser of each step. To light traffic paths, place lights high and direct them straight down or place several lights close to the ground to illuminate areas along the path, spilling light onto the pathway.

✔ **Light for work.** Use higher-intensity lighting for task areas, such as a cooking center or game area. Just as for paths, place several lights in trees or overhead structures and aim them straight down. Don't illuminate eating areas with harsh lighting. Use low-intensity lights or, if necessary, candles.

✔ **Trip the light fantastic.** Create special lighting effects. Place two or three lights, aimed downward, high in a tree to create interesting shadows from branches and leaves. Light other trees or plants along walls from below, using *well lights* set into the ground or low floodlights. Conceal the light source behind plants or rocks.

✔ **Avoid overlighting.** You don't need to illuminate the entire outdoor landscape or light every feature or point of use with its own light. Plan light schemes so that pools of light spill over into other areas. Instead of lining a path with lights that shine directly onto it, for example, light the garden areas along one side of the path enough to illuminate the path, too.

✔ **Avoid underlighting.** A common mistake is to illuminate a deck or patio beautifully but ignore the rest of the yard. Rather than surround your deck with darkness, create variety and security by spotlighting a few trees and bathing distant flower beds in soft light.

Installing Low-Voltage Lighting

Low-voltage lighting systems consist of light fixtures, cable (or wire), and a transformer, which you plug into a standard 120-volt receptacle (see Figure 25-2). Because the wire between the transformer and light fixtures carries low-voltage current, you don't need to bury it or enclose it in a conduit (although you may want to conceal it). Simply run it along the ground, up tree trunks, under deck railings, or wherever needed, securing it by using staples or clips. Avoid suspending wires overhead.

Figure 25-2:
A transformer converts house voltage to low-voltage DC current. You can connect many different types of light fixtures to the system.

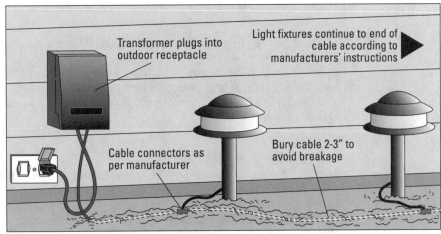

Transformer plugs into outdoor receptacle

Light fixtures continue to end of cable according to manufacturers' instructions

Cable connectors as per manufacturer

Bury cable 2-3" to avoid breakage

Low-voltage fixtures produce a fairly low level of light (three to five *foot-candles,* in the lingo), which is desirable for most outdoor lighting needs. Adequate lighting, however, requires many fixtures — for example, eight to ten for an average deck; two to three for a short run of stairs; three per tree for effective downlighting; and one for every six to eight feet of pathway.

Because transformers have a limit to the number of fixtures they can power and the distance the wire can run, divide the lighting load into several circuits of six to ten lights each (depending on the size of bulbs and transformer — consult the manufacturers' specifications). No run should be longer than 100 feet.

To install the system, follow these steps:

1. **Start by mounting the transformers.**

   Mount each transformer next to an electrical outlet, which must have *ground-fault circuit-interrupter* (GFCI) protection (unless it's indoors, away from a concrete floor or water faucet). Transformers have weatherproof cases that enable you to locate them outdoors, but try to find a protected place. Although your choice of locations is limited by available outlets, locate each transformer as close to the lights it powers as possible. A central location, where you can place all the transformers, is ideal because then you can change settings for the whole system easily.

2. **Install the lights.**

   Some lights have plastic or metal stakes for support, which you simply drive into the ground. Some have brackets that you can attach to posts, branches, walls, and other structures. Set well lights into holes in the ground. (Don't backfill yet.)

   Recessed fixtures require cutting a hole into the stair riser, post, railing, or other surface in which you place each one. These in-wall lights come in several sizes, but the most versatile fit into the same-sized opening as a standard light switch box, two inches by four inches. If you install recessed lights in masonry, install the boxes and run wire as you build the wall or steps.

3. **Run the cable.**

   After installing all the light fixtures, run the cable. Make sure that you use cable that's compatible with the transformer and light fixtures. Attach one end to the terminals on the transformer. Then run it to the nearest light fixture, fastening it or burying it as necessary. Most fixtures have a clamp — something like a clamshell — that you lay the cable into and close tightly over the cable. The clamp has metal prongs that penetrate the insulation of the cable to make contact with the copper core. You don't need to strip or cut the cable. Simply enclose it in the clamp and continue running it to the next fixtures.

4. **After hooking up all the lights, plug in the transformer, turn it on manually to test the system, and set the timer.**

Extending House Wiring

Some lighting, especially near high-traffic areas by the back door and at a cooking center or sport court, requires fixtures powered by 120-volt house current. Because a 120-volt circuit has the capacity for many more fixtures than a low-voltage circuit, you may need only one circuit for all your outdoor lighting needs. Place a few lights on at least one additional circuit, however, so that all the lights don't go out at once if a circuit breaker trips.

The easy option

The simplest way to bring electricity outdoors is to place a fixture or outlet on the exterior side of a house wall near an electrical outlet on the interior side. The following list tells you how to install these items:

- ✔ For a new outlet, run nonmetallic cable (known by the trade name Romex) from the existing outlet to a new fixture box on the exterior wall. Install a ground-fault circuit-interrupter (GFCI) receptacle in the new box and connect the wiring to the existing wires in the interior box (making sure that the circuit is turned off first).

- ✔ For a new light, run nonmetallic cable from the exiting outlet to a new switch box and then into a fixture box on the exterior wall. Install the light fixture, wire in a switch at the switch box, and connect the cable to the circuit wiring at the existing outlet.

Adding an outlet or light fixture to an existing general-purpose circuit is generally acceptable, as long as you tap into the circuit at a junction box or receptacle box. Tapping into the circuit at a light switch or light fixture is not acceptable, however, unless the box functions as a junction box for other circuit wiring.

Wiring the yard

If an outdoor light fixture already exists, you can extend the wiring to new locations for additional lights. Because the wiring for such an extension is exposed, you must protect the wires or cable with metal conduit. All connectors for the conduit must be liquid-tight (waterproof).

Another way to extend electrical wiring outdoors is to run a new circuit from the service panel. Use nonmetallic cable for runs inside the house (as long as they're concealed within walls or a crawlspace) and metal conduit wherever wiring is exposed outdoors. If you bury the wiring, enclose it in rigid metal conduit (buried at least 12 inches) or plastic conduit (buried at least 18 inches) or use Type UF cable for direct burial (buried at least 12 inches and covered by boards). Enclose the exposed wiring in rigid-metal conduit where it emerges from the ground and terminate it in a liquid-tight electrical box attached to a post or other support or an outdoor light fixture. If the fixture is free-standing, anchor the base in a concrete block that you bury and fill with concrete.

Don't undertake a wiring project yourself (except low-voltage lights) unless you have experience with electrical wiring and have obtained the necessary permit.

Irrigating Deck and Patio Plants

No matter how enjoyable they may be, watering plants around your deck or patio is a tedious chore and, if you go on vacations, a nightmare. Container plants are certainly convenient and beautiful, but the soil dries out quickly and requires frequent watering. Happily, these problems have an easy solution — *drip irrigation*. A complete system, especially with an automatic timer, is not cheap, but your savings in water consumption, dead plant replacement, and hassles should offset the cost (see Figure 25-3).

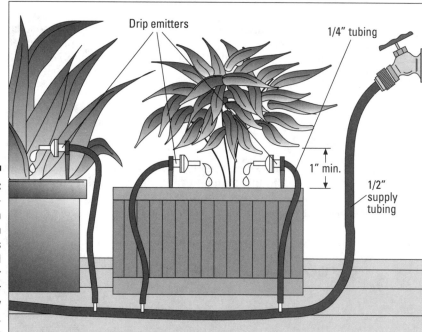

Figure 25-3:
A micro-irrigation system eliminates the need to water container plants by hand.

Planning a system

A drip-irrigation system is a network of tubing that delivers water to emitters, microsprinklers, or drip hoses that you place at the bases of individual plants or clusters of plants. A few "working parts" regulate the flow of water, including a filter, pressure regulator, backflow preventer, and valves. An optional (and expensive) component, which is really the beauty of the whole system, is an automatic controller that includes a timer and valve controls; after you dial or punch in the settings, the timer turns the water on and off automatically. Your only activity is periodic maintenance of the system. You can also add a device for introducing liquid fertilizer into the water stream at predetermined times and amounts.

Most manufacturers provide excellent step-by-step instructions for installing their systems. Before you begin planning yours, visit a home center or irrigation supplier and pick up product specifications and instructions.

Basic components of a drip system

The basic components of a drip system include the following items:

- ✔ A filter (to keep the tubing free of minute debris that can clog the drip holes)
- ✔ A pressure regulator (to keep the water pressure in the system constant for optimum performance)
- ✔ A backflow preventer (a simple device, usually a vacuum breaker, that prevents water in the drip system from backing up into the public water supply)
- ✔ Valves, manual or electronic (to control water flow to different circuits)
- ✔ An automatic controller (includes valve controllers and a timer)
- ✔ Tubing
- ✔ Emitters, microsprinklers, and a drip hose

You can buy components individually or in kits. Kits are less expensive than the same parts bought individually but may include components that you don't need. The major components, such as the pressure regulator and filter, may also be too small if you intend to expand your system beyond the kit size. For a small deck or patio, however, a kit is probably the best choice.

Your main planning task is to decide what type of drip emitter or microsprinkler to use at each plant. These devices are calibrated for different flow rates, such as half a gallon per hour, so that each plant receives an individualized amount of water. Manufacturers provide recommendations for the size and number of emitters to use for certain plants. Most container plants require one emitter rated at a half, one, or two gallons per hour (GPH), depending on size. Some plants, such as ferns or bromiliads, may also require *misters* (devices that create mist) to keep the leaves moist.

To facilitate planning, draw a schematic of all the containers and write down the size of emitter for each one. Next, draw a tubing circuit to connect the emitters. It doesn't need to be a continuous circuit; you can run a main supply line and connect branches to it, which enables you to use smaller-diameter tubing that's easier to conceal. Large patios or decks may require several circuits. Check the manufacturer's specifications for the maximum gallonage per circuit (the total GPH ratings of all emitters), which is typically 150. Also check for the maximum length of runs for the two common sizes of tubing, quarter- and half-inch. Typically, a single circuit should have no more than 50 feet of quarter-inch tubing, with no branch tube exceeding 25 feet. For small installations you can probably use quarter-inch throughout. For larger circuits, use half-inch tubing for the supply line (no more than 200 feet altogether) and quarter-inch branches.

Plan your layout so that all the circuits originate at the water faucet you intend to use.

Installing drip irrigation

Follow these steps to install your drip-irrigation system:

1. **Start by unrolling the tubing and setting it in the sun for half an hour.**

2. **Attach the components to the water faucet in the order that the manufacturer recommends.**

   Typically, the order is backflow preventer, timer (for single-circuit setups), filter, pressure regulator, and line connector.

3. **For multiple-circuit systems operated by automatic valves, connect each valve (which includes a vacuum breaker) directly to the water supply line.**

4. **Attach a filter, pressure regulator, and line connector to each valve.**

   Run concealed wiring from each valve to the main controller, which you can mount anywhere.

5. **Attach the main supply tubing (quarter- or half-inch) to the working parts and run it over, under, around, and through the patio or deck area, as necessary.**

   Secure the tubing with clamps.

6. **Attach the quarter-inch branch lines to the supply line, using *tee-connectors* for a quarter-inch supply line or *plunge connectors* for a half-inch supply line.**

   To connect plunge connectors to half-inch tubing, use a hole punch to make a hole and push the quarter-inch fitting into the hole until the barb at the end of the fitting is completely inside the half-inch tubing. Use a straight fitting for single branch lines and a tee-fitting to attach two branch lines at the same connection.

   Run the tubing for each branch line and secure it with clamps. Avoid kinking the tubing.

7. **Attach emitters to the branch lines at each plant or cluster of plants.**

   Use in-line emitters if the branch continues to an adjacent plant and end-line emitters where branch lines terminate. Support each emitter approximately one inch above the soil, using stakes provided by the manufacturer.

8. **After you connect all of the emitters and tubing, turn on the system for a few minutes to flush it out and then close off the end of the supply line by using a cap or clamp.**

9. **Turn on the system to test it for leaks.**

   Cap leaks with hole plugs and reconnect leaky connections.

10. **Finally, if the system is on an automatic controller, set the timing adjustments to determine the watering cycle.**

Part V
The Part of Tens

The 5th Wave   By Rich Tennant

"Well, that's the last soapstone patio I'll ever put in."

In this part . . .

The *...For Dummies* books have this strange section called "The Part of Tens." These pages virtually wrote themselves as I thought about ten answers to each of three intriguing questions people often ask: What are some interesting alternatives for deck and patio surfaces? What are some quick and simple ideas for dressing up any deck or patio? And how can I save money?

Chapter 26

Ten Unique Surfaces

*Y*ou can build most decks and patios from the materials that I present in this book, but if you're looking for something unusual, simpler, or more exotic, this chapter offers ten ideas for other materials that you may want to consider.

Decking Your Deck

Wooden deck surfaces, such as redwood 2x6s or preservative-treated $5/4$-inch decking, are what most people imagine when they think of a deck. A few other materials offer advantages over a wooden surface in certain situations. Check out the following sections.

Elastomeric membrane

Some decks, especially balconies and rooftop decks, function as roofs as well as decks. Such decks must be waterproof to keep rain and snow out of downstairs areas. They may still have wooden *duck boards* (portable sections of decking) for the finished surface, but you install these over the waterproof material. Until recently, built-up roofing, also referred to as *tar-and-gravel roofing*, was the preferred covering for flat roofs intended for use as decks. This type of material, however, wasn't suitable for walking on, and you needed to replace it every 10 to 15 years, which meant first removing any wooden decking that you laid over it.

Today, dozens of products are available for use in rooftop decks. Not only do they provide a waterproof covering, but you can also walk on them, and they're engineered to last for decades. Many come in colors that blend into landscape designs. Some you apply the same way as you do paint and require a stable underlayment. Others are membranes that you roll out in sections that you can seam together by using heat, a bonding agent, or other means. They all require solid sheathing, such as plywood, for the subsurface. The generic term for many of these products is *elastomeric membrane,* although this term is specific to certain formulations and may not apply to all products. To find dealers who carry these products, look for suppliers who specialize in waterproofing materials, roofing coatings, or even boat and marine products.

Tile

If wood feels too temporary or lacks the elegance that you seek for your deck, consider covering it with tile or cut stone, such as slate. You must slope the deck and possibly reinforce it to take the additional weight, but with modern "backer boards" to use for the underlayment, installing thin tile or stone veneers on a deck is entirely possible. You need to realize, however, that, even though the tile itself is impervious to moisture, the grout joints aren't. You must, therefore, completely waterproof the subsurface or moisture can seep into the wooden framing system, causing the deck to rot. To do so, install lightweight backer boards over $3/4$-inch thick plywood and seal all joints and screw heads with a sealant before installing the tile.

Carpet

Some carpeting is designed for outdoor use, as shown in Figure 26-1. Boats and miniature-golf courses are just two examples of its use. Visit your local carpet supplier and investigate the many style and color options available.

As with tile, carpet requires a waterproof substrate over the wooden sheathing, and you must slope the deck away from the house at a quarter inch per foot. Use preservative-treated plywood for the sheathing and cover it with a waterproofing compound, according to the carpet manufacturer's recommendations, before you lay down the carpet.

To install the carpet, roll it out over the deck and rough cut it around the perimeter so that it overhangs the edge by half an inch or so. Then, without moving it, fold one half over on the other, exposing the substrate. Spread the adhesive recommended for the carpet, according to the manufacturer's directions, onto the substrate. Then return the folded section of carpet, carefully smoothing it out from the center with a flooring roller (which you also use for vinyl flooring) as you go along. Do the same for the other half. Then, using the flooring roller again, smooth out the carpet. Trim the edges.

Figure 26-1:
This outdoor carpet looks good and feels nice under bare feet.

Patios without Paving

Although *patio* implies a solid surface, you don't necessarily need to install paving or pour a concrete slab to create the floor for an interesting outdoor room. Following are three nonpaving options — inexpensive and easy to install — that may work for you.

Gravel

First you have your basic gravel, and then you have . . . well, *gravel.* Some gravel, such as *pea gravel,* has rounded edges and the sound and feel of loose pebbles. Although this type looks attractive, drains quickly, and stays clean (see Figure 26-2), it doesn't compact into a tight mass. Pea gravel constantly moves underfoot. As a patio surface, gravel lacks the stability of other materials, but it has a satisfying "crunchy" texture that's almost luxurious. It makes you slow down. To install a gravel patio, prepare a base of compacted crushed stone (see Chapter 16). Then spread one to two inches of pea gravel over it.

Figure 26-2:
A gravel patio has a primitive attraction that makes you slow down and linger.

Crushed stone

Okay, this stuff is still gravel, but it *sounds* more exotic and has a much different texture than does pea gravel. Crushed stone has sharper edges than gravel, and if the stone's graded by size, you can control its placement to achieve different densities. A mixture of small rocks and *fines* (sand and fine particles), for example, compacts into a very dense mass that provides a surface almost as solid as paving. The smaller particles, however, are somewhat messy. A higher grade of crushed rock, with a larger aggregate, doesn't compact as tightly as the small size does but is "cleaner." As a patio surface, these materials have a classic, old-world feeling. Most come in tan and brown tones, giving them a natural look. To install crushed stone, simply excavate a few inches, fill the depression with the material, and compact it. Build a slope into the surface, as you would a paved patio.

Plant a patio

This idea may seem like cheating, but why not consider a lawn for a "patio?" I don't mean a lawn of coarse turf grasses but a tightly textured, low groundcover with the smooth, firm surface of a putting green. You need to conduct some research to find the ideal plant material for this patio. If your site is exposed to constant and direct sunlight, only a few grasses can stand up to the combination of harsh weather and hard use. Consult with a turf expert in your area, whom you can find through a nursery, golf course, or municipal groundskeeping service. You can also check out *Lawn Care For Dummies,* by Lance Walheim and the Editors of the National Gardening Association (IDG Books Worldwide, Inc.). Keep in mind that this type of patio is a high-maintenance option. You must weed, feed, and mow your patio. Other nonturf grass plants may work for a patio that doesn't have much traffic. Dichondra and creeping thyme are two examples of low ground-covers that can sustain light traffic. Again, you must water, feed, and weed your patio if you use one of these groundcovers, but not to the extent that turf grass requires.

Islands in the sea

A variation on gravel or groundcover patios is to "float" large flagstones or slabs of broken concrete in them. These solid stepping stones create islands of stability that relieve a plant patio from wear and a gravel patio from monotony. They also provide solid bases for chairs and other small furniture. To install such a patio, prepare the base as you would for a conventional patio (see Chapter 16). Then spread out a thin layer of gravel or soil, set the large stones into place, and fill in the areas around them with gravel or soil. Compact it and, if you're "growing" the patio surface, sow seed or set out seedlings. Plant densely to inhibit weeds.

Unusual Pavings

Using material that's not usually associated with paving for a patio surface creates some interesting patio effects. You can work any hard, durable, flat-surfaced material into a patio. The examples in the following three sections should get your imagination going.

Wooden patio pavers

Blocks of wood, installed with the end grain exposed, have been a substitute for bricks and cobblestones for centuries. They give a patio surface a warm, yielding texture. If possible, use hardwoods with a tight, uniform grain pattern. You need to treat blocks of softwood lumber, which wear out much quicker than hardwood does, with a clear preservative. To install wooden paving, build a base the same way you would for a brick-in-sand patio (see Chapter 16). Cut the blocks to a uniform length of four to six inches and install them with the end grain pointing up. Level them as you would bricks, and sweep sand between the blocks.

Architectural salvage

Floor pavers from an old building, curbstones, cobblestones, salvaged adobe, flat roof tiles, and similar materials all make excellent paving units because they're modular and durable. The patina of age, combined with quaint and dated shapes, lend charm to a patio made from such relics. Contact an architectural salvage firm, recycling organization, or demolition company to see what may be available. Acceptable materials are not easy to find. Just make sure that you have enough pieces — and avoid marble altogether. Marble is devilishly slippery when it gets wet.

Scrap iron — a real "steel"

Don't overlook steel. Iron manhole covers and pieces of plate steel from rusted machinery or raised ships are large enough to use for paving. This option presents plenty of challenges, starting with the availability of scrap steel. Most is spoken for and enters the recycling stream very quickly. But you may find a junkyard or scrap-steel company that's willing to work with you to obtain 20 or 30 chunks of flat steel plate that you could use as patio pavers. The second challenge is weight. The steel must be heavy gauge to withstand patio use. You can solve this problem by renting a forklift for a day to unload, transport, and place the "pavers" at your site.

Finally, the surface of steel can be too slippery or too rusty and messy. The ideal surface is rusted, with a pitted texture, and not dusty or powdery. Steel that's been underwater for a long time achieves this state. For other steel, you may be able to stabilize the metal by coating it with a clear, nonglossy finish. To install a complete patio, use the steel pieces as large flagstones and install them over a gravel base. Grow groundcover between the pieces or fill the spaces with crushed rock that compacts easily.

Chapter 27

Ten Special Deck and Patio Details

How can you make your deck special? Here are ten ideas for quick and easy deck details. (Some of these ideas also work for patios.)

Buy and Install

Recently, interest in garden design has exploded. Garden shops and mail-order catalogs abound in decorative art that you can use to dress up your deck and yard. Consider the four items that I describe in the following sections for your deck.

Fountain

You can buy a small fountain, install it on your deck or next to your patio, fill it with water, and plug it in the same day. Dozens of designs are available, from cast-concrete imitations of Classical wall fountains (as shown in Figure 27-1) to free-standing metal sculptures. The sound of trickling water is a welcome addition to any deck.

Figure 27-1:
This
fountain
adds flair.

Birdbath and feeder

Watching birds come to your deck offers endless hours of enjoyment for all family members. Buy a birdbath that you can mount on the railing or the wall of the house, away from the main activity areas but close enough to keep filled. For the ultimate in convenience, run a water line from the drip-irrigation system for your planters to the birdbath to keep the latter filled automatically (see Chapter 25). You can also attract birds by installing a feeder on your deck.

Tivoli lights

Buy strings of Tivoli lights and attach them to the underside of railings and benches (see Figure 27-2). Avoid clear bulbs that give off an intense light; choose a style with subdued light that casts glowing pools of light onto surfaces below.

Figure 27-2:
Concealed
Tivoli lights
create a
subtle
magic that
makes a
patio glow
at night.

Decorate the Deck Components

As you build your deck, you focus most of your effort on just getting the thing finished. You can add a great deal of pizzazz to the deck, however, with the help of simple details that you build into the components, either as you assemble them or after you complete the deck.

Rout exposed edges of boards

A *power router* is a versatile tool that's easy to use as soon as you pick up the basic techniques, such as cutting from right to left. (Make sure that you follow all the manufacturer's safety precautions.) You can use a router to shape the edges of boards by using one of several *piloted bits* (bits with a stationary roller tip that guides the bit along the edge of a board), which are designed for this purpose. *Round-over bits* (a type of piloted bit) produce a smooth, simple curve, called a *radius*. Other bits produce more intricate shapes, such as an *ogee* (shaped like the letter S) or a *beaded* (grooved) corner. For decks, shaped edges are very elegant and dramatic on cap rails, posts, and the decking boards themselves.

Decorate beam ends

As I discuss in Chapter 10, the exposed ends of beams offer an opportunity to add some style or even whimsy to your deck. You can draw a shape on paper, cut it out, and trace the outline onto each side of the beam end. Shapes can vary from straight 45-degree angles to a half circle, an S curve, or an animal head, such as that of a whale. After tracing the outline onto the beam, cut as close as you can to the outline, using several cuts of a hand-saw, circular power saw, or *reciprocating saw* (a heavy-duty, long-bladed jig saw). Then refine and smooth the shape by using chisels, a rasping plane, and a power sander.

Build fancy footings

Some people consider the feet the ugliest part of the human body, and many beautiful decks suffer the same indignity. The perfect solution to both problems is to use fancy shoes. As you build forms for footings, tack strips of wood or sheets of textured material — for example, bubble wrap or mineral-surface roll roofing — to the inside of the forms to create interesting textures and shapes in the concrete surface. You can chamfer (that is, bevel at 45 degrees) the top edges and corners; reproduce words or house numbers by using inverted alphabet blocks; or embed leaves, pebbles, or seashells into the concrete.

Inlay a border strip

You can accentuate the shape of your deck and give it a very dressy effect by installing a border at the edge of the deck surface, similar to borders in hardwood floors. Use the same material as you do for the decking or choose material of a contrasting color or size. Miter the corners. See Chapter 11 for more information.

Add gingerbread

Boards are boring. They're square, with rectilinear shapes and predictable dimensions. Of course, simple shapes and patterns are very effective design elements, but in some yards and for some homes such a deck feels too modern or out of place. You can give a period flavor to your deck by dressing it up with Victorian gingerbread molding or Classical architectural shapes. These include such gingerbread features as *finials* (doodads for the tops of posts), *knee braces* (braces with scrollwork that fit into the corner created by a post and a beam), *lattice screens, impediments* (ornamental triangles that fit over doorways), *dentil molding* (zigzag molding that resembles a row of teeth), and other classic styles. For some decks, gobs of the stuff work well; for other decks, only the light touch works. Avoid highly intricate combinations of pieces — multiple joints are moisture traps that enhance rot. Before installing pieces, treat them with a preservative sealer; after installing them, add a final coat of paint or sealer.

Build Into the Deck

You can build dozens of add-ons and amenities into your deck, limited only by your imagination. They don't need to be major projects, such as the overheads, screens, planters, spas, cooking centers, and other enhancements that I discuss throughout this book (see Chapters 1, 3, 22, 23, and 24). The following sections offer two ideas for projects that you can build if you have basic carpentry skills.

Build hidden compartments

You can hide hoses, garden tools, eating utensils, toys, and other paraphernalia in the deck itself by building hidden compartments into it. One approach is to cut out a section of four or five deck boards between joists. Build an enclosure between the joists, extending it below them as far as necessary for adequate storage space. Use preservative-treated plywood and drill holes in the bottom for drainage. Reassemble the cut sections of deck boards and attach cleats to the bottom of them to make a hatch. Mount the hatch on the deck surface by using hinges and attach a finger latch or hand pull to the free edge for lifting it. You can build the same kind of concealed storage in a bench.

Add a pass-through

If you don't have a convenient door between the deck and kitchen, build a pass-through to save steps, as shown in Figure 27-3. The easiest pass-through, of course, is simply to use an existing window. If you have one, but it doesn't open, replace the sash with a type that opens, such as a sliding window. Attach a shelf to the outside of the window, supporting it with diagonal cleats or knee braces. If no window is available, install one, if feasible, by using standard window installation techniques that any carpentry manual describes.

Figure 27-3:
A kitchen pass-through reduces traffic into the house and saves steps.

Chapter 28

Ten Money-Saving Tips

After you estimate the cost of your proposed deck or patio and factor in the incidental or "hidden" costs (see Chapter 8), you may find that the project is just out of reach of your budget. Before abandoning hope, consider the money-saving tips in the following sections.

Tips for Any Project

Whether you build a patio or a deck, certain principles should guide the process, such as designing the structure with a specific budget in mind and not overbuilding for your neighborhood (see Chapter 1). The following tips can also help you keep a project within budget.

Shop your list

Break down your project into an itemized list of materials and services, with precise quantities, and ask suppliers to bid on the entire list. Don't rely on discount pricing only at large retail stores. You may find specialty suppliers who can offer competitive pricing because you've done your homework and enabled them to fill one large order instead of many small orders. If bids exceed your budget, inquire about less-expensive alternative materials. Be reasonable and forthright in your negotiations. Avoid "cherry-picking" different materials from different suppliers unless you first clarify with them that the prices they give you aren't dependent on your buying the entire order. If you have neighbors or friends who are also building decks, you may find significant savings by consolidating your orders.

Shrink the project

Size is an illusion. A small deck doesn't feel small if it's in scale with its surroundings. A deck or patio doesn't need to be large to be successful, as long as it's beautiful. Review your design requirements (see Chapter 1) and look for activities that you can accommodate somewhere else to reduce the size of the deck or patio. If you need space for entertaining, for example, create a smaller deck that cascades down to a large open area covered with gravel or a smaller patio that flows onto the lawn.

Build in stages

Design the project so that you can build parts of it at a later time, when funds are available. If you want a combination spa, deck, and patio, for example, build the deck now to expand living space in the house and the spa and patio later. Or, if you're planning a patio with an overhead shade structure, build the patio now and use umbrellas until you have the resources to complete the project. Build the footings for the overhead at the same time that you construct the patio and use planters or benches to disguise the post anchors.

Hire a designer

Professional design costs money but can be the best money spent on a project. If you're strictly on a shoestring budget, this option isn't viable, but if you have a moderate budget that gives a designer something to work with, allocate some of that money to design.

Although many landscape designers, architects, and other design professionals make their mark by designing for the rich and famous or for large commercial and institutional projects, some designers find immense enjoyment in "bread-and-butter" work for clients with modest means. They enjoy the challenge and take pride in solving difficult problems. To find such a person, first be clear about your own budget and expectations. Make sure that potential candidates understand that you're hiring someone *to save money* and that you can't afford a dream project at this time. Clarify the scope of work you need, whether it's a concept design to shape the overall project or detailed working drawings to help you build it. Discuss fees and agree ahead of time on exactly how much you intend to spend and what that amount buys.

Expect to participate in the process by verifying measurements, pricing materials, and doing legwork. Above all, be flexible. You can't both get the deck of your dreams *and* save money. What you want is a tasteful, modest deck or patio with a flair about it that you couldn't have created yourself.

Tips for Decks

Most decks are already minimal structures with little "fat" to trim, so you can't save money by cutting out frills that aren't there. You can squeeze costs somewhat, however, by paying careful attention to each component of the deck and possibly redesigning the deck itself.

Use less-expensive materials

Go through your entire materials list and find as many cheaper alternatives as you can. If, for example, you plan to order a delivery of ready-mix concrete for deck footings and have it pumped, order instead a load of aggregate and some sacks of cement and plan on a few extra days of work to mix and pour your own — for example, doing one footing after work each day. Use a cheaper grade of decking lumber. Look for a used patio door instead of a brand-new set of French doors.

Design modest railings

Many railing designs are intricate and require a large quantity of clear, small-dimensioned wood, which is expensive. You can't very easily replace it with cheaper grades of lumber, because many knots and defects render small-dimensioned lumber useless. Instead, construct a railing out of wire mesh (see Chapter 12). Railings are also a good place to use recycled lumber, because few of the members are structural. You may find an old barn with redwood or cedar siding that you can rip into smaller dimensions or a fence that's being torn down.

Consider a detached deck

If your deck project involves substantial changes to the house, such as the installation of new patio doors or extensive alterations of the siding to accommodate a deck ledger, consider converting it into a detached deck, perhaps connecting it to the existing back door of the house with a small bridge. By placing the deck at a lower elevation, you may also save the cost of railings and a substantial framing system if the original deck was high. Some of the savings are offset, however, by the need for additional posts and footings to compensate for the absence of a ledger.

Redesign the deck

Add more joists so that you can use 1-by decking lumber instead of 2-by. Reduce dimensions to the nearest 2-foot increment — if the deck is 19 feet long, for example, which requires 20-foot lengths of decking, reduce it to 18 feet. Remove complex angles or wasteful bump-outs (protruding shapes), such as an octagon corner. Think through your furniture arrangements and traffic lanes to see whether you can find more-efficient ways to configure the deck to make it smaller.

Tips for Patios

Patios aren't as complex as decks and, therefore, hold less potential for nipping and tucking. They also aren't very expensive in the first place, unless you plan to use the most expensive paving materials. Not surprisingly, the first place to look for savings is in your choice of materials.

Choose cheaper materials

Masonry materials vary widely in cost. If you want a brick patio, consider concrete pavers, which are much cheaper. If you want flagstone, consider pouring a concrete slab and imitating flagstones by using a jointing tool to cut grooves into the fresh concrete surface to resemble joints between stones. After the concrete sets, fill the grooves with mortar of a contrasting color. You can also stain or color the concrete "stones." Consider alternatives to paving altogether, such as a gravel patio (see Chapter 26). Finally, look for free materials, such as chunks of broken sidewalk from a demolition site or a load of used bricks. If you know a cement contractor or concrete supplier, and have several months to follow through, build some forms for square pavers and ask him or her to fill the forms with extra concrete after deliveries. Another approach to saving costs is to build a "checkerboard" patio consisting of alternating sections of solid paving and loose gravel.

Build an expandable core

Start your patio project with a small patio and add sections to it over the years, as time and budget permit. Because concrete is impossible to match in color from batch to batch, choose an exposed aggregate surface or plan the patio as a "crazy quilt" of variable materials. For design flair and continuity, choose a more expensive material, such as brick or tile, for borders between separate sections.

Index

• *M* •

• *R* •

• *T* •

IDG BOOKS WORLDWIDE BOOK REGISTRATION

Register This Book and Win!

We want to hear from you!

Visit **http://my2cents.dummies.com** to register this book and tell us how you liked it!

- Get entered in our monthly prize giveaway.

- Give us feedback about this book — tell us what you like best, what you like least, or maybe what you'd like to ask the author and us to change!

- Let us know any other *...For Dummies*® topics that interest you.

Your feedback helps us determine what books to publish, tells us what coverage to add as we revise our books, and lets us know whether we're meeting your needs as a *...For Dummies* reader. You're our most valuable resource, and what you have to say is important to us!

Not on the Web yet? It's easy to get started with *Dummies 101*®: *The Internet For Windows*® *95* or *The Internet For Dummies*, 4th Edition, at local retailers everywhere.

Or let us know what you think by sending us a letter at the following address:

...For Dummies Book Registration
Dummies Press
7260 Shadeland Station, Suite 100
Indianapolis, IN 46256-3945
Fax 317-596-5498

BUSINESS AND GENERAL REFERENCE BOOK SERIES FROM IDG

COMPUTER BOOK SERIES FROM IDG